Assembly Design and Planning: Methodologies and Applications

Assembly Design and Planning: Methodologies and Applications

Edited by Abby Barnes

CLANRYE
INTERNATIONAL
www.clanryeinternational.com

Clanrye International,
750 Third Avenue, 9th Floor,
New York, NY 10017, USA

ISBN: 978-1-64726-593-9

Cataloging-in-publication Data

Assembly design and planning : methodologies and applications / edited by Abby Barnes.
p. cm.
Includes bibliographical references and index.
ISBN 978-1-64726-593-9
1. Assembly-line methods. 2. Assembling machines--Design and construction.
3. Automation. 4. Artificial intelligence. I. Barnes, Abby.
TS178.4 .A87 2023
670.427--dc23

For information on all Clanrye International publications
visit our website at www.clanryeinternational.com

Contents

Preface

This book has been an outcome of determined endeavour from a group of educationists in the field. The primary objective was to involve a broad spectrum of professionals from diverse cultural background involved in the field for developing new researches. The book not only targets students but also scholars pursuing higher research for further enhancement of the theoretical and practical applications of the subject.

Assembly design, formally known as design-for-assembly (DFA), refers to a set of best practices for manufacturing a product aimed at making it easier to assemble and manufacture a product, reducing the part count, minimizing the stages of assembly process, and mistake-proofing the assembly process as far as possible. The most important application of assembly design is product manufacturing. Assembly design techniques can be applied to products assembled manually or automatically. Assembly design makes use of one or the other type of assembly line for manufacturing products. In an assembly line, different machines and workers are arranged in a pre-defined sequence. Each location on the assembly line where a worker processes a product using the given machine is called a workstation. The products or the semi-finished products move from one workstation to another while they are being built. The use of assembly lines help in reducing the ergonomic strain and high labor costs. Automation of assembly lines is commonly done using highly rigid kinematic structures in special machines to ensure accuracy. There are two basic assembly design methodologies namely bottom-up design and top-down design. This book outlines the methodologies and applications of assembly design along with its planning aspects. It will help new researchers by foregrounding their knowledge in this area of study.

It was an honour to edit such a profound book and also a challenging task to compile and examine all the relevant data for accuracy and originality. I wish to acknowledge the efforts of the contributors for submitting such brilliant and diverse chapters in the field and for endlessly working for the completion of the book. Last, but not the least; I thank my family for being a constant source of support in all my research endeavours.

Editor

Towards the Automated Coverlay Assembly in FPCB Manufacturing: Concept and Preliminary Tests

Marcello Valori[1](✉) , Vito Basile[1] , Simone Pio Negri[1] , Paolo Scalmati[2], Chiara Renghini[2], and Irene Fassi[3]

[1] Institute of Intelligent Industrial Technologies and Systems for Advanced Manufacturing, National Research Council, Via P. Lembo, 38/F, 70124 Bari, Italy
marcello.valori@stiima.cnr.it
[2] Somacis S.p.A, Via del Lauro, 7, 20121 Milan, Italy
{p.scalmati,c.renghini}@somacis.com
[3] Institute of Intelligent Industrial Technologies and Systems for Advanced Manufacturing, National Research Council, Via A. Corti, 12, 20133 Milan, Italy

Abstract. In modern electronics, flexible and rigid-flex PCBs are largely used due to their intrinsic versatility and performance, allowing to increase the available volume, or enabling connection between unconstrained components. Rigid-flex PCBs consists of rigid board portions with flexible interconnections and are commonly used in a wide variety of industrial applications. However, the assembly process of these devices still has some bottlenecks. Specifically, they require the application of cover layers (namely, coverlays), to provide insulation and protection of the flexible circuits. Due to the variability in planar shape and dimensions, the coverlay application is still performed manually, requiring troublesome manipulation steps and resulting in undetermined time-cycle and precision.

This paper aims at the improvement of the industrial process currently performed, by proposing an approach for the automation of Kapton coverlay manipulation and application. Since these products are commercially provided as a film with a protective layer to be removed, the peeling issue is addressed, representing a challenging step of the automated process; the results of a systematic series of tests, performed in order to validate the peeling strategy, are reported in the paper. The overall assembly strategy relies on the development of a customized multi-hole vacuum gripper, whose concept is presented and contextualized in the proposed assembly process by outlining a suitable workcell architecture.

Keywords: PCB assembly · Film manipulation · Flexible electronics

1 Introduction

Modern electronics is moving fast, chasing market demands, towards miniaturization, flexible and stretchable electronics [1], embedded PCBs [2], molded interconnect devices (MIDs) and 3D electronic devices [3], environment friendly electronics [4]. Among these trends, flexible and rigid-flex PCBs are used in many applications due to their advantages compared to traditional rigid PCBs: by interposing flexible connections between rigid board portions, complex 3D arrangements can be achieved, complying with demanding volume constraints.

The main advantage obtained by the use of flexible printed circuit boards (FPCBs) is the possibility of 3D wiring, enabling the exploitation of the available volumes and complex routing requirements. In particular, exploiting their intrinsic lightweight and the possibility to be deformed and constrained into narrow volumes, flexible circuits are commonly used in biomedical applications [5], aerospace and smartphone industry. One fundamental feature of flexible circuits is the necessity of mechanical protection of the conductors; in order to comply with this requirement, coverlays are applied in addition to the solder masks. Among the various types of coverlay (film, screen printable, photoimageable) [6], film coverlay is generally preferred, due to its mechanical properties in terms of strength and durability. However, it is the most complicated solution from the point of view of the automation possibilities. Film coverlay thickness can span from 25 μm to 127 μm; the base material, polyimide (PI) or Polyethylene terephthalate (PET), is coated with an adhesive layer of epoxy resin or acrylic with thicknesses in the range 25 ÷ 75 μm. The adhesives are semicured, to be activated finally in the lamination phase. A further layer of release material is applied as adhesive layer protection for delivery and handling before application.

Figure 1 shows an example of rigid-flexible PCB layer stack-up. Figure 2 shows two examples of rigid-flexible circuits developed by the PCB manufacturer Somacis, Italy, as well as the effects of a final "routing" phase, referred in this case to the full-thickness trimming of the external frame to actualize the flexibility. Light brown, flexible circuits can be distinguished from green rigid circuits; the different color is due to coverlay surface. In some cases, flexible circuits enable signal connections between rigid circuits (Fig. 2, a), while in other cases they embody sensors or other devices (Fig. 2, b).

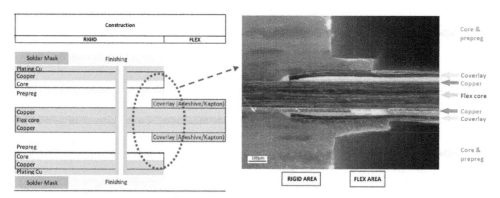

Fig. 1. Rigid-flexible PCB stack-up. Left: schematic of the layers. Right: a detail of the assembled circuit section acquired by a Zeiss Axio Imager M2m microscope. (Courtesy of Somacis, Italy).

In Fig. 3, a flexible circuit portion is shown, before and after the application of the coverlay; as highlighted, coverlay application is limited to flexible areas of the circuit, specific for each board design. The actual flexibility is obtained when, furthermore, the

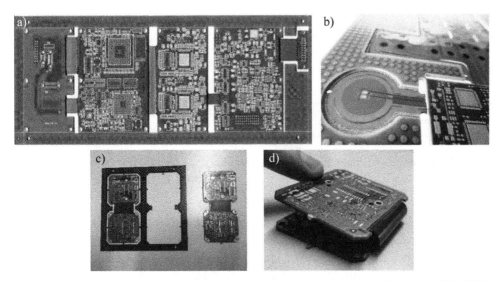

Fig. 2. Rigid-flexible circuits. a) Industrial application board, 14 layers (10 rigid + 4 flexible), thickness 2 mm. b) Device for human epilepsy monitoring. c) and d) The external frame furtherly eliminated, enabling the deformation of flexible circuits. (Courtesy of Somacis, Italy).

external frame, that is necessary for automated manipulation during the assembly of the other components, is removed. It is worth to highlight that the removal of the coverlay protective film can be troublesome, increasing process time, thus production costs, and inducing visual and mental stress for the worker.

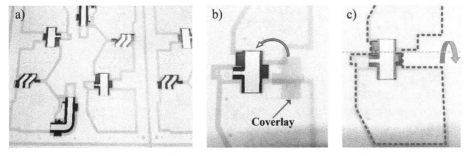

Fig. 3. Coverlay application. Flexible circuit before (a) and after (c) the application of the coverlay (b). In c) the red countour highlights the frame to be trimmed out and the blue line indicates the flexion axis of the final device. (Courtesy of Somacis, Italy). (Color figure online)

Flexible circuits layers are laminated together with rigid layers, according to the designed build-up (Fig. 4, left). In PCB fabrication, indeed, the layer stack-up is pre-assembled and then subjected to lamination and curing (pressure-heating cycle), aimed at the activation of the adhesive on coverlays and flexible circuits and the polymerization of epoxy resin in prepreg foils (Fig. 4, right).

The state-of-the-art application process of film coverlays is characterized by the following steps (Fig. 5): a) laser trimming of the specific contour, b) manual removal of the protective film, c) manual positioning on the PCB, d) manual application of one

Fig. 4. PCB fabrication: lamination and curing cycle. Pre-assembled stack-up (left) and 20 positions loader of a Lauffer press. (Courtesy of Somacis, Italy)

or more welding points to avoid displacements, e) lamination and curing for adhesive activation and/or polymerization of prepreg layers. Another option for increasing process accuracy is represented by the use of laser drilling after lamination: the coverlay film is applied without pre-drilling; after lamination, laser drilling is performed in order to selectively eliminate the coverlay film and obtain the designed geometry [6]. However, with this approach, there are no advantages for the automation of the peeling phase.

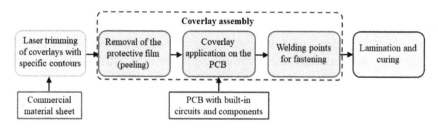

Fig. 5. Coverlay assembly: state-of-the-art process phases.

In panel-based processes of electronics industry, automating the peeling of flexible materials still represents an issue [7]. In this paper, a new concept is proposed for automated manipulation, positioning and assembly of coverlays in flexible and rigid-flexible circuit manufacturing, addressing in detail the peeling issue. Section 2 presents the conceived assembly procedure including gripping, peeling of the protective film and assembly on the current layer of the stack-up. Section 3 illustrates the concept of the automated assembly system with its architecture and main equipment, including gripper architecture. Section 4 reports the experimental tests performed for the peeling step of a typical coverlay and finally, conclusions are presented in Sect. 5.

2 The Proposed Assembly Approach

In this Section, a strategy for coverlay automated assembly is proposed, identifying firstly the process requirements, then the gripping features and the peeling strategy and, finally, the process phases are described.

2.1 Requirements

The requirements of the assembly procedure are determined based on the manual process currently carried out and the material properties.

Flexible Component Manipulation. Film coverlays are characterized by extremely low thickness. The system shall be able to manipulate these components, avoiding bending and ensuring flat positioning on FPCB surface.

Compliance to the Geometry. Depending on the specific FPCB design, coverlays are characterized by different dimensions and planar shapes, thus, the gripping strategy shall enable the compliance with a wide variety of geometries.

Removal of the Protection Film. In the assembly task, the protection film must be removed before coverlay application; therefore, a methodology for the peeling of such a film shall be implemented.

Thermal Bonding: Film coverlay shall be constrained to the FPCB by applying one or more bonding points, by locally activating the epoxy resin with a soldering tool.

Performance. Accuracy and repeatability of the assembly process shall be lower than the accuracy limit determined for flexible circuits with High Density Interconnect (HDI) PCB (100 μm) [6].

2.2 Gripping

In the manipulation of flat surfaces characterized by extremely low thickness combined with low stiffness materials, thus, deformable, the issue of preserving component configuration, avoiding undesirable bending, arises. This aspect can be even more relevant during the positioning phase, in which folds and air bubbles must be avoided. The use of a flat gripping surface as interface with the component represents a valid option to address these aspects.

Gripping strategy shall also comply with the requirement of the selective pick. Compliant grippers usually rely on the 3D shape of the object, in order to passively adapt to perform gripping, using different approaches and often implementing soft materials [8]; there are also commercial products available enabling the unconditional pick of objects with flat surfaces [9]. In the application dealt with in this paper, coverlays lie on a flat surface; due to the extremely low thickness, their 3D shape is not appropriate to be passively distinguished from the background by a compliant gripper. Thus, the necessity of a strategy for gripper "pre-shaping" arises.

Basing on these considerations, the gripper specifically designed for coverlay "pick-peel-place" is characterized by a flat interface surface and based on vacuum principle; a pattern of holes, representing themselves a matrix of suction cups, is realized in the flat surface. In order to avoid the uncontrolled pick of other patches lying on the same support, as well as the possible vacuum loss due to uncovered condition of one or more orifices, each suction cup is controlled individually, thanks to an upstream pneumatic valve module. With this approach, gripping pattern can be set depending on each specific coverlay contour, enabling the possibility of gripping different geometries.

2.3 Peeling Strategy

Peel strength represents one of the most important characteristics of coverlays, as it is a measure of component integrity in determined loading conditions. DuPont^{TM} Pyralux$^{®}$ LF coverlay material, for example, based on a Kapton$^{®}$ polyimide film, exhibits a peel strength of 1.6 kg/cm after curing, defined by the provider as per the applicable standard [10].

On the other hand, peeling represents also one phase of the assembly, as the coverlay is provided coupled with a release material; it is also the most demanding challenge to address in order to accomplish the whole task, due to the uncertainties in the peeling dynamics combined with the geometrical variability of the patches. Peeling dynamics has been widely investigated by the scientific community, and there are a number of patented machines, designed to be implemented in roll-to-roll production for different applications, performing tape peeling. In the majority of cases, peeling is triggered by the action of rolls [11] or insertion means acting as blades [12], combined with high bending angles of the release material. However, circuit board industry is mostly characterized by panel-based processing and coverlays may have very different shapes and dimensions. Therefore, the necessity of implementing a specific material removal method arises, studied for components characterized by planar dimensions in the order of few square centimeters.

In order to trigger the peeling of a film, adhering to another due to a substrate of a bonding agent, a mechanical action should be applied. With decreasing thickness, this task becomes more demanding, requiring precision and tools with appropriate edges. The detachment is achieved when the force, properly applied, is sufficient to trigger local fracture of the bonding agent. In the approach hereafter presented, the issue is addressed by an inverted perspective: instead of applying a detaching force when precise positioning occurs, the method relies on driving the film towards a source of mechanical action, working continuously at a high frequency; the approaching is stopped when detachment takes place due to the contact randomly occurred between the film and the source of the force.

In the practical implementation, a rotary tool with appropriate cutting profile can be suitable. In our experiments, a rotary sanding drum was used as a trigger for the peeling of the release material. As shown in Fig. 6, such a method, called hereafter "pre-peeling", exploits abrasive surface roughness to collide with the release material surface and detach it from the coverlay, thanks to the impulsive force obtained by high grinding speed and applied by one or more abrasive particles to the film to remove. Relying also on friction contact, mutual positions can be calibrated in order to guarantee that this force affects only the protective film. A specific setup, further described in this paper, was used to validate this method.

In Fig. 6, the most important process parameters are indicated. The a parameter is the unsupported overhanging portion of the coverlay (cantilever configuration) out of the clamp jaws, while e is the distance, along the x-axis, of the coverlay tip from the grinding tool axis, r is the radius of the sanding drum, rotating with angular speed ω and exerting a torque "T". Parameter e is straightly related to the approach angle ϑ to the cylindrical grinding tool, since $e = r \cos(\vartheta)$. These parameters have been chosen due to their direct relation with the physics behind the peeling process. Indeed, a is related to

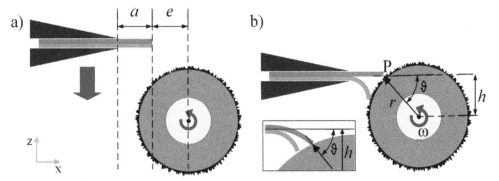

Fig. 6. Peeling trigger based on a sanding tool: a) the surface of the protective film approaches the rotating surface in a determined configuration; b) it is detached from the film coverlay. A magnification of the contact zone clarifies the definition of some parameters, considering the real operating conditions.

the coverlay flexural stiffness, so that stiffness decreases as a increases. Parameter e has influence on the peeling mechanism as it directly affects the direction of the interaction force applied by the tool on the component, due to the direct relation with angle ϑ. The combination of r and T determines the value of the force and ω affects the momentum. Finally, the whole process is closely linked to the roughness of the sanding drum.

Parameter h represents the distance, along the z-axis, between the sample and the grinding tool. The optimal set $[a, \vartheta, h]$ uniquely identifies the most suitable configuration of the coverlay and the rotating sanding drum for the pre-peeling phase. Regarding this aspect, it is relevant to point out that, in the practical implementation, coverlay samples preserve the curvature of the original material reel. The real h values differ from the theoretical value $h^* = r \sin(\vartheta)$ as they are affected by coverlay intrinsic curvature. According to this, ϑ is to be considered as the angle spanned between the radius connecting the center of the sanding drum with the contact point P and the axis of the clamp (or, in the automated task, of the end-effector), rather than the surface of the coverlay itself, as shown in the detail in Fig. 6-b).

2.4   Assembly Procedure

The assembly procedure is then defined in accordance with the chosen gripping and peeling strategy. With reference to Fig. 7, the following phases are identified:

a) Gripper Setup. With reference to the specific geometry of the coverlay to manipulate, an off-line setup is performed in order to activate selectively the vacuum orifices, thus modeling the gripping surface.

b) Coverlay Pick. Once the position of the component to manipulate is detected by an external sensing source, i.e. a vision system, the gripper can approach it and perform the pick on the coverlay side. A portion of the coverlay is kept on purpose outside of the gripping envelope.

c) Pre-Peeling. The unconstrained component portion is approached to the grinding tool, by the protective film side, thus triggering the detachment of the two films.

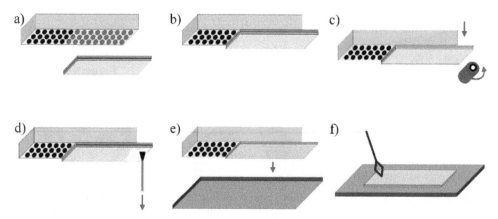

Fig. 7. The phases of the proposed assembly procedure: a) Gripper setup, b) Coverlay pick, c) Pre-peeling, d) Peeling, e) Coverlay positioning, f) Thermal bonding.

    d) Peeling. The whole protective film is pulled away by a suction cup, acting on the component portion detached in the previous phase.

    e) Coverlay Positioning. The coverlay is placed on the PCB.

    f) Thermal Bonding. The coverlay is bonded in one or more points in order to guarantee constrained precise positioning before lamination.

3   Assembly System Architecture

The whole assembly system under study is based on the approaches proposed for gripping and pre-peeling. In this section, a concept of the workcell and the design of the specific gripper for the task are presented.

3.1 Workcell Description

The workcell architecture for coverlay application, outlined in Fig. 8, is aimed at exploiting the proposed automation strategy to obtain the PCB assembly ready for lamination and curing. The inputs of the process are the flex or rigid-flex PCB with circuits and SMT (surface mounted technology) components installed in previous steps.

    In the assembly concept, the task is customized off-line, depending on the coverlay contour: a specific software tool is required for the pre-shaping phase. This setup is fundamental for task completion, since an appropriate portion of the picked coverlay has to remain outside of the gripper envelope, enabling peeling triggering.

    In the workcell concept there are two conveyors, one providing the laser-trimmed coverlays and one sliding the flex or rigid-flex PCBs to assemble. The "pick-peel-place" task is performed by a commercial manipulator, equipped with the specifically designed gripper. The implementation of a collaborative manipulator is foreseen, due to the advantages provided by including a human operator in the assembly environment [13], even for a mere on-site supervision. Within the collaborative robot scenario, several commercial models are suitable for the task, considering the extremely low payloads and the accuracy required, assessed 100 μm in Sect. 2.1. As an instance, in Figs. 8 and 9 the

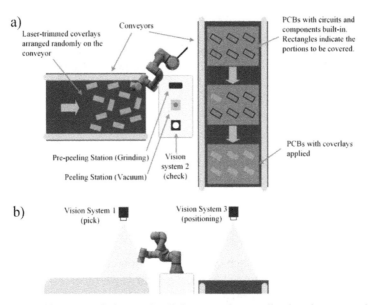

Fig. 8. Possible architecture of the workcell for coverlay application in a generic assembly scenario: a) top view and b) front view.

gripper is equipped on a Universal Robot UR5e. Regarding component pick and place, two vision systems are placed on top of the two conveyors, with appropriate fields of view (FOVs) to detect, respectively, position and orientation of the coverlay to pick, and the release position on the PCB. Within the robot reach, the pre-peeling and peeling stations are included, corresponding respectively to a rotating sanding drum and a fixed vacuum gripper; a vision system is necessary for gripping position check.

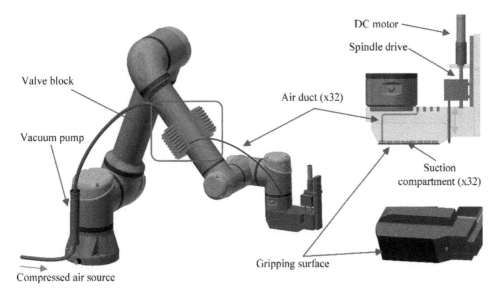

Fig. 9. Design of the specific gripper. On the left, the gripper equipped on a UR5e; on top, right, gripper components are highlighted: on bottom, right, the interface surface is indicated.

3.2 Gripper Architecture

A specific gripper is designed in order to perform coverlay film manipulation and comply with all the assembly phases. The overall design is shown in Fig. 9 and each subsystems is hereafter described.

Vacuum Pump. A vacuum pump, dedicated to gripper actuation, is installed on robot frame. In the design reported in Fig. 9, a vacuum generator is included.

Interface. The interface with the object consists of a flat surface; tiny holes provide vacuum source and a rubber coating guarantees adhesion and avoids undesired impacts with the board during the component placement. The diameter of the holes, 2 mm, has been experimentally determined as a trade-off between gripping force and deformation of the material due to suction force.

Valve Block. The interface surface covers the suction compartments, which are independent each from another provided by the vacuum valve block. The valve block consists in a series of 32 tiny 3/2 normally closed, cartridge solenoid valves, commercially available, supplied by common manifolds in parallel configuration, controlling, downstream, one duct each one; only one duct is highlighted in the Figure. Each duct ends up with a suction compartment. With this configuration, the goal of selectively shaping the gripping surface is achieved by modeling the gripping surface, controlling each valve individually.

Bonding Tool. The bonding apparatus consists in a retractile, metal solder tool. It can slide on the side of the gripper, in order to bond the coverlay once it is located on the PCB, while it is maintained by the gripper in the correct position. One spindle drive actuated by a DC motor enables tool sliding, as shown in Fig. 9. The bonding tool slides out from a flat surface adjacent to the gripping surface, inclined to it in order to work as a foothold for the vacuum peeling tool during peeling completion.

4 Peeling Tests

4.1 Experimental Setup

As stated above, the peeling of the coverlay is conceived in two steps: pre-peeling and peeling completion. In order to verify the effectiveness of the proposed method to trigger coverlay peeling, a series of experimental tests was performed. The following parameters are considered to mainly affect the process: thickness of the coverlay, grit designation and dimensions of the sanding drum, rotational speed, geometrical configuration of the coverlay/drum approach. In this phase, the feasibility is addressed, focusing on the individuation of the optimal geometrical configuration for a defined set of coverlay material (thickness), pre-peeling tool (grit designation and diameter) and rotational speed.

Coverlay material is DuPont Pyralux LF0110 made of 25 μm thick Kapton polyimide coated on one side with 25 μm proprietary modified acrylic adhesive. The adhesive side is covered by a protective film with thickness of 40 μm. Coverlays are IPC certi-fied by the supplier. Coverlay geometries are determined on the basis of an industrial case, currently object of study of the research group; such a geometry is rectangular with dimensions 25 × 40 mm; further materials and dimensions will be investigated in following experimental surveys. The samples are trimmed, which means full-thickness cut, by a 2D laser cut machine from a coverlay sheet with dimensions 610 × 454 mm, obtained by cutting a roll 610 mm wide and 76 meters long.

The laser trimming operation separates the coverlays from the sheet, then collected and loaded on a conveyor for the subsequent operation. The testing equipment is com-posed by two main parts: 1) apparatus for coverlay positioning; 2) pre-peeling stage. With regard to the first component, the coverlays samples are mounted on a three-axes high precision metric stage, actuated by three micrometer screws, with travel range of 15 mm on each axis and sensitivity 1 μm. The coverlay samples are held inside two small aluminum jaws mounted at the end of two cylindrical fixtures. In order to dis-tribute the clamping force on a higher coverlay surface, two stainless steel plates with thickness 0.45 mm are used as interfaces between the clamp jaws and the coverlays. The pre-peeling stage consists of an electrical drilling tool, mounted horizontally. The sanding drum is a cylinder with an external diameter of 8.78 mm and height 12.7 mm (1/2 in.) used for smoothing applications, with grit designation P80, corresponding to average particle diameter of 201 μm. The tool shaft has a diameter of 3.2 mm. The setup is showed in Fig. 10.

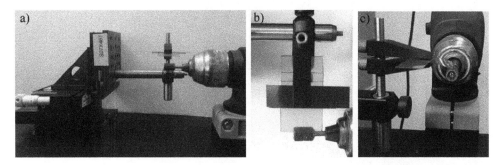

Fig. 10. Peeling initialization experimental set-up. Frontal (a), top (b), side view (c).

Preliminarily, the geometry of the set-up is verified: vertical stroke of the coverlay, alignments between grinding tool axis and coverlay profile, zeroing of the z-axis coin-cident to the first contact between the coverlay protective layer surface (bottom) and the side of the cylindrical grinding tool, centered position of the grinding tool with the coverlay width, etc.

The series of experimental tests was based on the variation of parameters a and e; ω was set at 800 rpm and the same sanding drum - thus, same radius and same sanding grade - was used. a was set at 10 and 15 mm, while e was set at 0, 1, and 2 mm; for a = 10 mm also e = 1.5 mm was considered as a further set of variables. Each of the 7 parameter sets is tested with 5 repetitions (sample labels A, ..., E). This value is reputed sufficient for the feasibility assessment. Each run is performed by setting the parameters (a and e) and driving the coverlay sample towards the grinding tool by slow vertical motion (approximately 2 mm/min), as schematically shown in Fig. 6; vertical motion is stopped when peeling is triggered. The outputs of each experiment are the peeling triggering success, the peeled area and the recorded value of the parameter h; the standard deviation characterizing this value for each set of runs is indeed used to assess the repeatability of the process. For each successful pre-peeling test, an image was captured and processed in order to calculate the peeled area, considered an important parameter, since peeling completion relies on the gripping of a film portion already peeled.

4.2   Results and Discussion

Figure 11 shows the results of image processing procedure previously described, obtained for two runs. The light brown portion of images are pre-peeled areas (Fig. 11, left). They have irregular contours which are identified by image processing algorithms (Fig. 11, right). The proposed procedure can also be automated and used real-time for peeled area detection and characterization. Accuracy can be increased by illumination and background optimization in the image acquisition step.

Fig. 11. Image processing applied to peeled samples. ROI (Region of Interest) original image (left) and processed image (right) for calculation of peeled area, in white. Runs reported: 100 A (a = 10; e = 0; sample A) on top and 150C (a = 15; e = 0, sample C) on bottom.

Table 1 reports the results obtained with the different parameter sets. At a first glance, it highlights that the grinding-based method can be a successful solution for peeling triggering in several configurations. It is important to point out that all the successful pre-peeling runs led to successful peeling completion, definitely validating the approach of splitting the peeling issue in two sub-phases.

Besides the validation of the approach, this preliminary series of tests was aimed at the definition of a reliable configuration for the automation of the pre-peeling phase,

Table 1. Experimental results of peeling triggering.

a [mm]	e [mm]	ϑ [deg]	Success Index	$<h>$ [mm]	σ_h [mm]	$<PA>$ [mm^2]	$<PA/TA>$ %
10	0	90°	5/5	5,54	0,17	129	52%
10	1,0	77°	5/5	5,91	0,27	93	37%
10	1,5	70°	3/5	6,02	0,17	171	68%
10	2	63°	3/5	5,22	0,07	115	46%
15	0	90°	5/5	6,79	0,22	174	46%
15	1	77°	2/5	7,40	0,23	31	8%
15	2	63°	1/5	6,40	–	89	24%

Success Index: number of successful pre-peeling runs; *PA: Peeled Area; TA: Total Area* (limited to the overhanging coverlay portion); $<h>$: mean h value and σ_h: standard deviation.

intended as the mutual position of an end-effector holding the coverlay and the grinding tool. The choice is the result of a hierarchical parameter analysis. The first parameter to consider is the *Success Index*: only configurations leading to 100% successful runs were considered. The Peeled Area PA (and, in particular, the ratio between PA and TA, the Total Area) was assessed as an important discriminating factor for the subsequent peeling completion phase; however, as already stated, all the successful pre-peeling runs were followed by successful peeling completion. From the pre-peeling automation perspective, acquired position standard deviation σ_h is then relevant: since the h value indicates a position suitable for the robot end-effector, a lower σ_h is directly translated in a better repeatability of the process, that represents a fundamental indicator in an automated task. According to this approach, the most suitable set of parameters for the batch of coverlays currently under examination, is represented by the "100" series (a = 10 mm; ϑ = 90°; h = 5.5 mm). It is worth to point out that, according to the discussion reported in Sect. 2.3, in the practical implementation, this particular configuration (ϑ = 90°) does not correspond to the protective film surface tangential to the sanding drum, due to the coverlay intrinsic curvature. As a further remark, in all the successful runs, no damages were observed on coverlay inner surfaces.

In the proposed approach, the process is considered stochastic, relying on the sand particles random distribution. The coverlay/particles contact frequency is directly related to the high rotational speed of the tool. Certain contacts lead to detachment, thus, success probability is strongly increased by high rotational speeds. However, coverlay/tool relative configuration is a fundamental factor to enable the engagement of the only protective film layer; in some cases, indeed, also the coverlay film is engaged itself, leading to a process fail. The experimentation led to the optimal configuration for the specific case-study.

5   Conclusions

The presented research activity deals with the automation of a specific task in electronic assembly, still performed manually. The topic is of outstanding interest, as it represents a critical phase in the production of flex and rigid-flex PCBs, whose implementation is incredibly growing in a wide range of application fields. Coverlays work as stiffeners, insulators and mechanical protection of the circuits; film coverlays present the most suitable mechanical properties, but they are characterized by low accuracy, as their application relies on operator skills. Furthermore, the removal of the protective film is troublesome and stressing.

The automation of the coverlay application phase is addressed by proposing an approach for the protective film peeling triggering, introducing a pre-peeling phase, based on a common workshop sanding tool. The whole assembly process is then outlined and the concept design of a suitable gripper is presented. Finally, the results of a series of tests, aimed at validating the peeling strategy and defining an optimal position for the automated pre-peeling phase, are reported.

The results demonstrate that the proposed peeling strategy can represent a successful methodology to be implemented in an automated process. Geometrical parameters need to be properly configured to ensure process reliability, defining the optimal relative position to promote the separation by engaging only the support material layer. In our experiments, indeed, some configurations led to 100% pre-peeling success, followed by successful peeling completion.

In future developments, the results obtained will be further validated in other experimental surveys; in particular, the variation of tool rotation speed will be considered, as well as the use of different sanding drums, corresponding to the variation of tool radius and sanding grade, and different coverlay materials. At the same time, gripper design will be refined, followed by the supply of all the components and realization. By equipping the gripper on a manipulator, it will be possible to validate the automation of most of process phases. Finally, the robot will be integrated in a complete workcell, as outlined in the paper.

Acknowledgments. This research was funded by the Italian Government through the National Operative Program H2020 PON 2014-2020, within the project "High-performance electronic Embedded Systems (HELMS)", grant number F/050507/02-03/X32.

References

1. Wong, W.S., Salleo, A.: Flexible Electronics: Materials and Applications. Electronic Materials: Science & Technology. Springer, Boston (2009). https://doi.org/10.1007/978-0-387-743 63-9
2. Jillek, W., Yung, W.K.C.: Embedded components in printed circuit boards: a processing technology review. Int. J. Adv. Manuf. Technol. **25**(3–4), 350–360 (2005)
3. Franke, J.: Three-Dimensional Molded Interconnect Devices (3D-MID): Materials, Manufacturing, Assembly and Applications for Injection Molded Circuit Carriers. Carl Hanser Verlag GmbH Co KG, Germany (2014)

4. Canal Marquesa, A., Cabrera, J.M., de Fraga Malfatti, C.: Printed circuit boards: a review on the perspective of sustainability. J. Environ. Manage. **131**, 298–306 (2013)
5. Khan, Y., et al.: Flexible hybrid electronics: direct interfacing of soft and hard electronics for wearable health monitoring. Adv. Funct. Mater. **26**, 8764–8775 (2016)
6. Coombs, C.F., Holden, H.T.: Printed Circuits Handbook, 6th edn. McGraw-Hill, New York, USA (2009)
7. Plovie, B., et al.: Stretchable mold interconnect optimization: peeling automation and carrierless techniques. IEEE Trans. Compon. Packag. Manuf. Technol. **9**(5), 955–962 (2019)
8. Shintake, J., Cacucciolo, V., Floreano, D., Shea, H.: Soft robotic grippers. Adv. Mater. **30**(29), 1707035 (2018)
9. Joulin Vacuum Handling. https://www.joulin.com/all-industries/standard/minigrip.html. Accessed on 30 Sep 2019
10. IPC-TM-650 Test Methods Manual, 2.4.9 - Peel Strength, Flexible Dielectric Materials. IPC Association Connecting Electronics Industries (2014)
11. Toyoda, Y., Nobuyuki, T. (NGK Spark Plug Co., Ltd.). United States Patent: Method and Apparatus for Producing a Wiring Board including Film Peeling. US 7,481,901 B2 (2009)
12. Ahn, K.H. (Samsung Display Co., Ltd.). United States Patent: Method and Apparatus for Peeling Donor Film from Substrate. US 8,877,006 B2 (2014)
13. Ruggeri, S., Fontana, G., Basile, V., Valori, M., Fassi, I.: Micro-robotic handling solutions for PCB (re-)manufacturing. Proc. Manuf. **1**, 441–448 (2017)

Improving Automated Insertion Task in Robotics by Reducing Registration Error

Geraldine S. Cheok[1], Marek Franaszek[1(✉)], Karl Van Wyk[1,2], and Jeremy A. Marvel[1]

[1] National Institute of Standards and Technology, Gaithersburg, MD 20899, USA
{cheok,marek,jeremy.marvel}@nist.gov
[2] NVIDIA, 4545 Roosevelt Way, Seattle, WA 98105, USA
kvanwyk@nvidia.com

Abstract. A peg-in-hole operation is representative of common tasks performed in assembly lines by robots. It requires registration of the coordinate frame where a part resides to the robot frame where it is acted upon. Poor registration causes misalignment of the peg and the hole which will result in a failed insertion of the peg. In this study, the dependence of the outcome of the insertion task on the quality of registration is investigated. It was shown in earlier studies that Restoring Rigid-Body Condition (RRBC) leads to decreased target registration error. This study quantifies the improvement in the Pass/Fail rate when the target registration error is reduced for a given peg-hole tolerance. A robot arm operated in position control mode was used to perform the insertion without performing any search algorithms or force/torque sensing. Results show that use of the RRBC method yielded substantial reduction in failed insertions, especially for tighter tolerances.

Keywords: Peg-in-hole · Rigid-body registration · Target registration error

1 Introduction

Accurate knowledge of an object's location is essential in manufacturing-based robotic applications. This is particularly important for the peg-in-hole task, which is an extensively studied robotic problem and the basis for many common tasks in assembly lines [1]. Research to improve this task has been conducted, and most of the proposed methods assume a peg can be initially tilted relative to the hole centerline and a search algorithm is used to guide the peg into the hole [2]. Many of the algorithms rely on feedback from force/torque (F/T) sensors [3, 4]. The premise of these methods is to improve performance given the errors (systematic and random) of the hole and peg locations [5]. The method described in this paper improves task performance by reducing the error in the registered hole location by applying corrections to the points transformed from world to robot frame. The method reduces registration error by restoring the rigid-body condition (RRBC) for point-based rigid-body registration [6]. This approach is similar to the Volumetric Error Compensation (VEC) technique, but it is easier to use as no advanced, analytical modelling of the error function is required [7–9]. It is reasonable to expect that improvement in the world-to-robot registration will have a positive impact on the peg-in-hole task; thus, increasing the likelihood for a successful insertion. However, the level of expected improvement has not been quantified. This paper quantifies the improvement in the peg-in-hole task that can be achieved by reducing the registration error. Recalibration of the perception system and/or remastering the robot arm (tasks which may require skills not readily available in small manufacturing companies) would reduce the registration error, but the method described in this paper is an easier task. Unlike some other approaches [10], the RRBC method does not require installation of additional hardware such as F/T sensors as it merely corrects the endpoints of the robot's path and no sensing is involved.

It was shown in [6] that RRBC method can substantially improve the quality of registration as gauged by the reduction of the Target Registration Error (TRE) – targets are points of interest to which registration is applied. To assess how the reduction of TRE improves the performance of a peg-in-hole task in a robotic application, three experiments were conducted. In these experiments, a robot arm, operated in position control mode, was commanded to move to a specified location and to insert a peg into a hole; that is, no modification of the preplanned path from a search algorithm or active force/torque feedback was used. This constitutes a very challenging test as the success of such an insertion depends almost entirely on accurate initial positioning. The coordinates of the hole were obtained by registering a world coordinate frame to the robot coordinate frame using a regular rigid-body registration. Then, automated insertions were performed using uncorrected hole locations and locations corrected by the RRBC method. A Pass/Fail metric was used to determine if the implementation of the RRBC method would increase the number of successful insertions. The RRBC method may be beneficial for insertion tasks when feedback from force/torque sensors is not available or sufficiently reliable or for other types of tasks such as automated drilling [11] or welding [12] where accurate positioning is crucial.

This paper summarizes the experiments, results, and conclusions from the three peg-in-hole experiments described in [13].

2   Related Work

Strategies used for peg insertion generally fall in two main categories: those which use active feedback from force/torque sensors to modify the preplanned path and those which complete the insertion task without such feedback.

In the first category, the methods rely on an active compliance strategy [14]. An example of such an implementation was shown in [15] where a vision system was used for part location together with a neural network processing data from a force/torque sensor in the wrist joint. Jokesch et al. in [16] used a generic algorithm to automatically connect electric vehicles with charging stations using a robot in impedance control mode. This task requires alignment of seven pins and an asymmetric peg and hole. Abdullah et al. [17] used data models created from F/T sensor data to search for the hole center using an algorithm based on human intuitive behavior. In [18], Bös et al. addressed limitations of admittance control schemes caused by the dependence of contact forces and torques on speed. Two iterative learning controllers were used to increase assembly speed and to reduce contact forces. Jasim et al. [19] used Gaussian Mixtures Model and F/T feedback in Contact-State modeling to identify accurate hole position. Xu et al. [20] divided the contact area around the hole into sixteen regions and used KD-Tree method to detect the right region for insertion using force feedback. While the use of force/torque sensors greatly improves insertion performance, this approach slows down the process, increases the cost of hardware, and may not be feasible when complex [21] or large scale parts [22] are mated.

In the second category, a passive or hybrid compliance strategy is applied, and a search algorithm is based on the profile of insertion depth [23–27]. For this type of strategy, rudimentary force feedback may be used only to ensure that a peg is in a constant contact with the surface of a part into which it is inserted. Strategies in both categories actively modify the preplanned trajectory as the search progresses and therefore, accuracy of the initial peg position is less critical for a successful insertion. However, an inaccurate starting point for the search algorithm will adversely affect the time spent in searching [28]. This positional accuracy depends on the quality of registration between the two coordinate frames.

Point-based rigid-body regisUtration is a frequently used procedure to determine the transformation, rotation $\mathbf{R}$ and translation $\boldsymbol{\tau}$, between two coordinate frames, for example: world or perception system frame and the robot frame. This procedure requires measurement of 3D common points in both frames. The procedure assumes that the rigid-body condition is satisfied, i.e. the distance between any two points in one frame is exactly the same as the distance between corresponding points in the second frame. However, due to noise and possible bias, this condition may not be preserved and corrective methods, like mentioned earlier RRBC, must be used.

3   Description of the RRBC Method

In this report, the first coordinate frame, from which points are transformed, is called the working frame (X). The second frame, to which points are transformed, is called the destination frame (Y). If the transformation $\{\mathbf{R}, \boldsymbol{\tau}\}$ from X to Y is known, it can be applied to the points of interest, $\mathbf{T}_X(k)$, $k = 1, \ldots, K$, which are measured only in X but must be accessed in Y. We call these points target points. Due to registration error, targets transformed from the working frame are not mapped exactly in the destination frame. To decrease the error of a transformed k-th target, a correction vector $\boldsymbol{\varepsilon}(\mathbf{T}_X(k))$ is added to the target measured in X

$$\hat{\mathbf{T}}_X(k) = \mathbf{T}_X(k) + \boldsymbol{\varepsilon}(\mathbf{T}_X(k)) \tag{1}$$

where $\hat{\mathbf{T}}_X(k)$ is the corrected target location in X. In RRBC, the correction $\boldsymbol{\varepsilon}(\mathbf{T}_X(k))$ is obtained by linear interpolation of corrections $\boldsymbol{\varepsilon}_n$ determined earlier at points X_n which are close to target $\mathbf{T}_X(k)$ and is given by

$$\boldsymbol{\varepsilon}(\mathbf{T}_X(k)) = \sum_{n=1}^{N} w_n(\mathbf{T}_X(k), X_n)\boldsymbol{\varepsilon}_n(X_n) \tag{2}$$

where weights w_n are based on the proximity of X_n to $\mathbf{T}_X(k)$, and $\sum w_n = 1$.

Corrections ε_n can be calculated from points $X_n, n = 1, \ldots, N$, measured in the working frame and the same points Y_n measured in the destination frame

$$\varepsilon_n = R_{inv} Y_n + \tau_{inv} - X_n \tag{3}$$

where $\{R_{inv}, \tau_{inv}\}$ is inverse of the registration transformation $\{R, \tau\}$, i.e., $R_{inv} = R'$ where R' is the transposed rotation matrix and $\tau_{inv} = -R_{inv}\tau$. Points measured in both frames are called fiducials, and the registration transformation $\{R, \tau\}$ was determined from at least three non-colinear fiducials using least-squares fitting algorithm [29].

If targets $T_Y(k), k = 1, \ldots, K$ are also measured in the destination frame (as in this research study), the Target Registration Error (TRE) can be calculated as

$$TRE(T_X(k)) = R T_X(k) + \tau - T_Y(k) \tag{4}$$

A reliable metric of registration is based on a representative set of K targets measured in both frames [30] and can be calculated as the Root Mean Square of *TRE* (RMS_T)

$$RMS_T = \sqrt{\frac{1}{K} \sum_{k=1}^{K} TRE^2(k)} \tag{5}$$

4   Description of Experiments

A six degree of freedom (6DOF) collaborative robot arm (UR5) operating under high stiffness, in position control mode, was used to insert a peg into a series of holes. The speed of the robot was set to about 0.35 m/s (i.e., 35% of its maximum tool speed). Three experiments, Exp. 1 to 3, were conducted; each with slight variations. The coordinates of the holes were determined by registering a world frame to a robot frame using conventional, rigid-body registration and three fiducials for Exp. 1 and 2 and five fiducials for Exp. 3 to obtain $\{R, \tau\}$. After transforming the target locations from world frame to robot frame using $\{R, \tau\}$, uncorrected hole locations and locations corrected by the RRBC method were sent to the robot controller. Insertion of a peg in each target hole was attempted, and a simple Pass/Fail metric was used to determine the effectiveness of the RRBC method. A Pass meant that the robot in position control mode was able to fully insert the peg into the hole (as determined by monitoring the robot's z axis coordinate) with a measured force less than 17 N; otherwise, it was considered a Fail. It was also considered to have failed if the peg was fully inserted but jammed while extracting the peg.

Each of three experiments was repeated at least seven times. Before each experiment, the locations of all holes were re-measured with the robot in compliance mode and the transformation matrix $\{R, \tau\}$ and corrections ε_n were calculated. Then, for each repeat, the insertion test was performed for two transformed, uncorrected and corrected, target locations. A third insertion test was performed using the raw measured positions of the targets. These insertions reflect the time-consuming process of lead-through programming and were nominally expected to always be successful as these were the actual measured positions in the robot coordinate frame. Any failed insertion in this category is attributed to a non-zero noise in robot which affects its repeatability. The performance using these insertions served as a baseline.

The purpose of these experiments was to determine the effect of the RRBC corrected vs. uncorrected position on the peg insertion rate. The main reason for the large number of insertions (7 runs with 88 holes per run) was to check that any improvement is not due to random effects such as noise and drift (see non-zero baseline curve in Fig. 3). The influence of systematic factors such as robot speed or stiffness was not investigated in this study.

4.1   Equipment

In the experiments, a 12.675 mm (0.499 in) diameter peg was used and was rigidly attached to the robot arm (see Fig. 1c). In practice, the pegs would likely not be rigidly mounted to the robot and would likely be held in a gripper. This removes a source of variability encountered in practice which can be either beneficial or detrimental to the insertion task depending on the gripper.

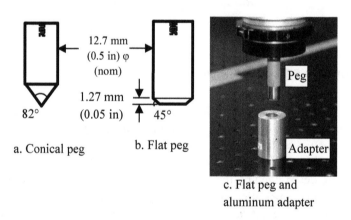

Fig. 1. Conical and flat pegs (a and b, respectively) and aluminum adapter (c).

For Exp. 1, the end of the peg was conical, and for Exp. 2 and 3, the end of the peg was flat with a slight chamfer (see Fig. 1a and b). From observations in Exp. 1, the peg was successfully inserted even though there was a visible initial misalignment of the peg and the hole; however, the "chamfer" of the conical peg allowed the peg to be inserted without exceeding the preset force threshold. After Exp. 1, it was decided that a flat peg may make the distinction between Pass and Fail more definitive, and flat pegs are more typical in practice.

The diameter of the hole allowed for a 0.051 mm (0.002 in) clearance with respect to the peg. The hole was drilled into a 28.575 mm (1–1/8 in) diameter cylindrical piece of aluminum (Fig. 1c) and will be called an "adapter," henceforth. Threaded holes at the bottom of the adapter enabled the attachment of the adapter to the optical plate.

The experiments were conducted using an optical breadboard plate mounted on a rigid aluminum frame. The plate had threaded holes spaced on a grid at 25 mm (0.98 in) intervals. The nominal locations of the holes were taken as ground truth locations. The work volume was essentially 2D with 17 rows by 21 columns of holes (Fig. 2).

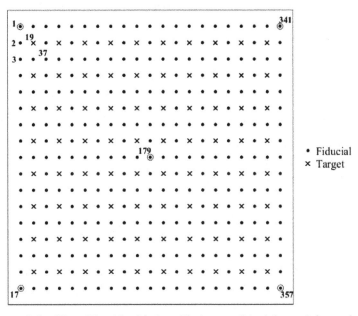

Fig. 2. Layout of the 17 × 21 grid of holes. Circles are fiducials used for registration. Dots represent Fiducials and crosses represent Targets in the figure.

4.2 General Procedure and Concept of Experiments

Given the manufacturing tolerances of the pre-drilled holes, the ground truth locations of the holes were set to the nominal locations of the holes in the world coordinate frame. The locations of all holes, in robot coordinate frame, were obtained by manually inserting the peg into the adapter with the robot in gravity compensation mode, and recording the values of $(x, y, z, \vartheta_x, \vartheta_y \vartheta_z)$, where (x, y, z) is a Cartesian position, and $(\vartheta_x, \vartheta_y \vartheta_z)$ are Euler angles representing the peg orientation. Each position was measured once. These manual measurements were obtained prior to the start of each experiment, and these measurements in robot frame along with the ground truth locations in world frame are required to calculate corrections $\boldsymbol{\varepsilon}_n$ in Eq. (3) for the RRBC method.

Since the experiments described in this paper are essentially 2D, only corrections to the x- and y-coordinates were calculated, and the z-coordinate was unchanged from the raw measured value. No corrections were made to the peg orientations.

As seen in Fig. 2, targets were located in every column and every other row, resulting in a total of 80 targets. Being a research study, the locations of the targets $\{\boldsymbol{T}_Y\}$ were measured beforehand in the robot coordinate frame using manual measurements – in practice, this may not be feasible and target locations are usually unknown. Target locations were treated as unknown positions in the calculations in this study to reflect practice, and the surrounding, manually-obtained fiducial locations were used in the calculations of corrections ε_n. The measured target locations $\{T_Y\}$ were only used to determine the registration error TRE in Eq. (4). The correction to a target location $\varepsilon(T_X)$ was estimated using $N = 8$ corrections $\{\varepsilon\}_N$ of the fiducials closest to the target. The weights w_n in Eq. (2) were based on distances between the target and N nearest fiducials. In our experiments, the same set of weights was used for all targets, but in practical applications, the location of target T_X relative to N nearest fiducials would vary.

The robot controller received $\left(x,\ y,\ z,\ \vartheta_x,\ \vartheta_y \vartheta_z\right)$ as destination poses for all 80 target locations, where $(x,\ y)$ were either the raw, transformed uncorrected, or transformed corrected Cartesian positions, and $\left(\vartheta_x,\ \vartheta_y \vartheta_z\right)$ were either "Original" angles (raw measured values for a given position) or "Fixed" angles. The Fixed angles, $\overline{\vartheta}_x$ and $\overline{\vartheta}_y$, were simply the average of all 357 raw angles for ϑ_x and ϑ_y, respectively, where ϑ_x and ϑ_y determined the perpendicularity of the peg to the table. ϑ_z defined the rotation about the centerline of the peg which was irrelevant in our setup as we used symmetric, cylindrical peg.

A summary of the parameters used in the three experiments is given in Table 1. As noted in Table 1, each experiment consisted of either 7 or 12 runs. A run involved insertion of the peg into 80 hole locations.

Table 1. Summary of parameters in experiments.

Exp. #	# of runs	Peg type	D_p, Peg diameter mm (in)	D_h, Hole diameter mm (in)	$\Delta = D_h - D_p$ mm	Angles $(\vartheta_x, \vartheta_y)$	# of fiducials for regular registration
1	7	Conical	12.675 (0.499)	12.751–12.776 (0.502–0.503)	(0.076–0.101)	Original	3
2	7	Flat	12.675 (0.499)	12.751–12.776 (0.502–0.503)	(0.076–0.101)	Original	3
	7	Flat	12.675 (0.499)	12.751–12.776 (0.502–0.503)	(0.076–0.101)	Fixed	3
3	7	Flat	12.675 (0.499)	12.700–12.725 (0.500–0.501)	(0.025–0.05)	Fsixed	5
	5	Flat	12.675 (0.499)	12.700–12.725 (0.500–0.501)	(0.025–0.05)	Fixed	5

5 Results and Discussion

5.1 Failed Insertions: Uncorrected vs. Corrected Target Locations

For each run, the number of times the peg failed to be inserted was determined, and the ratio of this number to the total number of insertions (80 targets) was calculated and plotted. The plots of the percent Fails for the three experiments are shown in Fig. 3. The data from these plots are summarized in Table 2. The columns labeled Unc/Cor in Table 2 quantify the improvement in performance of insertion task due to the RRBC corrections to the target locations. In Fig. 3 and Table 2, the baseline values are the results of attempted insertions using the raw (recorded in the robot's coordinate frame) positions. As mentioned in Sect. 4, there should be no failures for the baseline insertions, and the observed failures (about 2% to 6%) are likely due to measurement noise as the raw measurements were based on single measurements and to robot drift.

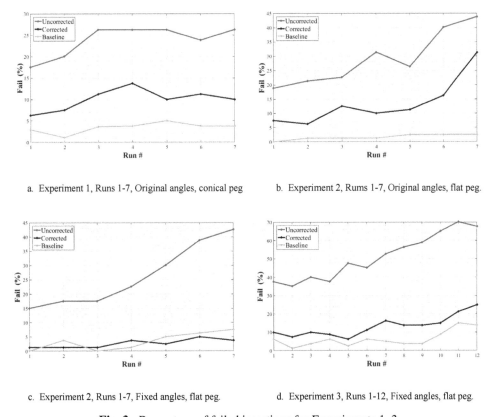

a. Experiment 1, Runs 1-7, Original angles, conical peg   b. Experiment 2, Rums 1-7, Original angles, flat peg.

c. Experiment 2, Runs 1-7, Fixed angles, flat peg.   d. Experiment 3, Runs 1-12, Fixed angles, flat peg.

Fig. 3. Percentage of failed insertions for Experiments 1–3.

Figure 3 shows that the RRBC increases the successful insertion rate as compared to the uncorrected targets locations. The average improvement was a 2.4 times reduction in the failure rate for the insertions with the Original angles (Exp. 1 and 2) and was approximately 11 and 4 times reduction in the failure rate for the Fixed angles, Exp. 2 and 3, respectively. This level of improvement should be analyzed in conjunction with the tolerances reported in Table 1, columns Peg diameter and Hole diameter.

Another trend observed in Fig. 3 is the increase in the number of failures with time, observable even with the baseline trials. Some possible reasons for this increase were thermal effects as the day wore on and turning the robot on/off each day. Therefore, a third experiment was conducted. The first seven runs in Exp. 3 (Runs 1–7) were conducted continuously in one shift without turning the robot off. However, as seen in Fig. 3d,

Table 2. Percentage of Failed Target Insertions.

	Failed insertions							
	Original angles				Fixed angles			
	Baseline (%)	Unc. (%)	Cor. (%)	Unc./Cor.	Base-line (%)	Unc. (%)	Cor. (%)	Unc./Cor.
EXPERIMENT 1								
Avg.	3.4	23.8	10.0	2.4				
Std. Dev.	1.2	3.6	2.5	0.3				
EXPERIMENT 2								
Avg.	1.6	29.1	13.6	2.4	3.4	26.3	2.7	11.0
Std. Dev.	0.9	9.6	8.5	0.7	3.0	11.0	1.5	3.0
EXPERIMENT 3								
Avg.					6.4	51.0	13.2	4.2
Std. Dev.					4.2	12.5	5.6	1.2

Runs 1–7, the number of failures still increased with time despite the robot not being power-cycled. This increase is therefore likely due to drift in the robot hardware, as it also affects the baseline results, which do not depend on the quality of registration. At this time, the only explanation that can be offered for this increased number of failures is that the robot, sensors, and mechanics, drift with the number of performed insertions. The observed drift should not be interpreted as a process of asymptotic approach to steady state but rather as a systematic departure from initial conditions due to the performance of a repeated task. However, even as the repeated use of robot increased the number of failures, the use of the RRBC was always beneficial.

After the initial seven runs in Exp. 3, five additional runs were performed over the next three days. As seen in Fig. 3d, the number of failures did not seem to be leveling off, and after 12 runs the percent of failures was about 70%. It needs to be stressed that the slow drift of robot parameters makes the calculated corrections ε_n in Eq. (3) progressively less accurate and increases the failure rate. Given the tight tolerances of the insertions, this drift need not be large to impact trial performance, and insertions with looser tolerances may not experience such failure growth trends.

5.2 Relationship Between Failures and TRE

In Fig. 4, the normalized failure values for each target are plotted against the differences $\Delta_{TRE}(T_X) = TRE(T_X) - TRE\left(\hat{T}_X\right)$ where $TRE(T_X)$ and $TRE\left(\hat{T}_X\right)$ are the TREs for the uncorrected and corrected targets locations, respectively. The normalized failure value, $\Delta_{Fail,nom}(T_X)$, is the difference between the number of failed insertions for uncorrected target location T_X and the number of failed insertions for corrected target $\hat{T}_X$ divided by the number of runs for that experiment. If $\Delta_{Fail,nom} > 0$ then more failed insertions are observed at uncorrected target location T_X and if $\Delta_{Fail,nom} < 0$ then more failed insertions were observed for target locations corrected by RRBC. The plots are divided into four quadrants:

1. Q-I, upper left: RRBC increases *TRE*, reduces failed insertions
2. Q-II, upper right: RRBC reduces *TRE*, reduces failed insertions
3. Q-III, lower left: RRBC increases *TRE*, increases failed insertions
4. Q-IV, lower right: RRBC reduces *TRE*, increases failed insertions

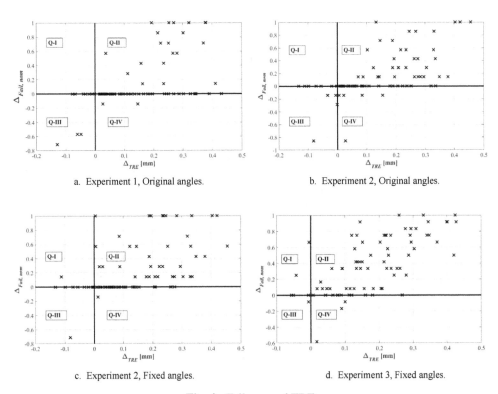

a. Experiment 1, Original angles.   b. Experiment 2, Original angles.

c. Experiment 2, Fixed angles.   d. Experiment 3, Fixed angles.

Fig. 4. Failures and TRE.

As seen in Fig. 4, the RRBC method either did not adversely affect the number of failures, or it reduced number of failures (Quad II). Also, the RRBC method reduced *TRE* for a majority of the targets (targets with $\Delta_{TRE} > 0$).

For Quads I, III, and IV, two possible explanations are offered for why the RRBC method increases *TRE* and/or increases failures. One reason is that the correction for the target is estimated based on the data of neighboring points. As discussed in [6], the data contains both noise and systematic bias. Although the noise is smaller than the bias, it affects the calculated corrections. The other reason is that linear interpolation is used to determine the corrections, and the correction may not be linear.

RMS_T (which is related to *TRE*) was calculated using Eq. (5) and is shown in Fig. 5. As seen in Fig. 5, the RRBC method reduces RMS_T and improves the registration performance. The average reduction of the RMS_T is about 60% when using the RRBC method compared to not using the RRBC.

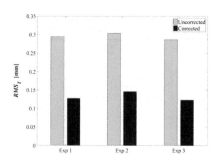

Fig. 5. Comparison of RMS_T for Experiments 1–3.

5.3   Tighter Tolerances

Because of the drift in the failure rate with time as described in Sect. 5.1, a valid comparison of failure rates between the corrected and uncorrected targets locations can only be made for the first runs in Exp. 2 and 3. From Fig. 3c, failure rates for Exp. 2 are 15% and 1% for the first run for the uncorrected and corrected by RRBC target locations, respectively. From Fig. 3d, failure rates for Exp. 3 are 37% and 10% for the first run for the uncorrected and corrected locations, respectively. The higher failure rate for the uncorrected locations contradicts the expectation that the use of five fiducials (Exp. 3) would result in a better registration than the registration with three fiducials (Exp. 2). A reason for the higher rate of failures for the uncorrected locations in Exp. 3 was because the diameter of the hole in the adapter used in Exp. 2 was between 12.751 mm and 12.776 mm (0.502 in and 0.503 in) while the diameters of the holes in the adapters used for Exp. 3 ranged from 12.700 mm to 12. 725 mm (0.500 in to 0.501 in). The diameter of the flat peg was 12.675 mm (0.499 in) at the start of Exp. 2 and 12.662 mm (0.4985 in) after Exp. 3. Thus, the higher failure rate for the uncorrected locations, an increase of about 22%, in Exp. 3 can be attributed to the tighter tolerance – a decrease of 0.025 mm (0.001 in). The tighter tolerance increased the failure percentage from 1% (1st run, Exp. 2) to 10% (1st run, Exp. 3) for the RRBC method.

The efficacy of the RRBC method applied to an insertion task depends strongly on the difference Δ (see Table 1) between the hole and peg diameters and the corrected mean target registration error RMS_T. If the peg diameter D_p is very small relative to the hole diameter D_h, then there is no benefit to using the RRBC method as the insertion will always be successful (unless there is a very large uncorrected error RMS_T comparable with the hole diameter D_h). In the other extreme when $D_p = D_h$, the use of the RRBC method is futile because the insertion will always fail. Thus, the largest benefit of using the RRBC method to improve the insertion task is when the difference Δ is comparable with the corrected RMS_T. In Exp. 1 and 2, the ratio Δ/RMS_T was between 0.536 and

0.842, for Exp. 3 the ratio was between 0.208 and 0.417, based on values of Δ in Table 1 and values of RMS_T shown in Fig. 5.

Another observation is that in Exp. 3, the percent of failed insertions for the uncorrected locations started out at about 37%. Since the baseline value was about 6% (i.e., 6% of the failures is due to noise), 31% of the Fails was due to the registration error. This rate of failure may be unacceptable for many applications. Thus, for insertions where tight tolerances are needed, the RRBC method may have to be used, as only 4% of the failure can be attributed to registration error, as shown in Fig. 3d, Run 1.

6 Conclusions

Peg-in-hole experiments were performed to quantify reduction in the failed insertion rate when the target registration error is reduced by using the RRBC method. No search algorithms or force/torque sensors were used to aid the insertion task. The successful insertion of the peg depended almost entirely on the accuracy of the hole location which, in turn, depends on the quality of world to robot registration.

The RRBC method improves registration by reducing the registration error, RMS_T, by 60% when compared to uncorrected targets locations. This study shows that this level of improvement in positional accuracy led to a 11-fold reduction in the failed insertion rate and a 4-fold reduction for a tighter tolerance.

Manufacturing tasks which require accurate positional data would be more efficient if the registration process was complemented by the application of small corrections to the target locations. The use of the RRBC method may be especially useful for part assembly with tight tolerances where search algorithms are commonly used. Reduced registration error should result in a starting point closer to the desired point, and thus, lead to a shorter search time and smoother assembly. Other tasks such as drilling, welding, or inspection where traditional control techniques based on force/torque feedback are not available, should also benefit from reduced positional error.

7 Disclaimer

Certain commercial equipment are mentioned in this paper to specify the experimental procedure adequately. Such identification is not intended to imply recommendation or endorsement by the National Institute of Standards and Technology, nor does it imply that the equipment is necessarily the best available for the purpose.

References

1. Nevins, J.L., Whitney, D.E.: Computer-controlled assembly. Sci. Am. **238**, 62–74 (1978)
2. Abdullah, M.W., et al.: An approach for peg-in-hole assembling using intuitive search algorithm based on human behavior and carried by sensors guided industrial robot. IFAC-PapersOnLine **48**(3), 1476–1481 (2015)
3. Newman, W.S., Zhao, Y., Pao, Y.-H.: Interpretation of force and moment signals for compliant peg-in-hole assembly. In: International Conference on Robotics & Automation ICRA. IEEE, pp. 571–576 (2001)

4. Yamashita, T., et al. Peg-and-hole task by robot with force sensor: Simulation and experiment. In: Proceedings of the International Conference on IECON (1991)
5. Lin, L.L., et al.: Peg-in-hole assembly under uncertain pose estimation. In: Proceedings of 11th World Congress on Intelligent Control and Automation. Shenyang, China (2014)
6. Franaszek, M., Cheok, G.S.: Improving rigid-body registration based on points affected by bias and noise. In: Ratchev, S. (ed.) Precision Assembly in the Digital Age, pp. 226–234. Springer, Chamonix, France (2018)
7. Bristow, D.A., Tharayil, M., Alleyne, A.G.: A survey of iterative learning control. IEEE Control Syst. Mag. 96–114 (2006)
8. Galetto, M., et al.: Volumetric error compensation for the MScMS-II. In: 12th CIRP Conference on Computer Aided Tolerancing. Elsevier (2013)
9. Cajal, C., et al.: Efficient volumetric error compensation technique for additive manufacturing machines. Rapid Prototyp. J. **22**(1), 2–19 (2016)
10. Huang, S., et al.: Applying high-speed vision sensing to an industrial robot for high-performance position regulation under uncertainties. Sensors **16**(8), 1195 (2016)
11. Zhu, W., et al.: An off-line programming system for robotic drilling in aerospace manufacturing. Int. J. Adv. Manuf. Technol. **68**, 2535–2545 (2013)
12. L.Tingelstad, et al.: Multi-robot assembly of high-performance aerospace components. In: 10th IFAC Symposium on Robot Control, Dubrovnik, Croatia, pp. 670–675 (2012)
13. Cheok, G.S., et al.: Improving automated insertion applications by restoring rigid-body condition in point-based registration. National Institute of Standards and Technology Report NISTIR **8198r1** (2017)
14. Whitney, D.E.: Quasi-static assembly of compliantly supported rigid parts. J. Dyn. Syst. Meas. Contr. **104**(1), 65–77 (1982)
15. Navarro-Gonzalez, J.L., et al.: On-line incremental learning for unknown conditions during assembly operations with industrial robots. Evolving Syst. **6**(2), 101–114 (2015)
16. Jokesch, M., Suchý, J., Winkler, A., Fross, A., Thomas, U.: Generic algorithm for Peg-In-Hole assembly tasks for pin alignments with impedance controlled robots. In: Reis, L., Moreira, A., Lima, P., Montano, L., Muñoz-Martinez, V. (eds.) Robot 2015: Second Iberian Robotics Conference. Advances in Intelligent Systems and Computing, vol. 418, pp. 105–117. Springer, Cham (2016) https://doi.org/10.1007/978-3-319-27149-1_9
17. Abdullah, M.W., et al.: Force/Torque data modeling for contact position estimation in Peg-in-Hole assembling application. In: Proceeding of 4th International Conference on Advances in Mechanics Engineering. MATEC Web of Conferences (2015)
18. Bos, J., Wahrburg, A., Listmann, K.D.: Iteratively learned and temporally scaled force control with application to robotic assembly in unstructured environments. In: IEEE International Conference on Robotics and Automation (ICRA, Singapore, pp. 3000–3007 (2017)
19. Jasim, I.F., Plapper, P.W., Voos, H.: Position identification in force-guided robotic peg-in-hole assembly tasks. In: Conference on Assembly Technologies and Systems, Procedia CIRP. Elsevier (2014)
20. Xu, Y., Hu, Y., Hu, L.: Precision peg-in-hole assembly strategy using force-guided robot. In: 3rd International Conference on Machinery, Materials and Information Technology Applications (ICMMITA), Qingdao, China (2015)
21. Song, H.C., Kim, Y.L., Song, J.B.: Guidance algorithm for complex-shape peg-in-hole strategy based on geometrical information and force control. Adv. Robot. **30**(8), 552–563 (2016)
22. Liu, Z., et al.: Laser tracker based robotic assembly system for large scale peg-hole parts. In: Proceedings of 4th IEEE Annual International Conference on Cyber Technology in Automation, Control, and Intelligent Systems, Hong Kong, China (2014)
23. Polverini, M.P., et al.: Sensorless and constraint based peg-in-hole task execution with a dual-arm robot. In: ICRA, pp. 415–420. IEEE, Stockholm, Sweden (2016)

24. Park, H., et al.: Compliance-based robotic peg-in-hole assembly strategy without force feedback. IEEE Trans. Ind. Electron. **64**(8), 6299–6309 (2017)
25. Luo, R.C., Chang, A., Li, C.: A novel peg-in-hole approach based on geometrical analysis for inclined uncertainty. In: IEEE International Conference on Advanced Intelligent Mechatronics (AIM), Munich, Germany. pp. 891–896 (2017)
26. Su, J.H., et al.: Study on dual peg-in-hole insertion using of constraints formed in the environment. Ind. Rob. Int. J. **44**(6), 730–740 (2017)
27. Sharma, K., Shirwalkar, V., Pal, P.K.: Peg-in-hole search using convex optimization techniques. Ind. Rob. Int. J. **44**(5), 618–628 (2017)
28. Wyk, K.V., et al., Comparative peg-in-hole testing of a force-based manipulation controlled robotic hand. IEEE Trans. Rob. (2018)
29. Arun, K.S., Huang, T.S., Blostein, S.D.: Least-squares fitting of two 3-D point sets. IEEE Trans. PAMI **9**(5), 698–700 (1987)
30. Fitzpatrick, J.M., West, J.B., Maurer, C.R.: Predicting error in rigid-body point-based registration. IEEE Trans. Med. Imaging **17**(5), 694–702 (1998)

Automated Information Supply of Worker Guidance Systems in Smart Assembly Environment

Gerhard Reisinger[1,2]([⊠]), Philipp Hold[1,2], and Wilfried Sihn[1,2]

[1] Fraunhofer Austria Research GmbH, Theresianumgasse 7, 1040 Vienna, Austria
{gerhard.reisinger,philipp.hold,wilfried.sihn}@fraunhofer.at
[2] Institute of Management Sciences, Vienna University of Technology,
Theresianumgasse 27, 1040 Vienna, Austria

Abstract. The global megatrends of digitization and individualization substantially affect manufacturing enterprises. Assembly workers are exposed to increased process complexity resulting in physical and cognitive workload. Worker guidance systems (WGS) are used to overcome this challenge through output of information regarding what should be done, how it should be done and why it should be done. An unsolved scientific challenge in this context is efficient information supply of WGS. Information such as worker's instruction texts, pictures or 3D representations are created by employees of the work preparation department and transferred to the WGS. Manual information supply is a time-consuming and complex process, which requires a high (non-value-adding) effort as well as comprehensive knowledge in handling 3D CAD modelling and software programming. This paper presents a novel approach to reduce the required manual effort in information supply process. A knowledge-based model is proposed that enables an automated information supply of WGS in smart assembly environment by means of algorithms and self-learning expert systems, which pursues a holistic and consistent approach without media breaks. The automated approach assists employees of work preparation department, which means they can concentrate on their essential core competencies instead of being busy, for example, creating assembly plans, instruction texts or pictures for individual WGS. Finally, the technical implementation as a software-based proof-of-concept demonstrator and sub-sequent integration into the IT environment of TU Wien Pilot Factory Industry 4.0 is outlined.

Keywords: Digital assistance · Worker guidance · Smart assembly ·
Human-machine interaction · Assembly planning · Algorithms · Pilot factory

1 Introduction: Background and Definitions

Production systems and especially assembly systems in developed industrial countries are faced with the challenge of tackling rising product and process complexity in terms of individualized customer needs as well as productivity at the same time [1]. This is particularly true in the area of precision assembly, where workers must perform manual assembly processes precisely, cost-effectively and with high quality. By networked data and modern forms of information and communication technologies with physical production processes, so called cyber-physical production systems (CPPS) will become real. Cyber-physical systems are described as a combination of physical objects ("physical") and an embedded digital system ("cyber"). This embedded system collects and processes data and interacts with surrounding environment via actuators. By integrating equipment with CPS characteristics into an assembly environment, cyber-physical assembly systems (CPAS) are established [2].

In addition to cost pressure in global competition, more frequent changes of work contents as a result of higher product variance, reduced lot sizes (lot size 1 production) and shortened product life-cycles make it more difficult for operators to build-up task routine [2]. This leads to increasing cognitive workload of operators and increasing risk of human errors and product quality problems [3].

Worker guidance systems (WGS), connected tools and systems in the work environment collaborating with human workers, have been used already in the past e.g. to automate certain tasks for improved production and assembly as well as to relief operators from rough and strenuous working conditions [4, 5]. In this way, information provision was used to deliver operators with instructions and details required to successfully fulfil manually executed tasks [6]. Today CPPS and CPAS are characterized by increasing digitalization and automated information flow. Thereby information systems control technical processes (e.g. plants, tools) and orchestrate the interaction with operators on the shop floor in a holistic way [7].

One of the central challenges here is to provide various decentralized database systems with up-to-date information and control commands at all times. Connection and interoperation with higher-level planning and control systems is seen by industry as a successful solution. However, even higher-level planning and control systems show a significant bottleneck of information supply and their granularity in order to orchestrate work systems and to illustrate operators the right information at the right time in the right quality regarding the right work task [8]. In order to enable a comprehensive use of intelligently networked CPPS and CPAS, work preparation departments are confronted with the challenge of incorporating missing and supplementary information into corresponding systems. Thereby the manual effort and waste of (human) resources is relatively high [9].

Taking the above discussion into account, this paper presents a design concept and a software-based implementation of an automatic information supply of WGS as an interface between construction, planning and control systems as well as decentral information databases of various production and assembly technologies.

2 Related Work

2.1 Worker Guidance Systems

Digital assistance systems (DAS) are used within a CPAS as interface between humans and technical systems [10]. The primary goal is to provide optimal worker support to increase productivity, reduce execution times, minimize error rates and enable end-to-end traceability [11]. DAS comprise basic functions including documentation of process data, monitoring of processes, decision support and information output [12]. For information output, the term "worker information systems" (WIS) is used in literature of production management. WIS provide information such as step-by-step assembly instructions, security hints or warnings of potential errors without the need of printed paper media [13].

For step-by-step guidance of workers through assembly processes, also the term worker guidance, respectively WGS is used. WGS allow workers to overcome difficulties in performing complex precision assembly processes and reduce cognitive burden in assembling small lot sizes of ever increasing product variants [14]. The most significant difference between WIS and WGS is the feedback loop: WIS only supply information assistance according to a given set of rules, while WGS additionally support the input of information and data manually through graphical user interfaces or automatically through different sensors [15]. Aehnelt et al. stated that "information assistance in form of guiding can be understood as an informal way of mediating and learning facts (what), procedures (how) and concepts (why) required for a specific assembly task". Therefore a worker has to remember, understand and apply the information to execute the assembly task [16].

Lušić et al. differ between static and dynamic provision of information as well as real versus virtual information. Text and pictures are time-invariant and therefore static information, leading to additional cognitive load of the worker. Dynamic provision of information, e.g. videos or 3D animations lead to less cognitive load, but the duration of these have to be adapted to individual worker's needs. Real information require real objects for their creation and include recorded photos or videos, while virtual information can be derived digitally e.g. using a 3D Computer-Aided Design (CAD) software [17].

2.2 Information Supply of WGS

The information provided by WGS can be in form of texts, pictures, videos, virtual 3D objects or simple light signals and must be prepared, programmed and transferred to databases or storage media of an individual target system prior to production [18]. This preparation process is very time consuming and usually requires a specialized knowledge in programming and 3D CAD modelling [19]. In case of a small or single lot size production, the described preparation process has to be carried out often and represents a significant cost factor, which furthermore prevents an efficient usage of WGS [20]. To cope with the aforementioned challenges, different approaches have been presented in recent studies, which can be clustered into following categories:

(i) automation of assembly sequence planning [21], (ii) automation of instruction information creation [22], (iii) automated entry of created information into target systems [23] and (iv) support the human assembly planner where automation is not possible [24]. These four categories are described in detail:

(i) **Automation of assembly sequence planning:** Since the early 1990s, various algorithms and heuristics have been developed to automatically derive feasible assembly sequences of a product variant from product data or 3D CAD models, e.g. [25, 26]. This research area evolved with more computing power: The original approaches considering a simple listing of assembly sequences were developed successively, so that modern solutions allow an automatic feasibility study with regard to stability and available space at the joining position of each part [27], but also the average required assembly time can be calculated [28]. All of the aforementioned approaches relate to the general assembly planning process, but are not designed to create, process or distribute information for WGS.

(ii) Automation of instruction information creation: Mader et al. describe an approach to be able to automatically create work instructions in textual form and as pictures based on geometry and workstation data [22]. More recent work describes the preparation of videos and assembly animations using virtual prototypes [13]. Sääski et al. describe a concept to automatically create 3D objects for Augmented Reality (AR) worker guidance. Hereby the focus has been set on the integration of a wide variety of information systems as consistently as possible [29]. The created information has to be entered manually into databases of target WGS using a graphical user interface (GUI). This step is also associated with high manual workload during preparation phase.

(iii) Automated entry of created information into target systems:

To ensure that assembly workers on shop floor can use the created instruction information, it must be entered into the database of WGS through software interfaces. Müller et al. describe an exchange of information between agents and modules. While a WGS can be seen as a module, an "agent acts as a mediator or coordinator" between these modules and the virtual assembly planning environment [23]. A similar approach is pursued by Fischer et al., who describe the data flow between virtual assembly planning and the WIS database. Data is exported from the planning environment, translated into the desired target structure via an associative array and can be imported into the WGS [30].

(iv) Support the human assembly planner where automation is not possible: Zauner et al. describe the use of domain specific wizards, so-called "authoring wizards" in order to create visual information in a user-friendly way and without any programming knowledge [31]. Through a GUI, an assembly planner defines the required assembly information, such as assembly sequence, parameters and required tools [32]. The described approach is widely used in context of AR solutions and is applied in research and industry [33]. Despite support by means of authoring software, high manual effort remains in creation and entry of the information for each product variant. In addition, these software packages are usually limited to AR worker guidance and are designed for specific output devices or an individual WGS solution. Sensors for detecting depth information and movements enable teach-in of work instruction content at the assembly stations directly [34]. Funk et al. have developed a projection based WGS, which allows a complex assembly process to be trained by experienced workers. During the assembly process, the system recognizes the required part containers as well as joining positions and derives all the information required for projection-based worker guidance automatically. However, the authors themselves point out that this system is not mature and further development must be made, e.g. optimization of workpiece detection [20]. In addition, such a system cannot be used in lot size 1 production, since the entire assembly process has to be taught in with at least one piece.

In summary, the state of the art includes partial solutions, which favour a reduction of expenses in the supply of instructional information e.g. through automation of preparation tasks or support of human assembly planners. However, the lack of a holistic and consistent approach in order to achieve a fully configured WGS even at complex products and small lot size is evident. In this paper, we present an approach for the automated information supply of worker guidance systems, which helps to significantly reduce content creation efforts and to relieve assembly planning staff, especially in smart assembly environments. The approach differs from the state of the art by a continuous processing chain from product development to the output of digital content information on assembly shop floor. The activities of information supply of worker guidance systems are divided between human and computer according to their respective strengths and weaknesses. While human planners contribute product-, process- and resource-knowledge by means of optimally designed input interfaces, a computer takes over time-consuming creation activities for instruction elements, e.g. texts, pictures or optimised 3D models for AR. In order to further relieve assembly planners, they are supported by machine learning at the time-consuming task of planning assembly sequences. Case-based reasoning is used to derive assembly sequences for the new product variant based on earlier planning knowledge of similar product variants automatically. The following sections describe a conceptual design for an automated information supply and the technical implementation in a test environment.

3   Conceptual Design for Automated Information Supply

3.1   Automated Information Supply of WGS

In the context of WGS, the authors propose a definition for the term "information supply" as combination of "information creation" and "information entry". Hereby, the task of information creation contains the following subtasks:

- Definition of assembly plan, including assembly sequence, relevant parts and subassemblies as well as tools to be used.
- Derivation of virtual instructional information, including screenshots (static), animations (dynamic), textual descriptions (static) as well as 3D data for worker guidance through AR (static or dynamic).
- Creation of real instructional information, including photos (static), videos (dynamic) as well as recorded – e.g. spoken – textual descriptions (dynamic).

In order to provide instructions to workers on the shop floor, the instructional information has to be transferred into a database or file system of the target WGS. Most WGS provide a backend editor or a similar GUI, which can be used by assembly planners in order to convert created information to the required format and to enter it into the database. The information supply process should be carried out for each individual product variant and thus leads to high manual effort and costs for small lot sizes. This paper proposes a holistic knowledge-based approach, which includes entire information supply process, taking over routine tasks through algorithms and supporting assembly planners with a self-learning expert system. The result is a division of tasks between human and algorithm. While humans provide their domain and process knowledge, algorithms take repetitive tasks such as derivation of virtual information as well as transfer of created instruction information to databases.

Figure 1 illustrates the approach and describes how data is processed so that a 3D CAD model of a product variant can be used to adequately supply information to a WGS. The blue boxes symbolise automated algorithms, while green boxes designate GUIs for interaction with human planners. The approach builds upon earlier developments by Reisinger et al. [35] and has been extended by additional concepts to further reduce manual effort.

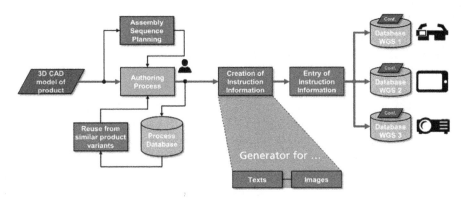

Fig. 1. Proposed approach for automated information supply of WGS

3.2 Authoring Process

In first step "Authoring Process", human assembly planners define assembly sequence ("what has to be done") and work methods ("how is it done"). An authoring tool with 3D user interface is provided and visualizes the 3D CAD model of current product variant. By selecting parts and subassemblies, assembly steps as well as an assembly sequence are defined. Individual steps can be enriched with additional information, e.g. required tools, screwing torques or parts. Furthermore, the assembly planner specifies intermediate steps that cannot be automatically extracted from a 3D CAD model, e.g. missing parts like springs or pipes. During this authoring process, the assembly planner is assisted through various functions, e.g. suggestion of correct torque depending on dimension of the screw. In summary, the main purpose of the authoring process is to enter process- and resource-knowledge of human assembly planners in an efficient way. Previous work in literature describing similar authoring tools – e.g. [31, 36] or [24] – show a significant weakness: The authoring process has to be conducted for each product variant, even in case of similar 3D product models. This leads to a high manual effort for assembly planners and thus a low efficiency is resulting.

3.3 Assisting Assembly Planning

To deal with the described weakness of conventional authoring processes, additional system features in planning new product variants are considered:

- **Case-Based Assembly Planning (CBAP):** In advance to the authoring process, similarity between the new product variant and earlier planned product variants is measured. In case of high similarity, the assembly plan from similar earlier product variant is reused for the new product variant. This is done through a rigorous allocation of parts and subassemblies of the new product variant by comparing more than 30 geometrical features. The computer reasoning method "Case-based Reasoning" [37] has been adapted for assembly planning. This is part of a self-learning expert system which assists human assembly planners. At the beginning of the authoring process, the assembly planner receives information, which earlier product variant was selected as case, a list of parts the algorithm was able to allocate automatically as well as a list of parts the algorithm was not able to allocate automatically. The human assembly planner can build upon the pre-generated process plan and allocate missing parts and subassemblies, leading to a significant saving of manual effort.
- **Assembly Sequence Planning (ASP):** If CBAP is not possible, multiple methods from ASP are used to propose the optimal assembly sequence for parts and subassemblies of new products [38]. The number of possible assembly sequences increases with the number of parts exponentially. Thus, even for a simple product, millions of different assembly sequences are possible, whereby 25–40% can be eliminated by reason of geometrical constraints. Including criteria such as stability and handling, only 5–15% of these remain as feasible assembly sequences. By evaluating remaining possibilities with regard to the required assembly time, a final assembly sequence can be selected and proposed to the assembly planner [21].

3.4   Creation of Instruction Information

Creating virtual instruction information for individual assembly steps is conducted automatically and requires the following domain knowledge elements:

- Product knowledge can be derived from 3D CAD model, e.g. geometries, structure of the product, required special treatment of parts or options like colours and material. Additional data can be gathered from external sources like Product Lifecycle Management (PLM) or Enterprise Resource Planning (ERP) systems.
- Process knowledge is entered manually by the assembly planner using the authoring tool. The assembly planner can use his/her experience concerning optimal sequence, required intermediate steps as well as evaluating, if the proposed process is realistic for assembly.
- Resource knowledge is provided by the assembly planner, e.g. which tools, measuring instruments and additional equipment to be used.

The textual description of individual assembly steps is automatically derived using previously manually defined text modules and contains information about assembled components, the operation and needed tools. Defined colour codes enable a differentiation of small and big parts, standard parts as well as a differentiation of tools.

The pictures for worker guidance are automatically derived as CAD screenshots for each assembly step and relevant components are highlighted in colour. To ensure optimal visibility of every component, pictures are derived from two different perspectives: A fixed position and viewing angle, in order to provide overall orientation to the assembly worker, as well as a picture from a view perspective previously defined in the "Authoring Process". To guarantee a high standardization of instructions, the colour coding of the pictures is the same that is used for the textual descriptions.

3.5 Entry of Instruction Information

The required information for worker guidance has to be prepared and entered into a database or file system of the target WGS so that worker guidance information on shop floor can be used to support assembly workers. The data structure of the database and file system is defined differently for each WGS and no standardized interface for entering worker information exists. At this point, the principle of post-processing is taken from Computer-Aided Manufacturing (CAM) information chain [39] and we propose the following definition analogously for WGS: A post-processor in context of worker guidance systems is an algorithm for automated translation of prepared worker information (assembly sequence, texts, pictures) and entry of these information into a database or file system of a target WGS. A post-processor is developed once for each target system and has to be adapted in regard to new data structures in case of updates. The development requires direct writing access to the respective database or file system as well as a good knowledge of data structure of the WGS.

4 Technical Implementation

In order to make the concept applicable, it was implemented as a software-based proof-of-concept demonstrator (PoCD) and integrated in the laboratory of TU Wien Pilot Factory Industry 4.0 (PFI40) with existing information systems and WGS.

4.1 Software-Based Proof-of-Concept Demonstrator

During implementation, individual modules have been developed using suitable programming languages and existing frameworks, e.g. authoring tool, generator for texts and pictures as well as post-processors. In order to ensure an efficient planning process, attention was paid to easy maintainability of the data structures as well as a high user-friendliness of the GUI.

Figure 2 presents the GUI of the developed authoring tool, which is used by the assembly planner to enter process- and resource-related information. The open source software "FreeCAD" is used to provide a 3D environment. FreeCAD and authoring window together form the authoring tool. Through python scripts as well as a provided Application Programming Interface (API), FreeCAD is able to communicate with the developed authoring window, which is displayed at the right side of above screenshot. The parts and components of the product variant are selected by the assembly planner for each assembly step through a list or by directly clicking parts and components in 3D environment. Screws are automatically identified by part name and appropriate screwing parameters such as torque, depth and pitch are suggested.

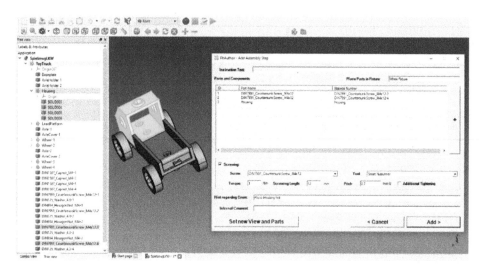

Fig. 2. GUI of developed authoring tool, using FreeCAD as 3D environment

Once the authoring process is completed and the information is released, it is passed to a virtual machine connected to local area network (LAN) via a Representational State Transfer (REST) API. The virtual machine acts as a container for various algorithms running automatically as well as a SQL database for data storage. The worker information is automatically processed as described in previous chapter. The automatic generation of instruction texts is carried out by algorithms, which have been implemented in Java Programming Language. The creation of instruction pictures is done by a self-developed media generator. Because of high resource usage, the media generator is implemented as a cloud service and can be controlled via a REST API. The assembly plan in XML form (created by authoring tool) and a 3D CAD model of the product variant to be assembled serve as input for the media generator. The output are generated pictures from different perspectives, which are automatically downloaded after the creation process is completed.

4.2   Integration in TU Wien Pilot Factory Industry 4.0

The developed software-based PoCD has been integrated into PFI40 and linked with existing information systems and WGS. The PFI40 is located in Vienna (Austria) and "serves both as a research platform and a teaching and training environment with regard to a human-centered cyber-physical production system" for lot size 1 production [40]. It combines development and testing of prototypes (Pilot Factory), demonstration and communication of findings (Demonstration Factory) and transfer of knowledge to students and course participants from practice (Learning Factory). The production of a plastic 3D printer is demonstrated in a realistic environment of approximately 900 m^2 space. Industrial machines, 3D printers, logistics systems and a cyber-physical assembly line are available [41]. The assembly line of PFI40 consists of four cyber-physical assembly stations, which in turn consist of various assistance systems, including visual worker guidance, an intelligent screwing system as well as collaborative robots.

Figure 3 shows the integration of the software based PoCD in the IT landscape of PFI40 [42]. Red coloured elements represent already existing systems of the PFI40 and contain an ERP system, a 3D CAD environment as well as two WGS of different manufacturers. The green ellipse indicates the virtual machine and contains a central database of the PoCD, implemented algorithms as well as passive and active interfaces for communication with the system environment. The authoring window is not part of the virtual machine but is executed on desktop computer of the assembly planner and communicates with 3D CAD environment FreeCAD and via a REST API with the virtual machine. After successful planning and preparation of the worker information, it is transferred towards two target WGS "Armbruster ELAM" [43] and "Sarissa QA" [44] using developed post-processors. Precision assembly staff on shop floor is now able to use these instructions for step-by-step worker guidance.

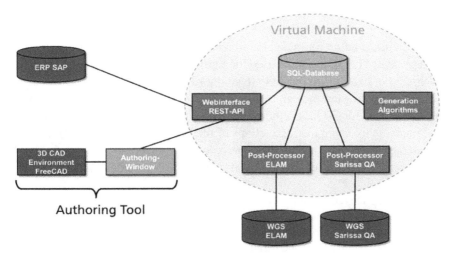

Fig. 3. Integration of software based PoCD in PFI40 IT landscape (Color figure online)

5 Conclusion and Future Research Agenda

5.1 Conclusion and Recommendations

This paper presents a novel knowledge-based approach to reduce the required manual effort in information supply process by dividing preparation tasks between human and machine. This involves the use of pre-defined rule-based algorithms for generating instructions, self-learning expert systems for transferring assembly plans to similar product variants and agent-based interfaces (post-processors) for automated entry of created information. The development of the proposed post-processors requires intensive knowledge of the data structure of the target WGS. Therefore, we recommend that the manufacturer of WGS should do the development of the post-processors.

The approach has been implemented as a software-based PoCD, integrated into IT environment of PFI40 and is used for information supply of two WGS of a cyber-physical assembly line. Previous findings show that preparation efforts per product variant could be reduced significantly and the system works efficiently even if there are computationally intensive algorithms. A comprehensive user study with both experienced and inexperienced participants is planned in order to measure actual effects, such as a reduction in planning times or an increase in worker satisfaction.

5.2 Limitation and Outlook

The approach presented in this paper is limited to providing information to WGS for assembly activities. Due to a recognizable evolution of conventional assembly systems into cyber-physical assembly systems, we recommend further research in the field of automated information supply of these environments. In addition to WGS, this also includes creation and linking of configuration sets for devices, tools, machines and measuring equipment. A further starting point for development is the expansion of the field of application so that, in addition to assembly activities, WGS can also be automatically supplied with information for manual maintenance, set-up and servicing processes. The approach presented here can also be used for mutual (reciprocal) learning between human and machine. For example, a machine (e.g. algorithm) can learn from human (e.g. process planner) how to plan precision assembly processes and how to create associated worker instructions for WGS. Furthermore, a precision assembly worker can also learn from the machine by using the instructions of the WGS [45]. A transfer and adaptation of the presented approach towards the creation of CNC machine tool code is also worth researching and would make work preparation of cutting machine tools more efficient.

Acknowledgment. This research is funded by the Austrian Research Promotion Agency (FFG) in the project MMAssist II, grant no. 858623 as well as in the project TAI-VW, grant no. 870667. The TU Wien Pilot Factory Industry 4.0 is also partly funded by the Austrian Research Promotion Agency (FFG) and several private industrial companies.

References

1. Dombrowski, U., Wagner, T., Riechel, C.: Analyse eines Konzepts zur Montageplanung auf Basis cyber-physischer Systemmodule. ZWF **108**(5), 344–348 (2013)
2. Hold, P., Ranz, F., Sihn, W., Hummel, V.: Planning operator support in cyber-physical assembly systems. IFAC PapersOnLine **49**, 60–65 (2016)
3. Bubb, H.: Human reliability: a key to improved quality in manufacturing. Hum. Factors Man. (2005). https://doi.org/10.1002/hfm.20032
4. Krüger, J., Lien, T.K., Verl, A.: Cooperation of human and machines in assembly lines. CIRP Ann. Manuf. Technol. (2009). https://doi.org/10.1016/j.cirp.2009.09.009
5. Drust, M., Dietz, T., Pott, A., Verl, A.: Production assistants: the rob@work family. In: IEEE ISR 2013 (2013)
6. Wiesbeck, M.: Struktur zur Repräsentation von Montagesequenzen für die situationsorientierte Werkerführung. Dissertation (2013)
7. Ansari, F., Hold, P., Sihn, W.: Human-centered cyber physical production system: how does Industry 4.0 impact on decision-making tasks? In: IEEE TEMSCON 2018 (2018)

8. Johansson, P.E.C., Malmsköld, L., Fast-Berglund, Å., Moestam, L.: Enhancing future assembly information systems – putting theory into practice. Procedia Manuf. (2018). https://doi.org/10.1016/j.promfg.2018.10.088

9. Wang, X., Ong, S.K., Nee, A.Y.C.: A comprehensive survey of augmented reality assembly research. Adv. Manuf. **4**, 1–22 (2016)

10. Hold, P., Erol, S., Reisinger, G., Sihn, W.: Planning and evaluation of digital assistance systems. Procedia Manuf. **9**, 143–150 (2017)

11. Romero, D., et al.: Towards an operator 4.0 typology. A human-centric perspective on the fourth industrial revoluation technologies. In: 46th International Conference on Computers & Industrial Engineering 2016 (2016)

12. Keller, T., Bayer, C., Bausch, P., Metternich, J.: Benefit evaluation of digital assistance systems for assembly workstations. Procedia CIRP **81**, 441–446 (2019)

13. Fischer, C., Bönig, J., Franke, J., Lušić, M., Hornfeck, R.: Worker information system to support during complex and exhausting assembly of high-voltage harness. In: 5th International Electric Drives Production Conference (EDPC) (2015)

14. Galaske, N., Anderl, R.: Approach for the development of an adaptive worker assistance system based on an individualized profile data model. In: Schlick, C., Trzcieliński, S. (eds.) Advances in Ergonomics of Manufacturing: Managing the Enterprise of the Future. Advances in Intelligent Systems and Computing, vol. 490, pp. 543–556. Springer, Cham (2016). https://doi.org/10.1007/978-3-319-41697-7_47

15. Teubner, S., Merkel, L., Reinhart, G., Hagemann, F., Intra, C.: Improving worker information - proposal of a dynamic and individual concept. In: International Conference on Competitive Manufacturing, COMA 2019 (2019)

16. Aehnelt, M., Bader, S.: From information assistance to cognitive automation: a smart assembly use case. In: Duval, B., van den Herik, J., Loiseau, S., Filipe, J. (eds.) ICAART 2015. LNCS (LNAI), vol. 9494, pp. 207–222. Springer, Cham (2015). https://doi.org/10.1007/978-3-319-27947-3_11

17. Lušić, M., Fischer, C., Bönig, J., Hornfeck, R., Franke, J.: Worker information systems. State of the art and guideline for selection under consideration of company specific boundary conditions. Procedia CIRP (2016). https://doi.org/10.1016/j.procir.2015.12.003

18. Hold, P., Ranz, F., Sihn, W.: Konzeption eines MTM-basierten Bewertungsmodells für digitalen Assistenzbedarf in der cyber-physischen Montage. Megatrend Digitalisierung - Potenziale der Arbeits- und Betriebsorganisation – Berlin (2016). https://doi.org/10.15358/9783800645466

19. Wolfartsberger, J., Zenisek, J., Silmbroth, M., Sievi, C.: Towards an augmented reality and sensor-based assistive system for assembly tasks. In: Proceedings of the 10th International Conference on PErvasive Technologies Related to Assistive Environments, PETRA 2017, pp. 230–231 (2017)

20. Funk, M., Lischke, L., Mayer, S., Shirazi, A.S., Schmidt, A.: Teach Me How! Interactive Assembly Instructions Using Demonstration and In-Situ Projection. In: Huber, J., Shilkrot, R., Maes, P., Nanayakkara, S. (eds.) Assistive Augmentation, pp. 49–73. Springer, Singapore (2018). https://doi.org/10.1007/978-981-10-6404-3_4

21. Bahubalendruni, M.R.A., Biswal, B.B.: A review on assembly sequence generation and its automation. Proc. Inst. Mech. Eng. Part C: J. Mech. Eng. Sci. (2016). https://doi.org/10.1177/0954406215584633

22. Mader, S., Urban, B.: Creating instructional content for augmented reality based on controlled natural language concepts. In: International Conference on Artificial Reality and Telexistence (ICAT) (2010)

23. Müller, R., Vette, M., Hörauf, L., Speicher, C.: Consistent data usage and exchange between virtuality and reality to manage complexities in assembly planning. Procedia CIRP (2016). https://doi.org/10.1016/j.procir.2016.02.126

24. Li, B., Dong, Q., Dong, J., Wang, J., Li, W., Li, S.: Instruction manual for product assembly process based on augmented visualization. In: Chinese Automation Congress (CAC) 2018 (2018)
25. Homem de Mello, L.S., Sanderson, A.C.: A correct and complete algorithm for the generation of mechanical assembly sequences. IEEE Trans. Robot. Autom. (1991). https://doi.org/10.1109/70.75905
26. Hadj, R.B., Belhadj, I., Trigui, M., Aifaoui, N.: Assembly sequences plan generation using features simplification. Adv. Eng. Softw. (2018). https://doi.org/10.1016/j.advengsoft.2018.01.008
27. Bedeoui, A., Benhadj, R., Trigui, M., Aifaoui, N.: Assembly plans generation of complex machines based on the stability concept. Procedia CIRP **70**, 66–71 (2018)
28. Pintzos, G., Matsas, M., Triantafyllou, C., Papakostas, N., Chryssolouris, G.: An integrated approach to the planning of manual assembly lines. In: ASME 2015 International Mechanical Engineering Congress and Exposition (2015). https://doi.org/10.1115/IMECE2015-52962
29. Sääski, J., Salonen, T., Hakkarainen, M., Siltanen, S., Woodward, C., Lempiäinen, J.: Integration of design and assembly using augmented reality. In: Ratchev, S., Koelemeijer, S. (eds.) IPAS 2008. IIFIP, vol. 260, pp. 395–404. Springer, Boston (2008). https://doi.org/10.1007/978-0-387-77405-3_39
30. Fischer, C., Lušić, M., Bönig, J., Hornfeck, R., Franke, J.: Webbasierte Werkerinformationssysteme. Datenaufbereitung und -darstellung für die Werkerführung im Global Cross Enterprise Engineering (2014)
31. Zauner, J., Haller, M., Brandl, A., Hartmann, W.: Authoring of a mixed reality assembly instructor for hierarchical structures. In: The Second IEEE and ACM International Symposium on Mixed and Augmented Reality 2003 (2003)
32. Knöpfle, C., Weidenhausen, J., Chauvigne, L., Stock, I.: Template based authoring for AR based service scenarios. In: IEEE Virtual Reality 2005 (2005)
33. Roberto, R.A., Lima, J.P., Mota, R.C., Teichrieb, V.: Authoring tools for augmented reality: an analysis and classification of content design tools. In: Marcus, A. (ed.) DUXU 2016. LNCS, vol. 9748, pp. 237–248. Springer, Cham (2016). https://doi.org/10.1007/978-3-319-40406-6_22
34. Bannat, A.: Ein Assistenzsystem zur digitalen Werker-Unterstützung in der industriellen Produktion. Dissertation (2014)
35. Reisinger, G., Komenda, T., Hold, P., Sihn, W.: A concept towards automated data-driven reconfiguration of digital assistance systems. Procedia Manuf. **23**, 99–104 (2018)
36. Franke, J., Risch, F.: Effiziente Erstellung, Distribution und Rückmeldung von Werkerinformationen in der Montage. ZWF **104**(10), 822–826 (2009)
37. Aamodt, A., Plaza, E.: Case-based reasoning: foundational issues, methodological variations, and system approaches. AI Commun. **7**, 39–59 (1994)
38. Sunil, D.T., Devadasan, S.R., Thilak, V.M.M., Vinod, M.: Computer aided design-based assembly sequence planning: a next stage in agile manufacturing research. Int. J. Business Excellence **16**(4), 454–477 (2018)
39. Xu, X.W., He, Q.: Striving for a total integration of CAD, CAPP, CAM and CNC. Robot. Comput.-Integr. Manuf. **20**, 101–109 (2003)
40. Abele, E., et al.: Learning factories for future oriented research and education in manufacturing. CIRP Ann. (2017). https://doi.org/10.1016/j.cirp.2017.05.005
41. Hennig, M., Reisinger, G., Trautner, T., Hold, P., Gerhard, D., Mazak, A.: TU Wien pilot factory industry 4.0. Procedia Manuf. (2019). https://doi.org/10.1016/j.promfg.2019.03.032
42. Erol, S., Jäger, A., Hold, P., Ott, K., Sihn, W.: Tangible industry 4.0. a scenario-based approach to learning for the future of production. Procedia CIRP (2016). https://doi.org/10.1016/j.procir.2016.03.162

43. Armbruster Engineering: ELAM-Software (2020). http://www.armbruster.de/. Accessed 28 Jan 2020
44. Sarissa: Quality Assist (2020). https://www.sarissa.de/. Accessed 28 Jan 2020
45. Ansari, F., Hold, P., Mayrhofer, W., Schlund, S.: Autodidact: introducing the concept of mutual learning into a smart factory industry 4.0. In: 15th International Conference on Cognition and Exploratory Learning in Digital Age (CELDA 2018) (2018)

4

Development of a Low-Cost, High Accuracy, Flexible Panel Indexing Cell with Modular, Elastic Architecture

Robert Brownbill$^{(\boxtimes)}$ ⓘ and Adam Roberts ⓘ

Electroimpact UK Ltd., Hawarden, UK
`{robertb,adamr}@electroimpact.com`

Abstract. The global aerospace industry is driving a demand for flexible manufacturing systems to accommodate multiple programs with variable capacities within a modular, economical production cell [1]. Traditional manufacturing cells often involve bespoke, monolithic hardware limited to single program use. This inherent restraint results in significant incurred costs and program disruption when reacting to design and capacity changes. This paper describes the development of a reconfigurable panel-indexing cell with a dynamic cost architecture as an alternative approach to established, monolithic tooling structures.

Keywords: Flexible manufacturing · Modular architecture · Aerospace panel indexing · Reconfigurable tooling

1 Introduction

This paper narrates the mechanical design thought-processes of this fixture's development. The best-practice approach discussed, champions the move away from high-complexity, high-cost, bespoke engineering solutions towards a design philosophy maximizing the use of commercially available off-the-shelf components to reduce cost and lead-time. In suitable applications, the reduction in capital expenditure and expedited time to enter production surpass the associated disadvantages. This reversal in engineering mindset should prove lucrative across all engineering disciplines.

Electroimpact are a world-leading supplier of automation and tooling systems for the aerospace industry; supplying equipment and solutions to all of the major aerospace manufacturers across the globe.

In addition to the supply of industrial solutions, Electroimpact (EI) are increasingly prioritising the collaboration of manufacturing research directly with industry and through partnerships with research and academic institutions. Such collaborations have resulted in the development of industry leading technologies, most notably that of Automated Fibre Placement (AFP) [2] and Accurate Robot Technology [3].

More recently, a growing demand for flexible, elastic manufacturing systems has been observed. The drivers behind this demand are primarily rate flexibility, programme flexibility and modular architecture.

During the development phase of the Clean Sky 2, VADIS collaboration program [4], EI identified the opportunity to incorporate the indexing and metrology requirements alongside flexible, modular architecture, allowing precise indexing capability within a single, configurable tooling solution.

2   Objectives

2.1   Innovative Design Methodology

The design methodology used for this fixture was to reduce costs as far as practicable without compromising on accuracy, rigidity or functionality. This was done through the extensive use of commercially available off-the-shelf components from manufacturers. This is a reversal of the mindset from the 1990s/2000s where added complexity was seen to be the way forward.

This price reduction thus enables a greater target market for the fixtures, enables more budget to be spent on other areas such as increased automation and facilitates automation avenues into lower-rate aircraft programs.

The use of an mass-produced metrology system to set the tooling points opposed to a jig-integrated PLC controller is more cost-effective as not only is a typical laser tracker around half the price of a PLC control and servo system, the metrology equipment may be utilized in other areas of the facility between uses. A semi-skilled operator is required to use the metrology system and the fixture positioning will have a slight increase in set-up time. However, these limitations are far outweighed for low to medium-rate aircraft programs by the initial capital savings.

2.2   Functional Requirements

The initial requirement of the VADIS panel jigs in the early development phase was to accurately index and clamp the upper and lower covers in nominal form during the scanning operation of the key datum features (the final metrology solution being the Nikon MV331). With the context of this straightforward remit, initial concepts showed conventional tooling solutions with interchangeable indexing profiles, Fig. 1.

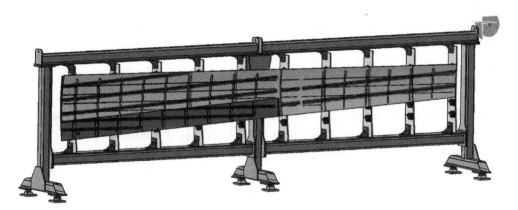

Fig. 1. Typical panel indexing concept using traditional rigid tooling methods

As the component design development progressed, it quickly became clear that a more flexible solution would be required to accommodate a broader selection of panel sizes. The design requirements ultimately converged to the following key criteria:

- Three upper panel assemblies indexed and clamped to nominal form:

  - Mid-Scale Upper Test Panel – 5 m × 1.4 m
  - Inboard Upper Panel – 5 m × 1.3 m
  - Outboard Upper panels – 4 m × 1 m

- High locational accuracy of indexing features with minimal tolerance stack between metrology and contact features
- Integrated metrology reference system for both index setting and for laser radar positional reference
- High structural and thermal stability
- Controlled, measured clamping forces

2.3   Commercial and Schedule Constraints

Following on from the functional requirements and taking into consideration the constraints of both the funding stream and the extended development time, EI expanded the design objectives to include:

- Manual adjustment of panel configuration (using a Laser Tracker)
- Prioritisation the use of standard purchased components
- Development a low-cost prototyping platform for the load cell monitoring

2.4   Modular Architecture

Once the functional and commercial requirements had been identified, EI realised the opportunity to integrate modularity and scalability within the tool design with the following aims:

- Modular base design able to function as a stand-alone jig or as a multi-base cell
- Upgradeability of drive systems allow future adaptation for semi-automated panel configuration

2.5   Cost Analysis

The following cost analysis is a rough order of magnitude (ROM) comparison between bespoke PLC-integrated fixtures and the low-cost altern ative discussed within the latter sections of this paper. Also included are scalability costs to double the space envelope.

Tooling Philosophy (Comparable Working Volume)	Cost* (GBP)	Lead Time (Months)
- Bespoke, semi-automated flexible panel indexing jig.		
- Integrated PLC control.		
- Servo driven actuators.		
TOTAL	**£ 700 k–900 k**	**12–18**
- Additional cost to double space envelope.	£ 250 k–400 k	
- Low-Cost, manually configurable, flexible panel indexing jig		
- Integrated PLC position feedback.		
TOTAL	**£ 400 k–650 k**	**9–14**
- Additional cost to double space envelope.	£ 200 k–300 k	
- Low-Cost, manually configurable, flexible panel indexing jig		
- Commercially Available Laser Tracker.		
TOTAL	**£ 300 k–450 k**	**4–10**
- Additional cost to double space envelope	£ 100 k–200 k	

* Correct ROM costs as of January 2020

3 Architecture

3.1 Overview

The modular concept of the jig's architecture lends itself to being easily reconfigurable. The concept consists of a fabricated steel base of a fixed length, the concept has chosen a nominal five metre base length. The base would be secured to the facility floor using industry standard, off the shelf, floor fixings. Each base would be capable of mounting up to four tooling posts.

A typical layout with three posts per base, Fig. 2, would be the recommended method. Current industrial applications see typical post spacing between one and two meters, to correspond with assembly feature locations. Owing to the module nature of the jig, several of these bases may be bolted together to create a larger panel cell, Fig. 3.

3.2 Structure

Both the bases and the posts are of welded fabrication from two-dimensional profiles, cut from steel sheet metal. Sacrificial material has been included in the weldment design such that the posts are machined, post fabrication, to add the precision features required for mounting the linear bearing rails, Y-drive supports and other tooling features.

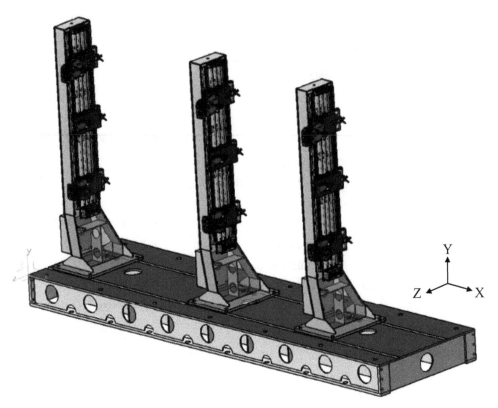

Fig. 2. Module base section with 3 tooling posts

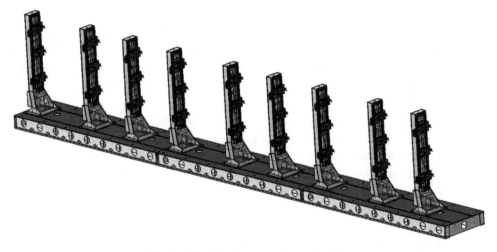

Fig. 3. Modular larger-scale application

The tooling posts are located to the base by means of T-bolts secured in T-slots. These longitudinal slots allow for the post X-position to be easily changed between applications by use of an overhead crane (2 lifting points are in the top of each post weldment). Positional tolerance of indexes in the span-wise, X direction, is typically an order of magnitude higher than the requirements for the cross-sectional profile indexes (Y & Z directions). Although methods could be employed to enable high precision location of each post in the X-direction, the posts would be set typically with a laser tracker and positioned using the overhead crane with some small manual input.

The before-mentioned concept would be that as implemented for an industrial application. Within the research budget allocated to the project, VADIS fixture posts were mounted directly to the floor, Fig. 4. This was chosen as the final installation location was a facility which includes floor mounted T-Slots. The industrial concept assumes a flat, basic concrete facility floor.

Fig. 4. VADIS fixture installed at electroimpact facility

The overarching function of the jig is to be flexible for a number of different panels configurations, Figs. 5, 6 and 7. The working envelope for the posts is a vertical range of 350 mm–1820 mm in Y and a horizontal range of 350 mm in Z. Post spacing can, of course, be varied in X to suit each application. A common post spacing was deemed suitable for the following three panels.

A thermal imaging camera was used on several occasions, in conjunction with a calibrated contact thermometer, to assess the thermal stability of the steel and aluminium components of the structure at several intervals during the day. It was found that on all occasions the jig temperature remained stable and uniform, Fig. 8, this was unless the external facility doors were left open for an extended period of time. It is therefore recommended that consideration be given to operations on the jig when any external doors are required to be open for extended periods.

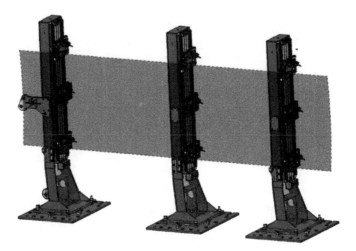

Fig. 5. Panel configuration 1

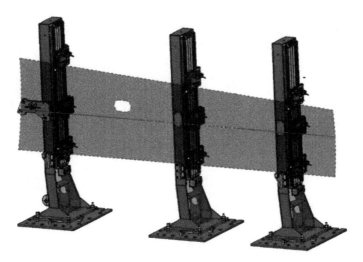

Fig. 6. Panel configuration 2

3.3 Drive Systems

One of the key objectives was to design the solution to be low-cost, as such, a high priority was placed on the use of off-the-shelf (mass produced) components. Not only is this highly beneficial in reducing costs but, should there ever be a need to replace or repair any of these components, the new parts can be on site in a matter of days. If they were to be of custom design, there would be the associated manufacturing lead time, typically in the order of four to eight weeks even for basic components. It was not possible to construct these assemblies entirely from bought out parts and as such, those

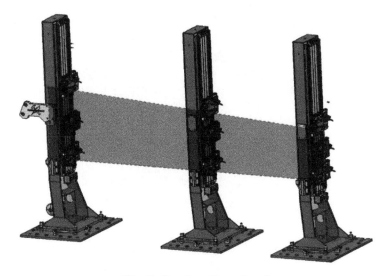

Fig. 7. Panel configuration 3

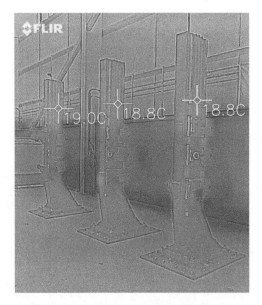

Fig. 8. Infra-red image of the VADIS Jig

custom parts were constrained to housings and non-wearing components. One example is the custom gearbox for the Y-drive, Fig. 9, although this is a custom machined 4-axis part, this was able to be manufactured from aluminium reducing machining time and costs as the rotating components selected were all off-the-shelf industry standard bearings.

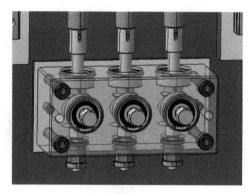

Fig. 9. Y drive gearbox

For the main Y-drive screws, it was chosen to select a trapezoidal thread form to reduce backlash as much as possible without the expense of ball screws. A bought-out screw was purchased and custom end operations added to interface with the gearbox spindle and the tensioning thrust bearing bracket.

Each of the three Y-drive screws allows adjustment of its corresponding Z-sled assembly, Fig. 10. The same utilisation of off-the-shelf drive components whilst minimising custom machined parts design methodology has been used here, two linear rails and trapezoidal drive screw assembly allow for adjustment in the Z-direction. These 2 degrees of freedom, coupled with the swivel index assembly allow the Optical Tooling Point (OTP) to be set to the panel

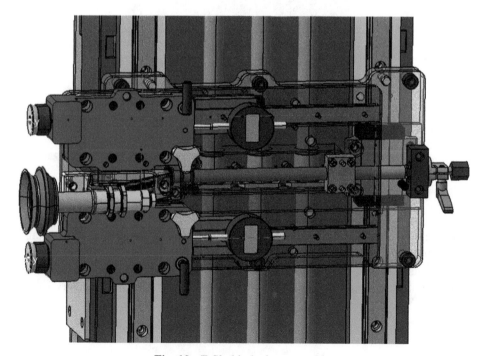

Fig. 10. Z-Sled indexing assembly

For the Y-drive assembly, the thread pitch of the drive screws along with the tensioning thrust bearing at the top of the post and the weight of the sled create suitable friction in the drive system to prevent the sleds from moving without the need for an interlocking brake. Whereas, on the Z-sled assemblies, their smaller screw diameter and higher applied forces from the clamp/panel loads, it was decided that an off-the-shelf hand clamp, shown orange, Fig. 10, would be required to prevent unintentional movement and creep during operation.

All adjustments can be made by the use of readily available metric tools in any standard engineering tool kit. Both Y & Z adjustments can be done using a 17 mm or 19 mm spanner/socket either by hand, ratchet spanner or with the use of power tools with the correct socket drive attachment, Fig. 11.

Fig. 11. Manual adjustment of the VADIS fixture with use of common power tools

3.4 Indexing

The swivel indexes used on this jig are of a tried and tested Electroimpact design. The cup and sphere method enables the indexing hemi-sphere to be removed and a Spherically Mounted Retroreflector (SMR) to be directly located into the cup, Fig. 12, retained with a magnet. The closer the SMR is to the final tooling contact surface, the smaller the tolerance stack up and the higher the accuracy of the system.

Although shown on a project specific, sliding assembly, Fig. 12, the actual swivel index mounts with a standard metric fine thread and is very compact assembly, Fig. 13.

As the SMR will set the centre point of the cup's semi-sphere, corresponding to the centre of the index hemi-sphere pad – this point only has to be on the surface of the part - no allowance needs to be made for the local angle of the panel at each location. The hemi-sphere can swivel through an angle of 20° to allow for Y & Z angular compliance, Fig. 14.

Fig. 12. Swivel index with SMR

Fig. 13. CAD scheme of EI swivel index

Fig. 14. EI swivel index assembly on the VADIS Jig

3.5 Metrology

As with all precision tooling cells, a robust and highly accurate metrology architecture is required to facilitate the high precision setting of the optical tooling points. Limiting the tolerance stack up between the OTP and the contact surface greatly improves the accuracy and repeatability of the system. Where possible the use of metrology tooling has been removed. This has been achieved, as previously discussed, by enabling the SMR to be located directly into the Swivel Index nest and retained for setting. Another way of achieving this is to implement a similar scheme for the Jig Reference System (JRS). The JRS enables the laser tracker or metrology equipment to be located within the jig reference frame. The use of fixed nests, opposed to tooling holes requiring the use of a pin nest, reduce the tolerance stack up. These nests are screwed into the jig base and secured in place with high strength epoxy compound. An anodised aluminium ring with laser etched point ID numbers was put around these nests, Fig. 15, to easily identify the JRS points and protect the nests from damage during jig operation.

Fig. 15. Jig reference system nest and ID ring with SMR

To ensure a high quality JRS, the Unified Spatial Metrology Network (USMN) [5] feature in the Spatial Analyzer software was used to analyse the measurements of the actual JRS points from several stations. These point clouds were then run through the algorithm and scaled for temperature to obtain high accuracy values for the actual position of the JRS points. It took seven stations, Fig. 16, to ensure that each point was shot sufficient times to yield a reliable JRS valuation.

To set each of the swivel indexes the metrology operator would book into the JRS then, with the SMR positioned in the swivel index cup, use the Y & Z adjustability to precisely position the OTP. This process would be repeated for all OTPs on the jig. Although this process would take longer than an automated system with inbuilt absolute scales, a semi-skilled operator would be able to reconfigure the jig in a relatively short of time. It is currently estimated that with a competent operator the cell could be reconfigured with less than a thirty minutes disruption to production (for the VADIS fixture or similar).

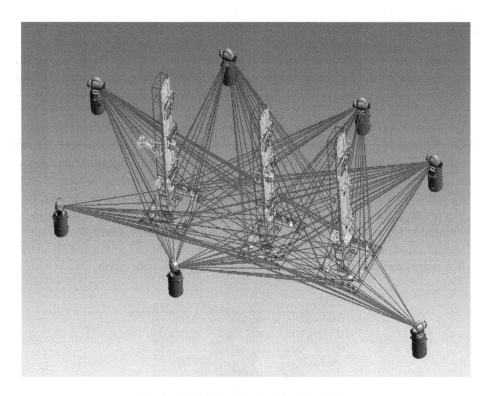

Fig. 16. USMN analysis of the VADIS Jig

Other benefits are such that the cost for the manually adjustable jig and the associated metrology system (laser tracker) are more cost-effective than a semi-automated cell with the added benefit that the metrology system is portable and can be used across multiple applications in the same facility.

3.6 Force Sensing Clamps

One of the key requirements from the Leonardo design department was for the application of a controlled, measured clamping force at predetermined locations across the panels.

EI's solution was a manually operated, screw-driven clamp assembly containing a 500 lb-f load cell directly behind the clamping pad, Fig. 17. To monitor the load cell values, a portable load cell amplifier was developed using a commercially available Arduino microcontroller, using a standard USB-B male-male interface cable.

Using a single interface across multiple load cells required the controller, Fig. 18, to be able to apply specific scaling factors to each individual load cell. Each clamp was given a unique identification (in this case, 'Upper Jig 1', 'Lower Jig 2' etc.) and is calibrated offline using measured calibrated masses. The scaling factors are then calculated and stored to the Arduino's internal non-volatile memory.

Fig. 17. Manual panel clamp with load cell feedback

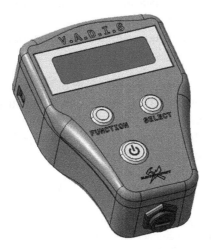

Fig. 18. VADIS hand pendant design

4 Next Steps

Following the successful implementation of the VADIS panel cell, EI intend to explore the subsequent developments:

Dynamic Cost Models. The jig architecture has been developed with scalability in mind. The configuration outlined within this paper is the most cost-effective solution, suitable for low rate with minimal configurations. EI propose the following levels of scalability:

- Manual configuration of index and clamp locations – using portable laser tracker
- Semi-automated configuration using permanently mounted laser tracker and handheld HMI
- Semi-automated configuration using integrated absolute scales, central PLC control and handheld HMI
- Fully automated configuration using integrated servos for each drive and a central PLC control

Modular Panel Interfaces. This paper describes the use of swivel indexes in a modular sub-assembly to control panel contours. EI propose to develop interchangeable sub-assemblies to increase the range of indexing methods. Typical sub-assemblies would include stringer profile indexes, manhole clamping and datum hole pin locations.

Lateral Post Adjustment. One of the major limitations of the proposed jig is the lateral (Z) adjustment of the drive systems. EI propose to pursue an additional drive system within the post weldment base to allow lateral movement of the entire post assembly. This would increase the indexing envelope to include panels with significant sweep angles.

Non-contact Metrology Inspection. With the latest advancements of metrology hardware, high-accuracy non-contact measurement of key index locations is possible. This allows for remote measurement without the need for the operator to move an SMR to metrology features. Speeding up configuration time and whilst also allowing for in-process inspection of the component.

Smart Manufacturing. Within the development of flexible manufacturing systems is the desire for Smart Manufacturing – gathering relevant manufacturing process data and using advanced analytics to improve manufacturing efficiency [6]. EI have identified several features of the flexible jig which could be developed: recording of panel clamp load data, panel identification, panel in-jig process time, panel configuration time, pareto of the major planned and unplanned downtime.

Acknowledgements. This project has received funding from the European Union's Horizon 2020 research and innovation programme under grant agreement No 738221. We are incredibly proud to work as part of this consortium. These developments would not have been possible without the hard work and support of Dr. Joseph Griffin, Dr. Konstantinous Bacharoudis, Dr. Alison Turner and Professor Svetan Rachev of the Centre for Aerospace Manufacture at the University of Nottingham along with Mr. Salvatore Cascella and his team at Leonardo Aircraft in Pomigliano d'Arco, Italy.

References

1. Millar, A., et al.: Reconfigurable Flexible Tooling for Aerospace Wing Assembly, Aerospace Technology Conference and Exposition (2009)
2. Electroimpact Inc.: Composite Manufacturing. Electroimpact (2019). https://electroimpact.com/Products/Composites/Overview.aspx
3. DeVleig, R., et al.: Improved Accuracy of Unguided Articulated Robots. SAE International, Warrendale, PA (2009)
4. University of Nottingham Centre for Aerospace Manufacturing, Leonardo Aircraft, Electroimpact UK Ltd.: Variance Aware Determinate assembly Integrated System (VADIS), Nottingham, Pomigliano D'Arco, Hawarden (2019). https://cordis.europa.eu/project/id/738221
5. New River Kinematics: Unified Spatial Metrology Network, New River Kinematics (2018). https://www.kinematics.com/spatialanalyzer/usmn.php
6. Davis, J., et al.: Smart manufacturing, manufacturing intelligence and demand-dynamic performance. Comput. Chem. Eng. **47**, 145–156 (2019)

5

Augmented Reality in Assembly Systems: State of the Art and Future Perspectives

M. Dalle Mura and G. Dini[✉]

Department of Civil and Industrial Engineering, University of Pisa, 56122 Pisa, Italy
dini@ing.unipi.it

Abstract. Assembly represents a fundamental step in manufacturing, being a time-consuming and costly process, on which the final quality of the product mostly depends. Augmented Reality (AR) may represent a key tool to assist workers during assembly, thanks to the possibility to provide the user of real-time instructions and information superimposed on the work environment. Many implementations have been developed by industries and academic institutions for both manual and collaborative assembly. Among the most remarkable examples of the last few years are applications in guidance of complex tasks, training of personnel, quality control and inspection. This keynote paper aims to provide a useful survey by reviewing recent applications of AR in assembly systems, describing potential advantages, as well as current limitations and future perspectives.

Keywords: Augmented reality · Assembly systems · Manual assembly · Collaborative assembly

1 Introduction

Assembly represents a key element in the whole fabrication process. The total cost of a product, the time requested for completing it and its quality strictly depend on the efficiency and accuracy of execution of the different assembly steps.

Very often, these operations can be complex and require fine adjustments in order to obtain an acceptable final result. The sequence can be lengthy, with many parts to be assembled together in a specific order, so as to assure the product to function as it should.

For these reasons, the workers should be skilled and trained to do that within the cycle time imposed by the production rate. In many cases, the sequence can be dependent on the variant to be assembled and can request the consultation of paper manuals, reference tables that could lead to time inefficiencies, distractions and, therefore, safety problems.

Typically, in manual assembly, the tasks are performed by human operators aided by tools or by semi-automated machines. Set up and maintenance operations should be provided and planned in advance for all equipment, so as to allow workers a proper use and avoid problems related to unexpected breakdowns, with consequent inactivity of the production system.

A relevant problem in assembly is also represented by human errors. Obviously, an error should be prevented by using different methods such as training sessions, sensing devices or poka-yoke solutions. These approaches are often expensive and in many cases do not give a complete assurance of avoiding these inconveniences. Human errors in assembly may result in increased production wastes or higher processing time and costs, also worsening the quality level of products because of manufacturing defects. To avoid possible damage to the entire production system, the probability of human errors in assembly should be reduced.

That said, the need of integrating the traditional manual assembly with a tool able to enhance the efficiency and the efficacy of the process becomes evident. The operator must be supported and guided in his/her actions through the accomplishment of assembly operations by non-invasive devices, which allow the user not to deflect attention and distract from the process. The tool should also be connectable to the hardware employed in the system, such as sensors, and able to access and consult software databases, in order to help the operator in executing the tasks as efficiently and effectively as possible.

Augmented Reality (AR) technology could be particularly suitable to address these issues. The possibility of replacing paper manuals with interactive instructions allows the worker to interact with both the real environment and the virtual information, also receiving a feedback on the operations made.

2   Basics on Augmented Reality

Augmented Reality (AR) can be defined as a hardware-software system able to overlay virtual images or objects on the real world visual, in order to give to the observer information that he could not obtain by using only the interaction of his/her physical senses with the workplace.

The main objective of an AR system is therefore to create virtual elements in the optical path linking the user's eyes with the real scene in front of him/her. To do that, the following steps have to be implemented:

- *real image acquisition*, through a video camera that captures the images from the real world;
- *tracking*, necessary to identify and record the position and orientation of objects in the environment, so as to properly align the virtual image. Widely employed are vision-based tracking systems, namely fiducial marker identification, which uses artificial markers to identify components in space, and markerless identification, which uses object features;
- *virtual image generation*, through a computer that uses 3D CAD models to create digitized contents;
- *composite image generation*, obtained by combining the real images captured by the camera with the virtual images generated by the computer, so as to produce the augmented content.

2.1 AR Techniques

The composite image can be generated using 3 different approaches which deeply characterize and influence the performance of a specific application:

- *optical see-through*, virtual images are projected in a transparent display positioned between the user's eyes and the real scene (Fig. 1a);
- *video see-through*, real and virtual images are mixed and visualized on a monitor display positioned in front of the user (Fig. 1b);

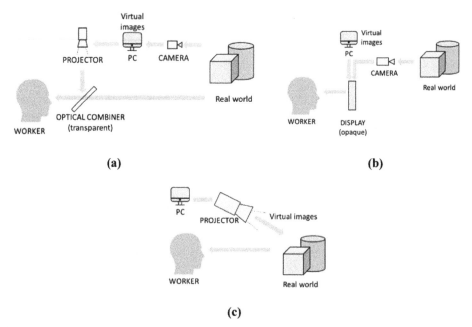

Fig. 1. Different approaches used to obtain the augmented real scene in front of the worker: (a) optical see-through; (b) video see-through; (c) image projection.

- *image projection*, virtual images are directly projected onto the surfaces of the objects in the real world (Fig. 1c).

2.2 AR Devices

An AR device identifies the hardware tool by which an operator can visualize the real scene in front of him/her enriched by the virtual elements. This device represents a very important element of the whole AR system since it constitutes the mean that gives to the human the perception of an augmented workplace.

In order to fulfill the previous conditions, an AR device should be:

- *realistic*: an AR system which operates interactively in real time and in three dimensions should give a "real" interpretation and sensation of the augmented environment;
- *immersive*: virtual objects and information are integrated with the real environment, in order to give a 3D perception of the scene and therefore an immersive feeling to the worker to be surrounded by a mixed real-virtual environment;
- *comfortable*: wearable devices must ensure portability and be non-invasive, so as not to detract the attention from the process.

Many solutions have been proposed in the last decade by different manufacturers and tested by researchers and industries. Four categories can be identified to be used in a workplace, depending on their position with respect to the user and to the real environment:

- *head mounted devices* (HMD): these visual displays are worn on the user's head. Advantages on using an HMD are that they are hands-free and give an immersive perception to the user, since the display with AR scene is positioned to the eye-level, while a current drawback is that they may be uncomfortable and the user could suffer of eye strain, especially after prolonged use. Among most well-known HMD, there are AR glasses, such as Microsoft HoloLens, Magic Leap One and Google Glasses;
- *hand held devices* (HHD): among these, there are smartphones and tablets. The main advantage with respect to an HMD is the possibility to be held only when necessary. However, they are less immersive, not hands-free and this could limit the worker in his/her actions;
- *spatial devices* (SD): they consist of displays of different sizes placed statically within the environment, not suited for mobile solutions;
- *projection devices* (PD): these solutions have the advantage of giving a very good mobility to the user. However, they need to be calibrated, they request flat and wide surfaces in the work area for projecting images and suffer of user obstructions.

Some of these types of devices are best suited to operate with certain visualization approaches of AR contents, as presented in Table 1. In particular HMDs can effectively operate either in video see-through and optical see-through modes.

Table 1. AR devices capability to be used in the three composite image generation approaches.

	Video see-through	Optical see-through	Image projection
Head mounted devices	X	X	
Hand held devices	X		
Spatial devices	X		
Projection devices			X

Other manufacturers are proposing innovative and more powerful devices, nowadays under development, such as AR contact lenses (or smart lenses) to be used as accessory to smartphones or as a separate device. Smart contact lens technology aims to project images into the wearer's eyes, through little display, camera and antenna inside the lens, where sensors are controlled by wearer's blinking [1]. Other researches are working on the development of new AR hardware, such as head-worn projectors [2] and Virtual Retinal Displays (VRD), which create the augmented images by projecting laser light directly into the worker's eye.

These last solutions, even if they aim at obtaining a more immersive impact to the user, at the current stage of development are far from a practical use and the absence of risks for the worker has to be proved.

2.3   AR Applications in Production Engineering

In recent years, AR techniques are spreading out in any field, from retail to military, from healthcare to education, gaming, travel, tourism, etc.

Production engineering, in particular, represents an area having a more and more increasing interest in this kind of tools able to be used in many activities, such as:

- *worker support in performing complex operations*, using virtual instructions during particular tasks and preventing the user from doing wrong actions that may involve errors, with time-related costs;
- *guided training*, accomplished through AR tools for teaching procedures and instructions conceived and addressed to unexperienced personnel;
- *remote support and maintenance*, thanks to the possibility of providing the composite image to the worker on the field and, remotely and simultaneously, to the expert maintenance technicians [3];
- *other potential applications*, such as real-time factory diagnostics or colleague collaboration and communication.

As said before, assembly represents a typical area of production engineering where this kind of technique may be profitably used, due to the strong need of supports and interactive tools in performing complex and articulated tasks, which can be encountered in assembly procedures.

The aim of this survey is therefore to provide a comprehensive insight on the state of the art of AR applications in assembly systems, as well as some current open issues that need to be overcome.

3   Applications in Manual Assembly Systems

Many applications have been experimented in manual assembly systems, mainly to support operators in performing correctly an assembly sequence. Extensive surveys have been published in 2012 and 2016 [4, 5], which demonstrate that from the beginning of this century, augmented reality is receiving increasing attention by researchers working on assembly problems.

In this wide literature scenario, a first rough subdivision can be made considering that the contributions can be addressed to "real industrial" and to "demonstrative" cases. The former concerns the implementation of an AR systems for supporting a real industrial problem (e.g.: assembly of an engine or a car body) and represents the main topic of this survey paper, the latter represents the experimental demonstration of procedures by using simple parts or toys, used as benchmarks.

These last contributions are often used to test specific hardware or software, such as in [6, 7], where the use of a smartphone, a Microsoft HoloLens and an Epson Moverio BT-200 smart glasses are compared with the use of paper-based instructions. Nevertheless, the contribution demonstrates that, on the one hand, users are able to solve the task of assembly a Lego Duplo set fastest when using paper instructions, but, on the other, made fewer errors with AR support (Fig. 2).

Fig. 2. HMD used to support simple assembly tasks of LEGO® bricks (source: [7]).

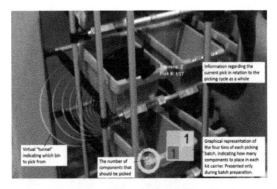

Fig. 3. Guidance in taking an object from a bin (source: [9]).

Other "non-industrial" cases often concern the assembly of furniture, which are very good as demonstrators, such as the research described in [8], where Microsoft HoloLens are used. The tests show that good results are achieved for assembly with high complexity.

3.1 Guidance in Assembly Tasks – Optical and Video See-Through Approaches

Guidance in performing assembly tasks undoubtedly represents the typical objective of many AR applications. In most cases, optical or video see-through approaches are used to guide assembly operations.

An example of a system used to substitute paper list in assembly operations is given in [9] and illustrated in Fig. 3. The AR application is developed for a Microsoft HoloLens hardware and the information is presented to the worker via a head-mounted display. The system is able to show a virtual "tunnel" indicating to the worker the bin where the part is placed, demonstrating its time-efficiency both for single kit and batch preparation.

Other applications concern the use of AR devices for guiding the correct execution of assembly operations. In [10], a prototype system is developed for providing different modality of guidance based on the different cognition phases of the user, i.e. perception, attention, memory and execution, in order to give appropriate information during assembly tasks. The prototype adopts an HMD and a 3D bare-hand interface, free from any devices, such as mouse or keyboard. In experiments concerning a motorbike alternator assembly, users proved to execute operations more quickly and accurately in comparison to a digital documentation on an LCD.

The study presented in [11] is focused on an AR video see-through support that associates different visual features to explain assembly operations with different difficulty level: the more the task to perform is complex, the easier to understand is the instruction given by the visual feature (Fig. 4). The results show that the method outperforms paper instructions.

A voice-based interaction technique is integrated with an augmented reality system for car assembly and disassembly in the work proposed in [12]. The speech signal is used to interact with the augmented reality environment, made of the virtual car's components visualized in the real scene. The voice commands, converted into textual commands, leave both hands free, so as to allow the user to manipulate the various components.

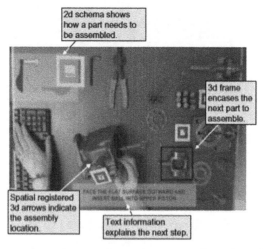

Fig. 4. Example of instructions given to the worker concerning: a) a scheme of the assembly operation; b) the assembly location; c) information regarding the next step; d) the next part to assemble (source: [11]).

In addition to hearing, AR has been combined with other human senses to overcome some drawbacks that may occur when only using this technology. An example is presented in [13], where a real-time vibrotactile guidance method is developed to support assembly tasks. The system uses a web camera, located on top of the workstation, to recognize components and user hands, and a vibrotactile wristband to give the user a feedback on the action made in the form of vibration.

3.2 Guidance in Assembly Tasks – Image Projection Approaches

Image projection is often used in assembly workplaces for its intrinsic capability of leaving the worker free of moving without carrying AR devices on his/her body. These systems, as the previous ones, eliminate the need for hard copy or monitor-based work instructions, and create a sort of digital "operating canvas" on a work surface.

A projector-based AR tool is in general more simple with respect to a video see-through or an optical see-through system and also more intuitive as regards its use by the operator, throughout every step of a manual process: what they have to do is follow the lights projected on the workbench or on the parts, as illustrated in Fig. 5 [14].

Fig. 5. Assembly instructions projected on the workbench and on the parts (source: [14]).

At Dassault Aviation, an image projection AR system named Diota's [15] is used to guide operators in complex assembly tasks performed inside the panels of fuselage structures. Instructions related to operations to be performed and machine types to be used are displayed on the assembly. Figure 6 demonstrates how the system works, also showing the obstruction generated by the presence of the worker, typical problem in these kinds of systems.

Fig. 6. AR projection systems used at Dassault Aviation (source: [15]).

Another approach of image projection is shown in Fig. 7 [16]. The system uses a panel placed near the operator, where instructions are projected to avoid major drawbacks of an HMD, such as poor comfort, need for special versions for users who wear eyeglasses and limited field of view. To step through the assembly sequence and review previous instructions, the worker uses foot pedals; in this way, hands are kept free from the AR device and the worker does not interrupt the assembly process.

Fig. 7. Presentation of picking information and assembly instruction on a projection-based AR assembly station (source: [16]).

3.3 Guidance in Complex Assembly Tasks

Guidance in complex assembly tasks is essential for performing this kind of operations and for avoiding errors or time consuming procedures. Usually, these tasks are accomplished by using reference manuals and forcing the worker to read several pages of paper instructions.

Fig. 8. Head-mounted display used at NASA for assembling spacecraft parts (source: [17]).

Typical complex assembly tasks can be encountered in aerospace industry. NASA uses HoloLens AR headsets [17] to faster build a new spacecraft and assemble the crew capsule Orion, as shown in Fig. 8. Boeing has developed smart glasses and an AR application for wiring harness operations. The system enables assemblers to easily see where the electrical wiring goes in the aircraft fuselage and this allows a significant reduction of errors and production time [18].

A particular situation of complex assembly is represented by performing operations in areas not directly visible by the user. The work proposed in [19] uses a tracking method to acquire information on the position of target objects in real time, to be combined with the digitized model of parts and human hands in the invisible area, superimposed on the assembly scene (Fig. 9). The method demonstrated an improved efficiency and accuracy compared to the assembly without augmented reality assistance.

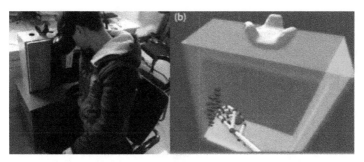

Fig. 9. Screw positioning, aided by AR system, inside a box in area not directly visible by the worker (source: [19]).

Complex assembly tasks can be also encountered in mounting electrical components. A tutoring system for motherboard assembly has been developed in [20]; the prototype uses an HMD to teach novice users the assembling of hardware components on a computer motherboard.

3.4   Order Picking

Order picking is a fundamental process in any production plant, to find and take the correct parts and products from a warehouse, just before assembly tasks. Companies are continuously looking for new methods to improve such a costly process, for which AR can represent an innovative solution.

In an application made in automotive industry, workers can automatically receive all the information they need directly in their field of vision, such as storage locations or part numbers, by using smart glasses (Fig. 10). The camera mounted in this device can be also used as a barcode reader: when a worker selects the correct part, the barcode is shown in green, if not, it is illuminated in red [21].

Fig. 10. Smart glasses used in order picking operations (source: [21]).

3.5   Quality Control and Inspection

Quality control and inspection represent important steps in an assembly sequence. In many cases, they could request instruments and a comparison with reference values.

For these reasons, AR systems are very suitable for this kind of application and can efficiently support operator in this critical phase.

An example is reported in Fig. 11, where an HHD using a video see-through system is employed to determine the correct position of the rear light of vehicle and its alignment with respect to the surrounding body panels [22].

Fig. 11. A video see-through method for inspection of parts after assembling (source: [22]).

Also Renault Trucks is using AR for quality control in assembly lines [23]. Quality control operators wear Microsoft HoloLens smart glasses to improve inspection operations during engine assembly, as shown in Fig. 12.

Fig. 12. Microsoft HoloLens smartglasses used for quality control of Renault Trucks engines (source: [23]).

In the aerospace industry, an AR tool for quality control was developed by Airbus Group, for fuselage section inspection during assembly. The tool consists of an HHD that quickly detects errors, in order to optimize inspection time, while reducing the risk of deviations in conformity [24].

3.6 Integration with Sensing Devices

Since the sole use of AR could not provide feedback signals for a closed-loop control on the tasks executed by the operator, in manual assembly lines AR-based systems are strongly requested to be integrated with sensors, able to give to the user appropriate physical values of the process [25]. Indeed, AR can be integrated with sensing devices to create a synergistic system in which the limits of one may be filled by the other. AR can thus be employed to guide the operator in carrying out the correct action and to provide a support to recover any committed errors.

For this purpose, the contribution described in [26] proposes a configuration of a manual assembly workstation integrating the use of a sensing device and augmented reality equipment, in order to guide the actions performed by the worker. Figure 13 shows the scheme of the system obtained by the integration of a force sensor, able to detect a part of assembly errors not relievable by the AR camera.

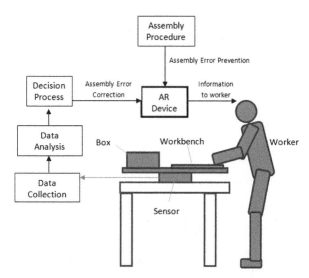

Fig. 13. A workstation integrating AR with a force sensor for error detection during assembly (source: [26]).

3.7 Training

Starting from the consideration that an AR system, in principle, can be used both for guiding expertise workers and for training unexperienced users, the difference between these two applications relies in the level of instructions given by the system.

In an AR system used for training, the sequence of instructions and the virtual objects used to guide the operator take into account the fact that he/she does not have any experience on a given assembly procedure. In this case, even very simple assembly tasks are explained in detail, showing also elementary information about the use of a tool or safety principles.

For example, the assembly line shown in Fig. 14, equipped with AR projectors, provides different assembly instructions according to the skill level of workers [27].

Other examples are described in [28], where the training platform has been tested on an actuator assembly, and in [22, 29] where an HMD-based training system is used at the BMW Group Production Academy on an engine assembly (Fig. 15).

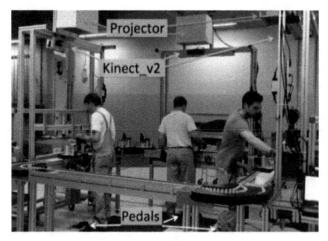

Fig. 14. AR assembly line equipped with PDs (source: [27]).

Fig. 15. AR-assisted training developed at BMW Group Production Academy (source: [22]).

Training can be also efficiently performed through virtual assembly. An example of augmented reality system developed for training, which uses a low-invasiveness hand tracking device, is reported in [30]. The proposed methodology enables the user to interact with the virtual objects, acquiring the pose of all the fingers of both hands by a markerless optical triangulation, as reported in Fig. 16.

4   Applications in Collaborative Assembly Systems

The recent introduction of collaborative robots in assembly lines has led to the development of new fields of study, mainly concerning the safety of the work environment shared between human and robot. Also in this regard, AR may be beneficial, particularly in providing virtual information on the real workplace, to enhance situational awareness for the worker, to support spatial dialog among human and robot and to enable even remote collaboration.

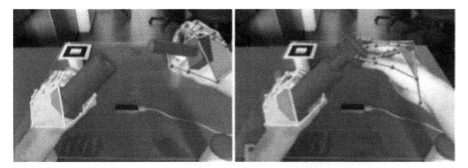

Fig. 16. Sequence of virtual assembly by augmented reality (source: [30]).

The main topics currently treated in the field of AR applications for human-robot collaboration are in particular the development of Human Robot Interface (HRI) and the enhancement of worker's safety perception.

An application of AR in Human-Robot-Interface is given in [31]. The research focuses on the study of an AR solution for increasing human confidence and trust in collaborating with robots. The work describes the design and development of an interface system that shows virtual animation of the robot movements to the operator in advance on the real workplace, in order to improve human safety.

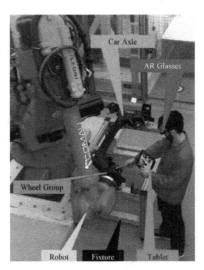

Fig. 17. Application of a see-through AR system to assist an operator in a cooperative work with a robot (source: [32]).

A typical application concerning the worker's safety perception when working close to an industrial robot is given in [32]. The main information provided by the system are assembly related instructions, robot workspace and trajectory visualization. The system, as illustrated in Fig. 17, was tested on a real case study derived from the automotive industry and demonstrated to optimize the time for assembly and the worker's safety perception in an HRC environment. Other examples can be found in [33], where an

AR system for collaborative cooperation between a robotic assembly unit and a human worker has been developed by EON Reality, or in [34], where virtual instructions are given to workers to perform simple assembly tasks in cooperation with a robot (Fig. 18).

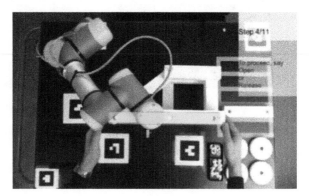

Fig. 18. Virtual instructions given during a collaborative work between a human and a robot (source: [34]).

5   Other Potential Areas of Application

AR techniques could be also useful in other areas concerning assembly process and assembly systems. Among them, the most promising and with the highest potential of development are:

– *assembly layout planning.* AR devices could be used for: i) obtaining a graphical overlay of the new equipment onto the existing ones; ii) performing visual check for collisions or for available spaces in transportation systems such as forklifts;
– *workplace ergonomics*, such as the detection of the reachability of objects in a manual assembly station using a digital human model superimposed on the real scene, or the graphical overlay of different workspace zones containing all elements within a grasping distance, with no need to bend or walk forward;
– *assembly process evaluation*, in particular the evaluation of aspects such as the assembly sequencing, the assembly path visualization, the assembly accessibility with collision detection among parts, the ergonomic use of tools, the co-working, all of them to be made thanks to the integration with sensing devices (e.g.: haptic interfaces).

6   Open Issues and Future Perspectives

Despite the significant progress of AR technology and applications in recent years, some limitations to be solved still occur. The main limits of AR implementation in assembly systems concern the following aspects:

– hardware and software performance,
– tracking methods,
– user's acceptance,
– authoring procedure.

They represent limits but, consequently, issues to be enhanced by the research community and therefore future perspectives for AR to more effectively assist assembly in the near future.

6.1 Hardware and Software Performance

Hardware performance is a key-element for obtaining efficient solutions. Nowadays this aspect presents some limits, even if it is increasingly improving. Features such as comfort for the user, wider field of view, comprehension of the environment, and, most importantly, more natural human machine interface through NLP (Natural Language Processing), hand and eye tracking are very important and many manufacturers are working on improving them.

Another open issue is "latency", which refers to the error of misalignment among virtual objects resulting from the delay between the movement of the user and the moment in which the changed image is displayed, with respect to the new position of the user [11]. To solve this problem, Waegel and Brooks [35] developed a low latency inertial measurement unit (IMU) and proposed new 3D reconstruction algorithms.

6.2 Tracking Methods

Among tracking methods, AR systems for assembly applications mainly use the marker-based approach, thanks to its stable and fast detection of markers in the entire image sequence. Valuable features are accuracy, flexibility, robustness, computation efficiency as well as ease of use. However, significant drawbacks of this tracking method are incorrect registration in the field of view due to marker occlusion and impossibility of using markers on many industrial components for their small size.

Tracking should be enhanced to create a good orientation of virtual contents with respect to the user's field of view. For example, Microsoft HoloLens 2 has implemented some tracking additions and improvements which are very beneficial to the workers. Gesture recognition, eye and hand tracking working together may provide to workers a more contextual interaction with virtual objects.

Marker-less tracking is considered the natural successor of marker-based approach. Among these techniques is Simultaneous Localization and Mapping (SLaM), which allows to build up a map within an unprepared environment, simultaneously keeping track of the current location, by extracting scene features.

The importance of this issue is also demonstrated by another contribution [36], where a method using the combination of point cloud and visual feature mechanical assembly system is used to create a tracking method. The accuracy is presented through a pump assembly case study and the results show that the tracking trajectory estimated by the method is very close to the real one and better than other methods, obtaining a good alignment of objects.

6.3 User's Acceptance

As far as the user's acceptance is concerned, research conducted in real work environment shows that operators could prefer AR over conventional methods of instruction [37]. Users generally give positive feedbacks when experiencing AR, especially for the possibility for non-experts to perform complex tasks and for the reduced mental workload on the user. However, this applies to AR systems implemented with care and attention to details on the interface and the content within presented to the user [37]. Moreover, to feel for the user that a task is worth using the AR support, its complexity must be high enough, as discussed in [38].

6.4 Authoring Procedure

Another important open issue is represented by the complexity of authoring in AR applications: an effective AR system requires a deep analysis of several aspects related to the assembly procedure (assembly sequence, instructions to be given to the operators, tools and fixtures, work environment, etc.) and its implementation in the AR platform and software.

A proposal of standard guidelines has been given in [39], with advantages to obtain time saving, error reduction and accuracy improvement.

Another contribution in this field has been given in [37] with the creation of AR work instructions for assembly using a new form of authoring, based on an expert recorded performing the assembly steps, automatically processed to generate AR work instructions.

An authoring tool has been also developed by BMW Group in order to support and simplify the design of AR training programs [22].

7 Conclusions

This paper presents a comprehensive survey of AR research and development in assembly systems. Many successful implementations made by industries and academic institutions, both for manual and collaborative assembly, are described, as well as current open issues to be overcome.

According to the analysis of the state of the art conducted, it is possible to conclude that augmented reality, after an important and still existing experimental stage, is becoming increasingly utilized in industrial applications and the sector is in constant expansion. The potential contribution of this technology to facilitate faster and correct operations encourages the market to a continuous evolution of hardware and software systems, including aspects related to the portability and comfort of AR devices, for a best users' acceptance. Furthermore, the latest developments in tracking and authoring procedures aim at more robust and sophisticated systems.

References

1. PerfectLens.ca Homepage. https://www.perfectlens.ca/articles/7-exciting-developments-aug mented-reality-contacts Accessed 15 Nov 2019
2. Soomro, S.R., Urey, H.: Augmented reality 3D display using head-mounted projectors and transparent retro-reflective screen. In: Advances in Display Technologies VII, vol. 10126, p. 101260E. International Society for Optics and Photonics (2017)
3. Dini, G., Dalle Mura, M.: Application of augmented reality techniques in through-life engineering services. Procedia Cirp **38**, 14–23 (2015)
4. Nee, A.Y.C., Ong, S.K., Chryssolouris, G., Mourtzis, D.: Augmented reality applications in design and manufacturing. CIRP Ann. Manuf. Technol. **61**(2), 657–679 (2012)
5. Wang, X., Ong, S.K., Nee, A.Y.C.: A comprehensive survey of augmented reality assembly research. Adv. Manuf. **4**(1), 1–22 (2016)
6. Blattgerste, J., Strenge, B., Renner, P., Pfeiffer, T., Essig, K.: Comparing conventional and augmented reality instructions for manual assembly tasks. In: Proceedings of the 10th International Conference on PErvasive Technologies Related to Assistive Environments, pp. 75–82 (2017)
7. Blattgerste, J., Renner, P., Strenge, B., Pfeiffer, T.: In-situ instructions exceed side-by-side instructions in augmented reality assisted assembly. In: Proceedings of the 11th PErvasive Technologies Related to Assistive Environments Conference, pp. 133–140 (2018)
8. Deshpande, A., Kim, I.: The effects of augmented reality on improving spatial problem solving for object assembly. Adv. Eng. Inform. **38**, 760–775 (2018)
9. Hanson, R., Falkenström, W., Miettinen, M.: Augmented reality as a means of conveying picking information in kit preparation for mixed-model assembly. Comput. Ind. Eng. **113**, 570–575 (2017)
10. Wang, X., Ong, S.K., Nee, A.Y.C.: Multi-modal augmented-reality assembly guidance based on bare-hand interface. Adv. Eng. Inform. **30**(3), 406–421 (2016)
11. Radkowski, R., Herrrema, J., Oliver, J.: Augmented reality-based manual assembly support with visual features for different degrees of difficulty. Int. J. Hum.-Comput. Interact. **31**(5), 337–349 (2015)
12. Aouam, D., Benbelkacem, S., Zenati, N., Zakaria, S., Meftah, Z.: Voice-based augmented reality interactive system for car's components assembly. In: 2018 3rd International Conference on Pattern Analysis and Intelligent Systems (PAIS), pp. 1–5 (2018)
13. Arbeláez, J.C., Viganò, R., Osorio-Gómez, G.: Haptic Augmented reality (HapticAR) for assembly guidance. Int. J. Interact. Des. Manuf. (IJIDeM) **13**, 673–687 (2019)
14. Light Guide System Homepage. https://lightguidesys.com/blog/projector-based-augmented-reality-new-form-enterprise-ar/ Accessed 15 Sept 2019
15. Dassault Systems Homepage. https://blogs.3ds.com/delmia/2017/07/error-free-manufactu ring-immersive-technologies-reduce-errors-and-detect-them-faster/ Accessed 15 Sept 2019
16. Funk, M., Kosch, T., Kettner, R., Korn, O., Schmidt, A.: An overview of 4 years of combining industrial assembly with augmented reality for industry 4.0. In: Proceedings of the 16th International Conference on Knowledge Technologies and Datadriven Business, p. 4 (2016)
17. Technology Review Homepage. https://www.technologyreview.com/s/612247/nasa-is-using-hololens-ar-headsets-to-build-its-new-spacecraft-faster/ Accessed 15 Sept 2019
18. Assembly Magazine Homepage. https://www.assemblymag.com/articles/94979-the-reality-of-augmented-reality Accessed 13 Jan 2020
19. Wang, Z., Zhang, S., Bai, X.: Augmented reality based product invisible area assembly assistance. In: 2018 3rd International Conference on Control, Automation and Artificial Intelligence (CAAI) (2018)

20. Westerfield, G., Mitrovic, A., Billinghurst, M.: Intelligent augmented reality training for motherboard assembly. Int. J. Artif. Intell. Educ. **25**(1), 157–172 (2015)
21. Assembly Magazine Homepage. https://www.assemblymag.com/articles/93129-vw-tests-smart-glasses-for-order-picking Accessed 13 Jan 2020
22. BMW Group Homepage. https://www.press.bmwgroup.com/global/article/detail/T02 94345EN/absolutely-real:-virtual-and-augmented-reality-open-new-avenues-in-the-bmw-group-production-system?language=en Accessed 09 Sept 2019
23. Next Reality Homepage. https://hololens.reality.news/news/renault-trucks-tests-hololens-vis ualize-quality-control-engine-assembly-operations-0181282/ Accessed 15 Sept 2019
24. Aerocontact Homepage. https://www.aerocontact.com/en/aerospace-aviation-news/47138-the-assembly-of-the-future-is-already-a-reality-with-testia-s-sart-system Accessed 15 Sept 2019
25. Iliano, S., Chimienti, V., Dini, G.: Training by augmented reality in industrial environments: a case study. In: Proceedings of 4th CIRP Conference on Assembly Technology and Systems, Ann Arbor (2012)
26. Dalle Mura, M., Dini, G., Failli, F.: An integrated environment based on augmented reality and sensing device for manual assembly worstations. Procedia Cirp **41**, 340–345 (2015)
27. Funk, M., Bächler, A., Bächler, L., Kosch, T., Heidenreich, T., Schmidt, A.: Working with augmented reality: a long-term analysis of in-situ instructions at the assembly workplace. In: Proceedings of the 10th International Conference on Pervasive Technologies Related to Assistive Environments, pp. 222–229 (2017)
28. Gavish, N., et al.: Evaluating virtual reality and augmented reality training for industrial maintenance and assembly tasks. Interact. Learn. Environ. **23**(6), 778–798 (2015)
29. Werrlich, S., Nitsche, K., Notni, G.: Demand analysis for an augmented reality based assembly training. In: Proceedings of the 10th International Conference on PErvasive Technologies Related to Assistive Environments, pp. 416–422 (2017)
30. Valentini, P.P.: Natural interface for interactive virtual assembly in augmented reality using leap motion controller. Int. J. Interact. Des. Manuf. (IJIDeM) **12**(4), 1157–1165 (2018)
31. Palmarini, R., Del Amo, I.F., Bertolino, G., Dini, G., Erkoyuncu, J.A., Roy, R., Farnsworth, M.: Designing an AR interface to improve trust in human-robots collaboration. Procedia CIRP **70**, 350–355 (2018)
32. Makris, S., Karagiannis, P., Koukas, S., Matthaiakis, A.S.: Augmented reality system for operator support in human–robot collaborative assembly. CIRP Ann. **65**(1), 61–64 (2016)
33. EON Homepage. https://www.eonreality.com/use-cases/augmented-virtual-reality-manufa cturing/ Accessed 28 Aug 2019
34. Danielsson, O., Syberfeldt, A., Brewster, R., Wang, L.: Assessing instructions in augmented reality for human-robot collaborative assembly by using demonstrators. Procedia CIRP **63**, 89–94 (2017)
35. Waegel, K., Brooks, F.P.: Filling the gaps: hybrid vision and inertial tracking. In: 2013 IEEE International Symposium on Mixed and Augmented Reality (ISMAR), IEEE (2013)
36. Wang, Y., Zhang, S., Wan, B., He, W., Bai, X.: Point cloud and visual feature-based tracking method for an augmented reality-aided mechanical assembly system. Int. J. Adv. Manuf. Technol. **99**(9–12), 2341–2352 (2018)
37. Bhattacharya, B., Winer, E.H.: Augmented reality via expert demonstration authoring (AREDA). Comput. Ind. **105**, 61–79 (2019)
38. Syberfeldt, A., Danielsson, O., Holm, M., Wang, L.: Visual assembling guidance using augmented reality. Procedia Manuf. **1**, 98–109 (2015)
39. Chimienti, V., Iliano, S., Dassisti, M., Dini, G., Failli, F.: Guidelines for implementing augmented reality procedures in assisting assembly operations. In: International Precision Assembly Seminar, pp. 174–179. Springer, Heidelberg (2010)

6

Resource Interface Matchmaking as a Part of Automatic Capability Matchmaking

Niko Siltala[(⊠)] ⓘ, Eeva Järvenpää ⓘ, and Minna Lanz ⓘ

Tampere University, Korkeakoulunkatu 6, 33014 Tampere, Finland
{niko.siltala,eeva.jarvenpaa,minna.lanz}@tuni.fi

Abstract. This paper presents a case study for capability matchmaking method and specifically focuses on interface matchmaking process. This method can be utilised during production system design or reconfiguration by system integrators or end users. They will benefit from fast and automatic resource searches over large resource catalogues. The paper binds together the process around the capability and interface matchmaking, which are presented more in detail in our earlier publications. In this paper, the use of matchmaking process is exemplified, and a verification of the method is provided with two test cases.

Keywords: Interface matchmaking · Assembly system design · System reconfiguration

1 Introduction

Responsiveness of manufacturing is an important strategic goal for manufacturing companies operating in a highly dynamic environment characterized by constant change. Such responsiveness and adaptivity is related to the need to reconfigure and adjust the production and corresponding production system as efficiently as possible to the required changes in processing functions, production capacity, and the dispatching of the orders. [1, 2] To do this, the production system needs an inherent ability to facilitate continual and timely change in its structure and in its functional operations.

Traditionally, the production system design and reconfiguration has been time-consuming process done by the human designer. It includes search for suitable and connectable resources, and it relies heavily on the expertise and tacit knowledge of the system integrators and the end users of the system [3]. Meeting the requirements of fast adaptation calls for new methods and solutions that would drastically reduce the time and effort put into system design [2, 4], both in brownfield and greenfield scenarios. Plug and play interfaces, modern information and communication technologies, formal information models representing resources and products, as well as simulations and other computer-aided intelligent planning tools can all contribute to such methods and solutions [2, 4]. During the system design and re-configuration, new structural configurations are built to fulfil the functional requirements set by the product [4]. Similar to the design of modular products [5] – consideration of interfaces plays an important role in enabling the interchangeability and independence of resource elements. Thus, in order to achieve a feasible structural configuration, the combined production resources must have compatible interfaces.

Within the past two decades, there have been multiple different projects and research [6–8] trying to provide computerized support for system design and reconfiguration planning process. According to [6], the modular architecture paradigm for new production systems, which focuses on the clear functional decoupling of equipment module functionalities and the use of standardized interfaces to promote interchangeability, presents the possibility for developing automated system design and reconfiguration methods. Important steps towards modular assembly equipment and standardized hardware and control interfaces was made, for example, in EU-funded project EUPASS [7]. The recently finished project ReCaM [8], which results this paper also reports, aimed to develop a set of integrated tools for rapid and autonomous reconfiguration of production systems. The approach relies on a formal unified functional description of resources [9], providing a foundation for rapid creation of new system configurations through capability-based matchmaking of product requirements and resource offerings [10].

This paper will present, through two case studies, how the capability matchmaking process operates. Emphasis is placed on the interface matchmaking. First objective is to present how the interface concept for production resources can be utilized as a part of the capability matchmaking [11] procedure. Secondly, we will present, through two cases, how the capability and interface matchmaking work in practise and how they sort out feasible resource combinations for the system designer.

The paper is organized as follows. Section 2 introduces shortly our overall capability matchmaking approach and its associated concepts and data models. Section 3 focuses on the interface matchmaking process in general. In Sect. 4 we present with two cases how the matchmaking process advances and provides the matching resource combinations. Section 5 discusses how we have verified the automatically gained matchmaking results. The specific focus is placed on interface matching viewpoint. In the Sect. 6 we conclude the work done.

2　Capability Matchmaking Process

2.1　Information Models Involved

The capability matchmaking relies on different information models that are used to describe the resources and products in a formalized way. For each different resource, a resource description (RD) file (in XML format) is created and published by the resource provider. These files are saved to different catalogues, either global or local, from where the potential users, in this case the capability matchmaking software, can then utilize the descriptions. The resource description represents the basic characteristics, capabilities, interfaces, and properties of the resource. It can contain links to documentation, CAD models and to illustrative figures. One essential part in the resource description is the capability description of the resource, which selects the relevant capabilities and their parameters from the Capability Model.

Central information model for the matchmaking is the Capability Model. The Capability Model is a formal ontology model which is used to model capabilities and their relations. Capability consists of concept name, such as "Drilling", "Milling", "Moving" and so on, and parameters, such as "payload", "speed" or "torque". The model consists of simple and combined capabilities, where combined capabilities are combinations of simple capabilities. For instance "Picking" is a combined capability which requires as an input "Moving", and some sort of "Grasping" capability. The capability model forms a capability catalogue, which is a pool of capabilities that can be assigned to resources to describe their functionality. [12]

The Resource Model Ontology imports the Capability Model and is used to describe manufacturing resources and their capabilities. An instance ontology of Resource Model can be automatically created and populated by reading in the information from RDs. The Resource Model can also be used to model systems composed of multiple resources. Based on the relationships between simple and combined capabilities, it is possible to identify potential resource combinations that can have a certain combined capability. [12]

The Resource Model imports another ontology, called Resource Interface Model, which describes the resource interfaces in detail. It is used during the matchmaking for checking the compatibility of the resources from interface perspective. In other words, it is utilized to assess if two resources can be connected physically together. It includes information about interface definition, including identifier, name, category, gender and purpose of the interface; Interface standard and its characteristics and the standardisation organization; Interface port implementation. [13]

Also, the product requirements are described using formal Product Model ontology. The Product Requirement Description (PRD) contains information about the parts, how they are connected to assemblies and what kind of processes and process parameters should be used. The Product Requirement Description uses the same concepts that are involved in the Capability Model. Thus, there is a link between the resource capabilities and process requirements of the product. [11]

2.2 Overview of Capability Matchmaking Process

Figure 1 represents the capability matchmaking process. The Capability Matchmaking is implemented as a service [14] that the System Designer may call through his desired planning system. When the designer wants to launch this service, he will have to give it certain inputs, for example the matchmaking search space. This input includes description of the resources that should be taken into consideration during the matchmaking, and description of the product (i.e. the PRD), for which a match will be looked for. Thus, the resources and product requirements need to be formally described before the capability matchmaking process can be initialised. These resources in specific search space are automatically processed and read in from RDs to form a Resource Model instance ontology. The input related to the resources may be either a description of the existing system layout (i.e. a resource hierarchy building a system layout) or pool of resources selected from one or various resource catalogues. In the latter case, the input is in form of a flat list of resources creating a resource pool. The Capability Matchmaking software will then process these inputs and provide the matchmaking result to the designer. The result includes information about the resources and resource combinations matching for each process step of the product requirement. This information can then be further processed in the system designer's planning tool where the desired resources are selected according to some company or situation specific criteria. [14, 15]

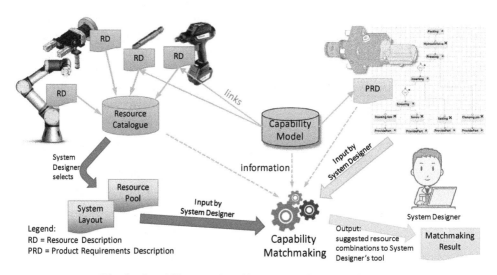

Fig. 1. Capability matchmaking process inputs and outputs

The capability matchmaking involves two aspects: Generation of new resource combinations and matching the capabilities of these combinations with the product requirements. The process flow is illustrated in Fig. 2 from left to right. First, the matchmaking system generates new resource combinations that have capabilities requested by the product, e.g. "Screwing". Next, the interface compatibility of the resources is checked based on the interface matchmaking rules [13, 16]. After that, the combined capability parameters are calculated for the remaining resource combinations based on the combined capability rules. Finally, when the resource combinations have been created and their combined capabilities have been calculated, these combined capabilities are compared to the characteristics and requirements of the product. For this purpose, capability matchmaking rules are used, which find out which resource combinations answer the requirements of the product. The combined capability rules have been introduced in [17] and matchmaking rules in [11]. Both have been implemented with SPIN rule language (SPARQL Inferencing Language).

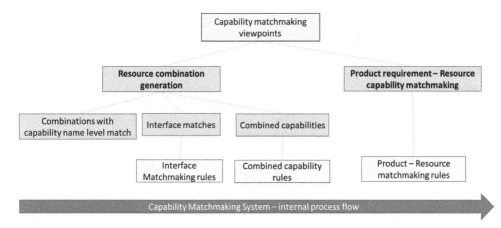

Fig. 2. Internal process phases in capability matchmaking

3 Interface Matching Process

The objective of the interface matching is to evaluate if a finite set of resources is connectable all together. The interface matching process and algorithm has been explained in detail in [16], and data models, namely Resource Interface Model, and rules guiding the interface matching process in [13]. The interface matching process is independent evaluation procedure working as one phase of capability matchmaking. Once capability matchmaking finds a potential combination of resources, it calls the interface matchmaking procedure with the found resources as a set of tested resources. With the call capability matchmaking provides populated Resource Model ontology as argument. At the end of the call, the interface matching procedure responses with simple true or false response, if the given set of resources are connectable from interface point of view or not.

The interface matchmaking algorithm has two main phases – coarse level and fine level interface matching. The former focuses on the interface code and the gender. The first checks only that the string label representing the coded name of the interface standard is the same at both resource sides. The second defines the polarity of the interface and evaluates it with simple rule – male and female or two neutrals can be connected. Only the coarsely connected resources can continue to fine level interface matching. It utilises the detailed interface characteristics. Each interface contains zero to many additional characteristics. These are properties with name, value and operator, which describes a rule how this characteristic should be compared with a counterpart in order to have successful connection between the resources. Each characteristic is defined as optional or mandatory. All mandatory ones must match with counterpart before resources are deduced connectable at fine level. If the interface does not have any additional characteristics defined, the coarse level match is directly valid at fine level.

The algorithm is implemented with Java. It makes several SPARQL queries to Resource Model and Resource Interface Model ontologies, in order to collect information and reason out connectable resources. It also uses internal data structures, where buffered information and intermediate results are stored for later use. At the end of both interface matching levels, algorithm uses intermediate results to create network out of tested resources. If and only if a single connected network containing all resources is created, it is determined that these resources are connectable. Detailed description of the algorithm is provided in [16]. The software module implementing the interface match-making process is now integrated as integral part of overall capability matchmaking process.

4   Case Examples

Two case examples are used to illustrate the capability matchmaking process, specifically focusing more deeply into the interface matchmaking phase. The first case focuses on screw driving and the second on pick and place operations. In practice, capability match-making processes all product requirements i.e. each process step one by one and provides output results for each process step at once. For illustration and simpler representation, the cases presented here focus only on a single process step and its requirements and results.

4.1   Screwdriving Solution

This case focuses on a single process step, which defines the requirement for fastening two parts with a M6 sized screw with socket head cap (socket size 5 mm). The required end torque is 13..17 Nm. The matchmaking for this process step is illustrated in Fig. 3, which shows only a subset of our complete test data. First, the matchmaking will create new resource combinations from the available resource pool for the required capability at capability concept name level, i.e. resource combinations that could provide "Screwing" capability. The available resources in the resource pool are illustrated in the up left corner in the figure, while the first phase presents four different combinations created by the matchmaking software. While creating these combinations, matchmaking software will simultaneously check that the interfaces of the resources match at fine level, and that the resources can be physically connected. In case of the resource combination (b) on the second phase, the tool bit does not fit into the screw driver's tool interface and thus incompatible combination from interface perspective is filtered out.

After that, the matchmaking system will calculate the combined capability param-eters for the remaining combinations and check that the capability parameters match with the parametric requirements of the product. During the combined capability calcu-lation, the matchmaking system considers each individual resource and calculates the viable range for the whole combination. I.e. if a tool bit can bear only a certain torque, it can be limiting the overall torque for the whole combination. The combined capability SPIN rules are used for inferring the combination parameters and matchmaking SPIN rules are used to compare the parametric requirements of the product with the capability parameters. In this example case the matchmaking system will check that the screw type and screw head size matches with the tool size and that the provided torque is within the range of the required torque. Unsuitable resources and resource combinations are again filtered out. In this case the combination possibility (a) (in phase three) does not provide enough torque, as it limits in maximum to 6 Nm, and it is eliminated from this

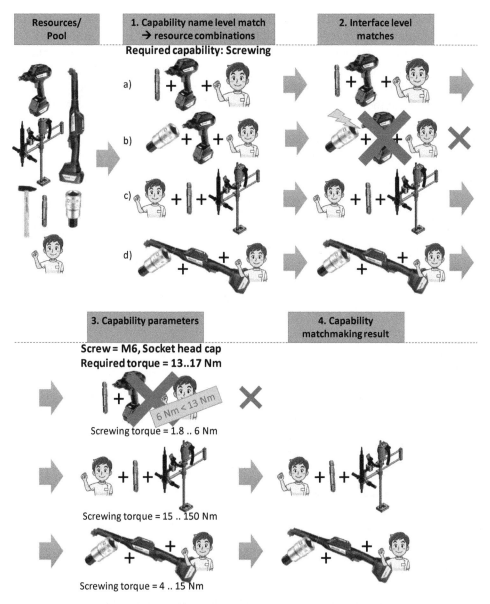

Fig. 3. Capability matchmaking process for screwing case

result. In the end, only the two suitable resource combinations are left as suggestions in the matchmaking result.

Within our practical test data, the resource pool used for this specific case had 68 resources. 530 resource combinations providing "Screwing" capability where found, and 36 out of those was found compatible from the interface point of view. Combined capabilities were calculated for these and finally two resource combinations were found feasible for the given product requirement. These were presented in Fig. 3.

Table 1 shows interface details for the resources used in this case example. Interface port is a placeholder for interface(s) used for a specific function. Interface standard identifies the code of the standard used. Gender sets the polarity of the interface implementation. Additional interface characteristics define properties characterising the interface, such as size and shape in this example. Comparison operator defines how a characteristic should be used in the compatibility evaluation. In this case operator is 'SAME_SET', which means that at both sides of the connection, the characteristic value(s) must be the same to allow successful connection.

Table 1. Listing of resource, their interfaces and interface characteristics for screwdriving case.

Resource	Port	Interface standard	Gender	IF characteristics	Operator
1. NXP pistolgrip nutrunner	IF1	ISO_1173:2001	F	C.Shape = HEXAGON	SAME_SET
				C.Size = 1–4	SAME_SET
	IF3	HUMAN.INTERACTION.GENERAL	M	–	
2. NXA right-angle nutrunner	IF1	ISO_1173:2001	M	C.Shape = SQUARE	SAME_SET
				C.Size = 3–8	SAME_SET
	IF3	HUMAN.INTERACTION.GENERAL	M	–	
3. Tightening system 350 - EC304	IF1	ISO_1173:2001	F	C.Shape = HEXAGON	SAME_SET
				C.Size = 7–16	SAME_SET
	IF3	COMP-A_MOUNT_0011	M	–	
	IF5	HUMAN.INTERACTION.GENERAL	M	–	
4. Tool bit for screwing - 1/4$''$ - HexSocket 4 mm	IF1	ISO_1173:2001	M	C.Shape = HEXAGON	SAME_SET
				C.Size = 1–4	SAME_SET
	IF2	ISO_4762:2004	M	C.NominalKeySize = 4	SAME_SET
5. Tool bit for screwing - 1/4$''$ - HexSocket 5 mm	IF1	ISO_1173:2001	M	C.Shape = HEXAGON	SAME_SET
				C.Size = 1–4	SAME_SET
	IF2	ISO_4762:2004	M	C.NominalKeySize = 5	SAME_SET
6. Tool bit for screwing - 3/8$''$ - HexSocket 5 mm	IF1	ISO_1173:2001	F	C.Shape = SQUARE	SAME_SET
				C.Size = 3–8	SAME_SET
	IF2	ISO_4762:2004	M	C.NominalKeySize = 5	SAME_SET
7. Tool bit for screwing - 7/16$''$ - HexSocket 5 mm	IF1	ISO_1173:2001	M	C.Shape = HEXAGON	SAME_SET
				C.Size = 7–16	SAME_SET
	IF2	ISO_4762:2004	M	C.NominalKeySize = 5	SAME_SET
8. Hammer	IF1	HUMAN.INTERACTION.GENERAL	M	–	
9. Human operator - expert	IF1	HUMAN.INTERACTION.GENERAL	F	–	

In Fig. 3. we have the first resource combination (a) from resources 1, 5 and 9. The interfaces allows the combination (See Table 1) – driver (1) has fitting interface (IF1) with the tool bit (5/IF1) at standard, gender and all interface characteristics. Driver (1) has also fitting interface (IF2) with the operator (9/IF1) moving the driver. But later, the combination (a) fails to fulfil the capability parameter requirement for generating enough output torque. The second resource combination (1, 6 and 9) fails at interface matching. The gender of driver (1/IF1) and tool bit (6/IF1) does not match, and even it would, the interface characteristics are not fitting (See Table 1). This would be the case if driver (1/IF1) is tried to connect with tool bit (7/IF1), when the interface characteristic C.Size will prevent the connection. In case of the resource combinations (c) and (d) both interface and capability parameter requirement are matching, leading to propose resource combinations (3, 7, 9) and (2, 6, 9) as a match and potential solution for this product requirement.

4.2 Pick and Place Solution

Another case example focuses on pick and place case. Similar kind of case was discussed as test case in [13]. The handled part is cylinder shaped having diameter of 44 mm and length of 30 mm and it weights 50 g. The product requirement defines following needs for the process step: grasping is done externally, maximum allowed compressive force is 10 N, transportation is needed in XYZ-directions (linear movements), and positioning accuracy is 0.2 mm.

Within our practical test data, the same resource pool with 68 resources is used as in the previous case. It contains two grippes and seven moving devices. The capability name level matchmaking found 12 potential combinations providing "pick and place" capability, and four out of those were found compatible also from the interface point of view. Combined capability parameters were calculated for these and finally three resource combinations were found feasible for the given product requirement. In this case three different robot arms are found mating with one of the grippers. Resource combination (a) from resources 4 and 1; (b) from 5 and 1; and (c) from 6 and 1 (See Table 2). The resource (4) demonstrates use of several standard interfaces for same interface port. In this case the Schunk-SWS interface is implemented with help of an adapter plate, thus a tool fulfilling either of these standards can be connected to this interface port. In case of resource combination (c) the gripper has two interface ports where the connection can take place – 6/IF2 and 6/IF3. The current version of interface matchmaking does not count or reserve the interface ports, but match is returned if there is any suitable position for connection. The fourth resource combination (d) is a manipulator (3) mating with the gripper (2) (See Table 2), but it provides motion only in two degrees of freedom, thus getting neglected from the result.

5 Verification of Capability and Interface Matchmaking Results

Important part of our SW development process was testing and verification. We used automatic unit tests for our SW development, but the verification of the end results was done mainly manually. We defined manually the expected resource combinations, and inferred and calculated the combined capability parameters from the input resource pool and the product requirement in question. This defined a target result, which was then compared with the result of automatic capability matchmaking process. The verification contained mainly two evaluation criteria: a) all resource combinations/resources compared to manually deduced matches are found, and b) no any false positive matches are included. I.e. resource combination is included to the result, even it is not solving the product requirement from whatever perspective or its resources are not connectable together.

In the development phase, we verified separately and gradually the operation of the different phases of our capability matchmaking process. I.e. starting from name level matchmaking and ensuring gradually, that correct sub-set or sub-result was passed on

Table 2. Listing of resources, their interfaces and interface characteristics for pick and place.

Resource	Port	Interface standard	Gender	IF characteristics	Operator
1. Gripper1.1	IF1	Schunk_SWS	F	C.Size = 005	SAME_SET
				C.Pneumatic = Pxx	SAME_SET
	IF3	General_Tool_TCP	M	–	
2. Gripper-disc1	IF1	COMP-A_GRIPPER_0001	M	C.Size = 30	SAME_SET
	IF3	General_Tool_TCP	M	–	
3. Lab_2-axis manipulator	IF1	SHAPE.FLANGE.CIRCULAR	N		
	IF2	COMP-A_GRIPPER_0001	F	C.Size = 30	SAME_SET
4. UR_UR10 ind	IF1	SHAPE.FLANGE.CIRCULAR	N		
	IF2	ISO_9409-1:2004	F	C.Pitch_circle_diameter = 50	SAME_SET
				C.Number_of_thread_holes = 4	SAME_SET
	IF2	Schunk_SWS	M	C.Size = 005	SAME_SET
				C.Pneumatic = Pxx	SAME_SET
5. UR_UR10 collaborative	IF1	SHAPE.FLANGE.CIRCULAR	N		
	IF2	ISO_9409-1:2004	F	C.Pitch_circle_diameter = 50	SAME_SET
				C.Number_of_thread_holes = 4	SAME_SET
	IF2	Schunk_SWS	M	C.Size = 005	SAME_SET
				C.Pneumatic = Pxx	SAME_SET
6. Dual-arm robot	IF1	SHAPE.FLANGE.CIRCULAR	N		
	IF2	Schunk_SWS	M	C.Size = 005	SAME_SET
				C.Pneumatic = Pxx	SAME_SET
	IF3	Schunk_SWS	M	C.Size = 005	SAME_SET
				C.Pneumatic = Pxx	SAME_SET
	IF5	SHAPE FLANGE RECTANGLE 4HOLE	M	P.Hole_pitch_in_X = 0.042	SAME_SET
				P.Hole_pitch_in_Y = 0.042	SAME_SET
7. Balancer device	IF3	General_Tool_TCP	M	–	
	IF4	HUMAN.INTERACTION.GENERAL	M	–	
8. Human operator - expert	IF1	HUMAN.INTERACTION.GENERAL	F	–	

the next phase. This was mandatory because of complexity of our system and eventually timely long run of complete capability matchmaking process.

The verification was comprehensive and truthful, because of the use of representative resources even the amount of resources was limited. We had different kind of resources providing the same simple capability, with good mix of interfaces and capability parameter values. The finite set made it possible to determine and calculate manually all possible resource combinations and their combined parameter values. The processes (capability name matching, SPIN rules, and interface matching algorithm) are expected to operate deterministically, thus the matchmaking should behave similarly and find correct results when the search space (i.e. size of resource pool) is enlarged.

6 Discussion and Conclusions

This paper presented interface matchmaking process and how it can be used to sort out resource combinations as a part of capability matching process. We have integrated the interface matching software module as integral part of the overall matchmaking process, and we have proven that the implementation of the prototype does work as desired. In this paper, the operation of the whole capability matchmaking process was demonstrated through two cases, focusing on interface matching. The presented cases illustrate how the capability matchmaking creates proposed resource combinations, and how interface and parametric matching filter out the non-fitting combinations, leaving eventually only the fitting matches as output. Sub-set of resources, which are involved within the cases, and the resources' interface definitions were described in the paper. The verification of results was discussed. The output of capability matchmaking corresponds with the manually deduced results for the given test resource pool containing 68 resources.

The capability matchmaking method can facilitate rapid system design and reconfiguration planning, by allowing computerised methods to find feasible system configuration scenarios to different product requirements. Use of automatic matchmaking reduces and speeds up the manual design efforts, as the system designer can focus his/her resource selection to truly connectable and fit resources, instead of searching for resources, and analysing their interfaces and properties. The matchmaking can be applied over large resource catalogues containing thousands of resources and their variants, which can be automatically screened to find the few appropriate resources and resource combinations. Additionally, the digital resource catalogues are expected to contain production resources from multiple vendors, which increases number of resources to study, but also increases the number of available alternatives. Thus, matchmaking opens possibilities for new and more innovative solutions to be found. The system designer is not bound to comfortable "old and known solution", which is almost solving the requirements, but he/she can select the optimum one.

As a future work, we have some ideas to continue the interface matchmaking procedure to still finer level of detail including resource matching at interface port level. This can extend the matchmaking procedure for suggesting also physical layouts, not only resource combinations. Testing of capability matchmaking tools and processes will be continued with more resources, and different assembly and manufacturing processes.

References

1. Koren, Y., Shpitalni, M.: Design of reconfigurable manufacturing systems. J. Manuf. Syst. **29**, 130–141 (2010). https://doi.org/10.1016/j.jmsy.2011.01.001
2. Wiendahl, H.-P., et al.: Changeable manufacturing - classification design and operation. CIRP Ann. **56**, 783–809 (2007). https://doi.org/10.1016/j.cirp.2007.10.003
3. Rösiö, C., Säfsten, K.: Reconfigurable production system design – theoretical and practical challenges. J. Manuf. Technol. Manage. **24**, 998–1018 (2013). https://doi.org/10.1108/JMTM-02-2012-0021
4. Westkämper, E.: Factory transformability: adapting the structures of manufacturing. In: Reconfigurable Manufacturing Systems and Transformable Factories, pp. 371–381. Springer, Berlin (2006). https://doi.org/10.1007/3-540-29397-3_19
5. Pakkanen, J., Juuti, T., Lehtonen, T.: Brownfield process: a method for modular product family development aiming for product configuration. Des. Stud. **45**, 210–241 (2016). https://doi.org/10.1016/j.destud.2016.04.004
6. Ferreira, P., Lohse, N., Ratchev, S.: Multi-agent architecture for reconfiguration of precision modular assembly systems. In: Ratchev, S. (ed.) IPAS 2010. LNCS, vol. 315, pp. 247–254. Springer, Berlin (2010). https://doi.org/10.1007/978-3-642-11598-1_29
7. EUPASS Consortium: EUPASS - Evolvable Ultra-Precision Assembly SystemS - Project. EU FP6, GA No 507978. https://cordis.europa.eu/project/rcn/75342/factsheet/en (2006). Accessed 11 Nov 2019

8. ReCaM - Rapid reconfiguration of flexible production systems through capability- based adaptation, auto-configuration, integrated tools for production planning - project. EU Horizon 2020, GA No 680759. http://www.recam-project.eu/ (2017). Accessed 11 Nov 2019

9. Siltala, N., Järvenpää, E., Lanz, M.: Formal information model for representing production resources. In: Nääs, I. et al. (eds.) APMS 2016. IFIP Advances in Information and Communication Technology, vol. 488, pp. 53–60. Springer, Cham (2016). https://doi.org/10.1007/978-3-319-51133-7_7

10. Järvenpää, E., Siltala, N., Hylli, O., Lanz, M.: Capability matchmaking procedure to support rapid configuration and re-configuration of production systems. Procedia Manuf. **11**, 1053–1060 (2017). https://doi.org/10.1016/j.promfg.2017.07.216

11. Järvenpää, E., Siltala, N., Hylli, O., Lanz, M.: Product model ontology and its use in capability-based matchmaking. Procedia CIRP **72**, 1094–1099 (2018). https://doi.org/10.1016/j.procir.2018.03.211

12. Järvenpää, E., Siltala, N., Hylli, O., Lanz, M.: The development of an ontology for describing the capabilities of manufacturing resources. J. Intell. Manuf. **30**, 959–978 (2019). https://doi.org/10.1007/s10845-018-1427-6

13. Siltala, N., Järvenpää, E., Lanz, M.: Creating resource combinations based on formally described hardware interfaces. In: Ratchev, S. (ed.) Precision Assembly in the Digital Age. IPAS 2018. IFIP Advances in Information and Communication Technology, vol. 530, pp. 29–39. Springer, Cham (2019). https://doi.org/10.1007/978-3-030-05931-6_3

14. Mital, A., Siltala, N., Järvenpää, E., Lanz, M.: Web-based solution to automate capability matchmaking for rapid system design and reconfiguration. Procedia CIRP **81**, 288–293 (2019). https://doi.org/10.1016/j.procir.2019.03.050

15. Järvenpää, E., Siltala, N., Hylli, O., Lanz, M.: Implementation of capability matchmaking software facilitating faster production system design and reconfiguration planning. J. Manuf. Syst. **53**, 261–270 (2019). https://doi.org/10.1016/j.jmsy.2019.10.003

16. Siltala, N., Järvenpää, E., Lanz, M.: A method to evaluate interface compatibility during production system design and reconfiguration. Procedia CIRP **81**, 282–287 (2019). https://doi.org/10.1016/j.procir.2019.03.049

17. Järvenpää, E., Hylli, O., Siltala, N., Lanz, M.: Utilizing SPIN rules to infer the parameters for combined capabilities of aggregated manufacturing resources. IFAC-PapersOnLine **51**, 84–89 (2018). https://doi.org/10.1016/j.ifacol.2018.08.239

7

Application of Advanced Simulation Methods for the Tolerance Analysis of Mechanical Assemblies

Konstantinos Bacharoudis$^{(\boxtimes)}$ ⓘ, Atanas Popov ⓘ, and Svetan Ratchev ⓘ

University of Nottingham, Nottingham NG7 2RD, UK
Konstantinos.Bacharoudis@nottingham.ac.uk

Abstract. In the frame of a statistical tolerance analysis of complex assemblies, for example an aircraft wing, the capability to predict accurately and fast specified, very small quantiles of the distribution of the assembly key characteristic becomes crucial. The problem is significantly magnified, when the tolerance synthesis problem is considered in which several tolerance analyses are performed and thus, a reliability analysis problem is nested inside an optimisation one in a fully probabilistic approach. The need to reduce the computational time and accurately estimate the specified probabilities is critical. Therefore, herein, a systematic study on several state of the art simulation methods is performed whilst they are critically evaluated with respect to their efficiency to deal with tolerance analysis problems. It is demonstrated that tolerance analysis problems are characterised by high dimensionality, high non-linearity of the state functions, disconnected failure domains, implicit state functions and small probability estimations. Therefore, the successful implementation of reliability methods becomes a formidable task. Herein, advanced simulation methods are combined with in-house developed assembly models based on the Homogeneous Transformation Matrix method as well as off-the-self Computer Aided Tolerance tools. The main outcome of the work is that by using an appropriate reliability method, computational time can be reduced whilst the probability of defected products can be accurately predicted. Furthermore, the connection of advanced mathematical toolboxes with off-the-self 3D tolerance tools into a process integration framework introduces benefits to successfully deal with the tolerance allocation problem in the future using dedicated and powerful computational tools.

Keywords: Tolerance analysis · Uncertainty analysis · Monte Carlo simulation · Stratified sampling techniques · Assembly design

1 Introduction

Low volume, high-value mechanical assemblies e.g. an aircraft wing needs a strict dimensional management procedure in place in order to control and manage variation stemming from the various manufacturing processes to fabricate the parts as well as to assemble them and form the final product. This task is quite critical and should be treated at the early stage of the design process in order to ensure functionality, high performance and

© The Author(s) 2021
S. Ratchev (Ed.): IPAS 2020, IFIP AICT 620, pp. 153–167, 2021.
https://doi.org/10.1007/978-3-030-72632-4_11

low manufacturing costs of the designed product. The main core of any dimensional management methodology is the ability to perform tolerance analysis and synthesis at the early design stage and thus, to predict the variance or the entire distribution of specified assembly key characteristics (AKC) as well as to optimise and allocate design tolerances for the assembly features in the various parts by minimising manufacturing cost. For the latter case, several studies have been performed, e.g. in [1], in which the optimisation problem in most of the cases was formulated using mainly one objective function, the manufacturing cost, and constraint functions based on the worst case error or on the root sum square variance of the AKC. Both formulations are given by

$$\Delta A = \frac{\partial f}{\partial d_1} t_1 + \frac{\partial f}{\partial d_2} t_2 + \cdots + \frac{\partial f}{\partial d_n} t_n \tag{1}$$

$$\sigma_A = \sqrt{\left(\frac{\partial f}{\partial d_1}\right)^2 \sigma_{d_1}^2 + \left(\frac{\partial f}{\partial d_2}\right)^2 \sigma_{d_2}^2 + \cdots \left(\frac{\partial f}{\partial d_n}\right)^2 \sigma_{d_n}^2} \tag{2}$$

where the AKC is denoted by A and it can be expressed as a function of the contributors d_i, i.e. other dimensions on the parts of the assembly formulating the tolerance chain, as $A = f(d_1, d_2, \ldots, d_n)$. The function f corresponds to the assembly model. $\frac{\partial f}{\partial d_i}$ is the sensitivity of the AKC to the contributors d_i, t_i is the tolerance i.e. the range that one dimension d_i can fluctuate about its respective nominal value $\overline{d_i}$ and $\sigma_{d_i}^2$ is the variance of contributor d_i used in statistical tolerancing. Usually, in statistical tolerancing, the contributor can be expressed as a random variable with mean value the nominal dimension value $\overline{d_i}$ and standard deviation defined such that N-sigma standard deviations to result in the tolerance range, i.e. $t_i = N\sigma_{d_i}$. This N-sigma standard deviation spread is also known as the natural tolerance range. Furthermore, considering geometrical tolerances, t_i can be associated with more than one random variables, for example the positional tolerance of a hole which is generally a function of two parameters, i.e. the magnitude and the angle of the positional vector, that gives the location of the varied centre of the feature with respect to (wrt) the feature frame in the nominal form. It is important to highlight that, in the case of Eq. (2), the estimation of the variance of the AKC assumes a linearization of the assembly function f whilst the probability distribution of the AKC is not taken into account in the estimation.

In an attempt to consider more statistical information about the AKC as well as the actual type of the assembly model function to the tolerance synthesis problem, constraint functions of the optimisation problem can be expressed based on the probability of defected products i.e. products that cannot meet the specification limits. Lending the terminology from the structural reliability analysis field, the tolerance synthesis problem thus, can be formulated as a Reliability-Based Optimisation (RBO) problem [2], its general form is given by

$$\begin{aligned} &\textit{minimise } C(t) \\ &\textit{subject to } P_D\big[g_j(\pmb{x_m}, d_i(\pmb{t}), SLs) \leq 0\big] \leq P_t, \, j = 1, .., m \end{aligned} \tag{3}$$

where $\pmb{t}$ is the vector of the design variables of the problem either deterministic parameters or random variables. For the tolerance synthesis problem, it corresponds to the dimensional or geometrical tolerances on the features of the various parts and are deterministic variables. $C(t)$ is the objective function to be minimized and has been mainly established by the manufacturing cost of the product including cost-tolerance relationships for every applied tolerance. P_D is the probability of defected products i.e. the probability of the event that the variation of the specified assembly key characteristic (AKC) do not conform to the specification limits, SLs, $g_j(x_m, d_i(t), SLs)$ stands for the limit state functions i.e. the relationship between the AKC and the specification limits, SLs. It is reminded that AKC is a function of the random variables $d_1, d_2, \ldots, d_n$ and the design parameters t i.e. applied tolerances. The mathematical formulation of the limit state functions can be an explicit mathematical expression or can be given implicitly e.g. by the use of a Computer Aided Tolerance (CAT) tool. P_t is the target probability of defected products and is usually calculated by the yield, i.e. the probability of the complementary event which generally equals to 99.7% following six-sigma quality approach. x_m is the uncertainty to which may some of the model parameters can be subjected to.

It is clear from the formulation of Eq. (3) that tolerance synthesis is an optimization problem with a nested reliability analysis problem in it, in which P_D should be estimated for every specified AKC in every iteration of the optimization algorithm. Currently, state of the art commercial CAT tools, e.g. 3DCS [3], use Crude Monte Carlo (CMC) simulation to perform the tolerance analysis. It is already common that crude Monte Carlo method can become very time consuming when estimation of small probabilities is involved. This probably explains the fact that tolerance synthesis is still treated in commercial CAT tools by using linearized assembly models and linear optimisation techniques e.g. in [3]. The problem of tolerance allocation becomes computationally very demanding whilst both appropriate optimization and reliability methods should be used to successfully deal with complex assemblies.

Thus, the focus of this work is on the tolerance analysis and the fast and accurate estimation of P_D using advanced simulation methods. A lot of work has been performed toward the development of advanced reliability techniques [4], nevertheless, mainly in the field of the structural reliability analysis rather than on the tolerance analysis field. Reliability methods can be categorized as approximate or gradient-based methods, simulation techniques and metamodeling based methods. It is interesting to notice that few of these methods have been implemented into the tolerance analysis field e.g. in [5] or more recently [6] whilst a systematic study needs to be carried out for their successful implementation in the field.

Therefore, in this work, state of the art reliability methods are explored in order to identify either the most suitable one or the gaps for further development of the probabilistic methods applied to this type of problem. Three simulation methods, namely the Latin Hypercube sampling technique (LH) [7], Quasi Monte Carlo simulation using Sobol's sequences (QMCS) [8] and the Subset Simulation method (SS) [9] are implemented to solve a tolerance analysis problem. The three methods are evaluated in terms of speed and accuracy against crude Monte Carlo simulation predictions. Initially, the case study is presented for an assembly consisted of two parts adopted from [10]. Although the example is elementary, it is adequate to highlight all the difficulties introduced in the estimation of the probability of defected products P_D. The rationale behind the selection of LH, QMCS and SS is explained by thoroughly examining the characteristics of the limit state function of the problem. A second case study is analysed in which the development of the assembly models is accomplished by building appropriate models using the commercial CAT software, 3DCS variation analyst. The ability to speed up the probability estimation of existed CAT tools using collaboratively off-the-self statistical tools gives the benefits to exploit the capabilities of each software to the maximum. That is, very complex assemblies can be analysed using professional CAT tools taking advantages of advanced mathematical toolboxes to implement the reliability analyses. This is the first step to establish a process integration and design optimization framework in order to deal with the more complex problem, the tolerance allocation one.

2   Tolerance Modelling

2.1   Case Study

Two examples were considered in this work to study and prove the efficiency of the selected reliability methods for tolerance analysis problems. More specifically, the first assembly was adopted from [10] and concerns a simple arrangement of two parts on a fixture. The assembly sequence and indexing plan has been thoroughly presented in [10].

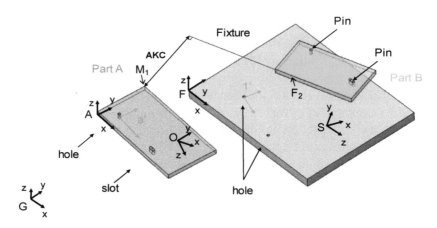

Fig. 1. Case study 1: two parts on a fixture along with the established frames and the AKC

The AKC of interest is depicted in Fig. 1 and comprises the distance between point M_1 in part A from the surface F_2 in part B. Variation was introduced by assuming positional tolerances for every assembly feature in the two parts and the fixture. In total eight tolerances were considered. The tolerance values were taken the same for all the features and are presented in Table 1.

For the second case study in which a 3DCS model has been built, a simple product of two parts was studied again. The two parts are presented in Fig. 2. The AKC is defined by the distance of the point M_1 in part A to the surface F_2 in part B. This example

Table 1. Tolerance specifications for the parts/fixture, first case study

ID	Parts	Tolerance zone	Value [mm]
t_{pos}	Part A/Part B/Fixture	Circular	0.4

is quite similar to the first one. It is presented, however, in order to test the successful implementation and collaboration of advanced reliability methods with commercial CAT tools defined by implicit limit state functions. Positional tolerances were assumed for all the holes with a value given in Table 1.

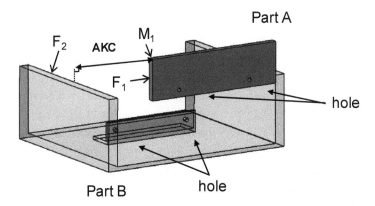

Fig. 2. Case study 2. Two pats forming the assembly in exploded view along with the defined AKC

2.2 Assembly Models

Assembly models were developed for both case studies. For the first example, the models were based on the matrix transformation method [11] and thus, mathematical expressions were formulated and programmed into MATLAB [12]. Briefly, an assembly can be described as a chain of frames [11] among the assembly features of the various parts using homogeneous transformation matrices (HTM). An HTM is defined by

$$T_{ij} = \begin{bmatrix} R_{ij} & p_{ij} \\ 0^T & 1 \end{bmatrix} \tag{4}$$

where R_{ij} is the 3×3 rotation matrix and p_{ij} the 3×1 translation vector. Variation is introduced using the Differential Transformation Matrix (DTM) [11] by multiplying the homogeneous transform T_{ij} by

$$T_{ij}' = T_{ij} DT_j \tag{5}$$

where DT_j is given by

$$DT_j = I_{4\times4} + \begin{bmatrix} 0 & \delta\theta_z & \delta\theta_y & dx \\ -\delta\theta_z & 0 & -\delta\theta_x & dy \\ -\delta\theta_y & \delta\theta_x & 0 & dz \\ 0 & 0 & 0 & 0 \end{bmatrix} \qquad (6)$$

where $\delta\theta_x$, $\delta\theta_y$ and $\delta\theta_z$ small rotations and dx, dy and dz small translations wrt frame j representing variation from the nominal form. It can be shown that the AKC specified in Fig. 1 is a function of two homogeneous transforms given by

$$T_{GO}^{var} = T_{GF}T_{SF}T_{F1'}DT_{1'}T_{1'a'}\left(T_{Aa'}DT_{a'}\right)^{-1}(T_{OA})^{-1} \qquad (7)$$

and

$$T_{GK}^{var} = T_{GS}T_{SF}T_{F2'}DT_{2'}T_{2'b'}\left(T_{Bb'}DT_{b'}\right)^{-1}(T_{KB})^{-1} \qquad (8)$$

where T_{GS} the homogeneous transform from the reference fixture frame S to the global frame G, T_{SF} the homogeneous transform from the auxiliary frame F to the reference fixture frame S, $T_{F1'}$ the homogeneous transform from the compound frame $1'$ to the auxiliary frame F, $T_{1'a'}$ the homogeneous transform from the compound frame on part A, a', to the compound frame on fixture, $1'$, $T_{Aa'}$ the homogeneous transform from the compound frame a' to the auxiliary frame A, T_{OA} the homogeneous transform from the auxiliary frame A to the reference frame A of part A and finally $DT_{1'}$ and $DT_{a'}$ the DTMs that take into account variation in the position of the features on the fixture and the part A respectively. For Eq. (8), transformation matrices are similar to the ones presented for part A by interchanging frames $2'$, b', B and K with $1'$, a', A and O respectively. An in depth discussion about the derivation of the assembly models can be found in [10]. It is important to notice that the AKC is a function of the imposed positional tolerances expressed by the definition of the DTMs. The interpretation of geometric tolerances into the appropriate DTM matrix format was performed according to [13].

For the second example, 3DCS variation analyst has been used to build implicitly the assembly model defining appropriate features, moves, tolerances and measures.

2.3 Probability of Defected Products and Limit State Function

An example of the probability of defected products, that is, the products that do not conform into the specification limits can be observed in Fig. 3. It corresponds to the area below the red curves at the tails of the histogram plot and is defined by

$$P_D = P(LSL > A \cup USL < A) = P(g_1 = A - LSL < 0) + P(g_2 = USL - A < 0) \qquad (9)$$

USL is the Upper Specification Limit and LSL is the Lower Specification Limit usually determined by customer requirements. Generally, the requirement for the assembly process is that six standard deviation of the AKC should result in the specification range as depicted in Fig. 3. Assuming a normal distribution for the AKC, each probability in the right hand side of Eq. (9) should be equal or less than 1.5E−03, a quite small probability value. The limit state functions g_1 and g_2 for the two events in the right hand side of Eq. (9) are given from the expressions inside the parentheses of the two probabilities. The definition of the limit state function has been given using the same approach with the one in the structural reliability field. That is, when the limit state function is negative then the system fails. In the tolerance analysis field, when the limit state function is negative then a defected product has been produced. It is reminded that the AKC, A, is a function of the contributors d_i or in reliability terms, the random variables.

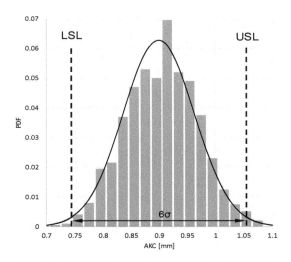

Fig. 3. AKC distribution in relation to the upper and lower specification limits

To explore more the nature of the tolerance analysis problem and visualise the limit state function of Eq. (9), the first case study presented in Fig. 1 is analysed by considering variation only for the pilot hole on part A. This assumption reduces the reliability problem in a two random variable reliability problem and thus, makes possible to visualise the limit state function. The two random variables of the problem are the magnitude (M) and the angle (φ) of the positional vector that gives the location of the varied centre of the pilot hole in Part A wrt the feature frame in nominal form of part A as depicted in Fig. 4.

A Rayleigh distribution is usually assumed for the magnitude, M, and a Uniform one for the angle, φ. The parameter of the Rayleigh distribution is defined such that three standard deviations result in half of the tolerance range depicted in Table 1. The parameters for the Uniform distribution are set equal to 0 and 360° respectively.

The magnitude and the angle of the positional vector are transformed into the appropriate DTM format as presented in [10]. The AKC is evaluated based on the HTMs of Eq. (7)–(8). The 3D graph and the contour plot for the limit state function g_1 in the physical space are presented in Fig. 5. For clearer visualization, the *LSL* was set to a higher value to result in a larger probability value of defected parts, i.e. $P(A - LSL < 0)$

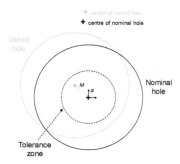

Fig. 4. Nominal and varied form of pilot hole assuming circular tolerance zone

greater than 1.5E−03. Additionally, only two contour lines were plotted in Fig. 5 whilst the axis limits were modified appropriately.

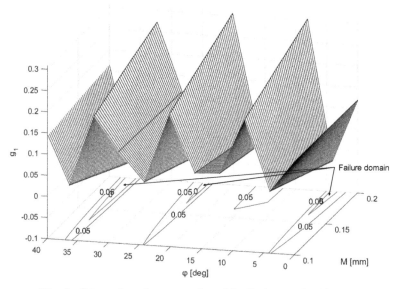

Fig. 5. 3D graph and contour plot of the limit state function g_1

It is interesting to notice that the limit state function is a non-linear/non-convex function even for this simple example that involves just one geometrical tolerance. This is due to the sin and cos function of the angle component when describing the positional tolerance in Fig. 4. Furthermore, the failure domain i.e. the design space where the limit state function becomes negative, consists of several disconnected areas as can be seen in Fig. 5. Thus, to summarise the characteristics of the statistical tolerance analysis problem, they are distinguished by the estimation of small probability values, involving a moderate to high number of random variables when considering complex assemblies in which tens of tolerances will be included in the tolerance chain of the AKC, exhibiting highly non-linear limit state functions as well as disconnected failure domains.

3 Advanced Simulation Methods

In order to select an appropriate reliability method and successfully implemented it to solve the tolerance analysis problem all the aspects discussed in Sect. 2.3 should be considered and addressed to some point. All the above mentioned observation make this task quite difficult.

The estimation of the probabilities in Eq. (9) is equivalent to the computation of specific integrals. That is, generalising the problem, the probability of the event that the limit state function $g(X)$ is negative can be obtained by:

$$P(g(X) \leq 0) = \int_{x \in F} f_X(x)dx = \int_{x \in R} I_{g(x) \leq 0}(x)f_X(x)dx \qquad (10)$$

where X is the vector of random variables (i.e. herein, the contributors d_i) with joint probability density function f_X and $I_{g(x) \leq 0}(x)$ the indicator function in which $I_{g(x) \leq 0}(x) = 1$ if $g(x) \leq 0$ and $I_{g(x) \leq 0}(x) = 0$ otherwise and $F = \{g(X) \leq 0\}$ the failure domain.

Due to the disconnected failure domains of the tolerance analysis problem depicted in Fig. 5, typical gradient-based reliability methods e.g. the First or Second Order Reliability Methods [4] (FORM or SORM), were not considered in this analysis because their typical formulation is inappropriate to deal with this type of problems. Nevertheless, further development of this type of methods should be explored in the future because of their fast probability estimation. Thus, herein, and as a first step, only advanced simulation techniques were assessed. Meta-modelling based methods were not further considered. Additionally, Importance Sampling methods [4], although very efficient and suitable for accelerating the probability estimations by sampling the design space at the region that contribute the most to the probability of interest i.e. probability of defected parts, they were not considered herein. This is because most of these methods consists of a searching algorithm based on the FORM and thus because of the nature of the failure domain, the implementation of Importance Sampling will be inappropriate in its current form. Further investigations need to be performed for this type simulation techniques as well.

3.1 Crude Monte Carlo

The method used as a benchmark in this work is the CMC. CMC is based on the random sampling of the vector of the random variables X. Samples of size N are formed for every random variable and repetitive simulations are performed through the developed assembly models. A sample of output values for each limit state function is obtained. Thus, the probabilities of Eq. (9) can be estimated by

$$P(g(X) \leq 0) = \widehat{P} = \frac{N_{fail}}{N} \qquad (11)$$

where N_{fail} is the number of times that the limit state function becomes negative. A major step in implementing the CMC method is the random number generators. CMC analysis was implemented, herein, using UQLab [14], an advanced general-purpose uncertainty quantification tool developed by ETH Zurich. The tool is based on MATLAB functions and thus, the respective generators were used. Although CMC is quite simple in its implementation and can handle complex, implicit and highly non-linear limit state functions, however, the coefficient of variation, $CoV[\cdot]$, of the probability estimator, $\widehat{P}$, in Eq. (11) i.e. the ratio of the standard deviation to the mean value of the probability estimator, depends on the probability that is being estimated and the sample size N. For a decent probability estimation, i.e. $CoV[\cdot] \approx 10\%$, as a rule of thumb, $\frac{P}{100}$ samples are in need. This indicates a large number of iterations to accurately estimate small probability values. Additionally, random sampling usually generates clusters and gaps as depicted in Fig. 6. This indicates that the random variable space is not efficiently searched. For disconnected failure domains as depicted in Fig. 5, this will introduce the need for more iterations to cover efficiently the entire random variable space.

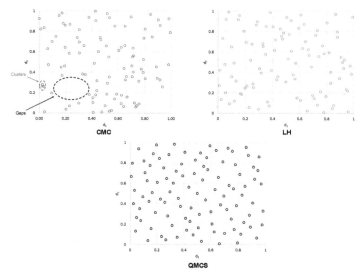

Fig. 6. Two sampled variables using different sampling techniques, namely random sampling (CMC), LH sampling and Sobol' sequences (QMCS).

To alleviate the computational burden associated with Monte Carlo simulation, variance reduction techniques have been proposed to deal with the issue [4]. Herein, a stratified sampling technique was explored, namely the Latin Hypercube simulation as well as a Quasi Monte Carlo simulation method based on Sobol' sequences. Additionally, an adaptive Monte Carlo technique namely the Subset Simulation method was also investigated.

3.2 Latin Hypercube Simulation Method

The basic idea behind LH simulation is to sample the random variables more efficiently by avoiding clusters and gaps generated in random sampling as depicted in Fig. 6. In order to achieve this, the range of each variable is divided into k non-overlapping intervals on the basis of equal probability. One value from each interval is selected at random with respect to the probability density in the interval. The k values obtain for the first random variable are paired in a random manner with the k values obtained for the second random variable and so on until $k*n$ samples are formed, where n is the number of the random variables. It is important to mention that even the random variables are sampled independently and paired randomly, the final samples can be correlated. In order to obtain samples with correlation coefficients matching the intended ones restrictions in the paired method are usually employed. Finally, the efficiency of the LH simulation can be improved by performing optimisation and iterating the LH method according to some criterion e.g. maximising the minimum distance between any two points. Having the final samples for the n random variables, the probability estimator that the limit state function is less than zero can be estimated by Eq. (11). UQlab has been used to implement LH simulation and thus, Matlab algorithms were used.

3.3 Quasi Monte Carlo Simulation Based on Sobol' Sequence

Sobol' sequences belong to the family of low-discrepancy sequences [8]. Discrepancy is the measure that characterises the lumpiness of a sequence of points in a multi-dimensional space. Samples made from a finite subset of such sequences are called quasi-random samples and they are as uniform as possible in the random variable space as depicted in Fig. 6. Thus, the random variable space is explored more efficiently, a good characteristic to deal with multiple failure domains. Additionally, the estimated probability in Eq. (10) is expected to converge faster than would the respective probability based on random sampling [8]. The quasi-random samples can be analysed as any other empirical data set and thus Eq. (11) can be used to determine the probability of interest. Herein, the sampling based on Sobol' sequences as well as the randomisation of the sample, i.e. scrambling of the sequence, were performed using appropriate MATLAB functions. The transformation of the sample points of the unit hypercube into the appropriate sample with prescribed marginal distributions and correlation as well as the Monte Carlo simulation were set up using UQLab.

3.4 Subset Simulation Method

The basic idea behind the subset simulation method is that the estimation of a rare probability, e.g. small probabilities involved in Eq. (9), can be performed by means of more frequent indeterminate conditional failure events F_j so that $F_1 \supset F_2 \supset \cdots \supset F_M = F$. Thus, the probability of interest can be estimated as a product of conditional probabilities

$$P(g(X) \leq 0) = P\left(\bigcap_{j=1}^{M} F_j\right) = \prod_{j=1}^{M} P(F_j|F_{j-1}) \qquad (12)$$

where $F_j = \{g(X) \leq y_j\}$ the indeterminate conditional failure events, y_j are decreasing threshold values of the limit state function whilst their values need to be specified, F_0 is the certain event and M the number of subsets. The threshold values y_j can be chosen, so that the estimates of the conditional probabilities $P(F_j|F_{j-1})$, corresponds to a sufficiently large value $p_o \approx 0.1$. Therefore, with an appropriate choice of the intermediate thresholds, Eq. (12) can be evaluated as a series of reliability analysis problems with relatively high probabilities to be estimated. The trade-off is between minimizing the number of subsets, M, by choosing relatively small intermediate conditional probabilities and maximizing the intermediate conditional probabilities so that they can be estimated accurately without much of computational burden. The probability $P(F_1|F_0)$ is estimated using CMC whilst the conditional probabilities $P(F_j|F_{j-1})$ are typically estimated using Markov Chain Monte Carlo based on Metropolis-Hastings algorithms [15, 16]. UQLab has already build-in functions to implement subset simulation method.

It is important to highlight that merging advanced statistical tools e.g. statistical toolbox of MATLAB or UQLab with off-the-self CAT software gives the capability to analyse complex assemblies efficiently by implementing advanced statistical methods to the problem at hand. Therefore, appropriate user defined interfaces were established herein by linking UQLab and 3DCS variation analyst. Taking advantage of the option of user defined samples into 3DCS, vectorised computing capability was made possible when linking UQLab and 3DCS for any type of simulation method. Therefore, running CMC through UQLab by calling externally 3DCS in a batch mode or using directly 3DCS software resulted in approximately the same computational time. The efficient process integration framework between advanced statistical tools and CAT software gives the opportunity to move one step forward, i.e. toward the direction of the implementation of the tolerance synthesis in terms of RBO.

4   Results and Discussion

To study the efficiency of the proposed reliability methods in tolerance analysis problems, the two case studies were analysed. Results are presented for the first case study in Fig. 7 in which the probability P_1 corresponds to the first probability of the right hand side of Eq. (9) with limit state function g_1. The graph in Fig. 7a depicts the $CoV[\cdot]$ of the probability estimator against the number of model evaluations for the selected reliability methods. The graph in Fig. 7b depicts the normalised mean value against the number of model evaluations. The normalisation was performed with respect to the expectation of the probability estimator evaluated by CMC for 1E+06 iterations. For the second case study similar results are depicted in Fig. 8. The mean value, $E[\cdot]$, and the coefficient of variation $CoV[\cdot]$, of the probability estimator for each method were derived by an empirical approach. That is, hundreds reliability analysis were performed and samples of the probability values of Eq. (9) were, thus, generated and statistically analysed obtaining the mean value and the coefficient of variation of each probability estimator.

It is apparent from Fig. 7 and Fig. 8 that advanced simulation methods perform better than CMC. More specifically, SS has the best performance in terms of computational effort and accuracy of the prediction. More specifically, the predictions shown in Fig. 7a framed with the black box correspond to $CoV[P_1] \approx 25\%$, a fair variation of the probability estimator. In order to achieve this variation, it turns out that it should be executed approximately 2,700 model evaluations implementing the SS method, 5,500 simulations using LH and QMCS and almost 10,000 evaluations for CMC.

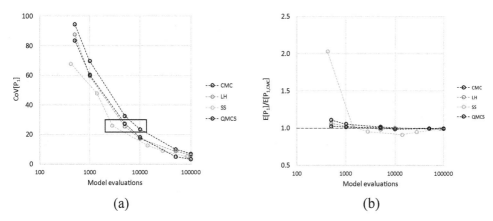

(a)   (b)

Fig. 7. Descriptive statistics for the probability estimator, $P(g_1 \leq 0)$, against the number of model evaluations for the first case study: (a) coefficient of variation (b) normalized mean value

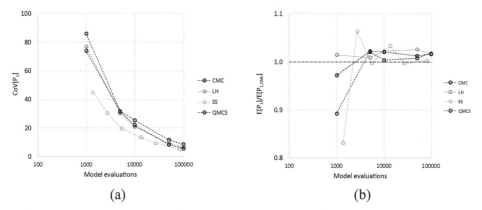

(a)   (b)

Fig. 8. Descriptive statistics for the probability estimator, $P(g_1 \leq 0)$, against the number of model evaluations for the second case study: (a) coefficient of variation (b) normalized mean value

Additionally, all the reliability methods converge to the CMC result (1E+06 iterations) as depicted in Fig. 7b. Similar results were obtained for the second probability P_2 of Eq. (9).

Figure 8 proves that advanced statistical tools can be linked successfully with professional CAT tools and further to accelerate the probability estimations. Similar observations for the efficiency of the reliability methods made for the first example can be stated for the second one. Both problems are analogous. Fig. 7 and Fig. 8 reveal that QMCS and LH methods produce quite similar results.

Finally, it should be stated that there is an advantage of the CMC, LH and QMCS method over the SS method with respect to their implementation. More specifically, for the first group of reliability methods, the sample generation procedure and the calculation of the AKC values need to be performed just one time, yet both probabilities P_1 and P_2 of Eq. (9) as well as any other percentile of the distribution of the AKC can be estimated quite fast. This is not the case for the SS method in its current form in which the assembly model should be evaluated for any new percentile that needs to be estimated. That is for

Eq. (9), two different analyses should be performed to estimate the two probabilities of Eq. (9). Nevertheless, SS still remains the best option in any case.

5 Conclusions

One major outcome of this work is that statistical tolerance analysis of mechanical assemblies can introduce multiple failure domains in the design space, i.e. separated groups of values of the contributors that result in defected products, as presented in Fig. 5. This is due to the nonlinearity inserted by geometric tolerances such as positional tolerances of cylindrical feature of size. In a fully probabilistic consideration of the tolerance allocation problem, this imposes serious issues on the selection of the most appropriate uncertainty quantification method to proceed.

Therefore, for the first time, a comprehensive guidance was provided and three state of the art simulation methods were critically evaluated with respect to their applicability to the tolerance analysis problems. From the analysis, the best option with a good compromise between performance and computational burden turns out to be the Subset Simulation method. It was proved that for the same variability in the estimated probability of defected products, the Subset Simulation performs 4 times faster than crude Monte Carlo. Quasi Monte Carlo method based on Sobol sequences indicated a good efficiency being approximately 2 times faster than crude Monte Carlo and followed by Latin Hypercube simulation technique.

Furthermore, the work indicated the successful connection of advance statistical tools such as UQLab with off the self CAT tools. The successful link realizes the possibility to adopt advanced uncertainty quantification methods in real complex tolerance analysis problem and accelerate the probability estimations. This makes feasible the reliability based optimisation approach for the tolerance allocation problem.

The work is part of an ongoing research in which advanced reliability methods need to be studied further in combination with appropriate optimisation algorithm for the identification of successful strategies to attack to the reliability based optimisation problem.

Acknowledgements. This project has received funding from the Clean Sky 2 Joint Undertaking (JU) under grant agreement No. 738221. The JU receives support from the European Union's Horizon 2020 research and innovation programme and the Clean Sky 2 JU members other than the Union.

References

1. Sandipan, K., Jhareswar, M.: A review on dimensional tolerance synthesis: paradigm shift from product to process. Assem. Autom. **32**(4), 373–388 (2012). https://doi.org/10.1108/014 45151211262438
2. Valdebenito, M., Schuëller, G.: A survey on approaches for reliability-based optimization. Struct. Multi. Optim. **42**, 645–663 (2010). https://doi.org/10.1007/s00158-010-0518-6

 3. Dimensional Control Systems, 3DCS variation analyst. www.3dcs.com
 4. Morio, J., Balesdent, M.: Estimation of Rare Event Probabilities in Complex Aerospace and Other Systems: A Practical Approach. Woodhead Publishing, Sawston (2016)
 5. Nigam, S., Turner, J.: Review of statistical approaches to tolerance analysis. Comput. Aided Des. **27**(1), 6–15 (1995)
 6. Mazur, M.: Tolerance analysis and synthesis of assemblies subject to loading with process integration and design optimisation tools. Ph.D. thesis, RMIT University (2013)
 7. McKay, M., Beckman, R., Conover, W.: A comparison of three methods for selecting values of input variables in the analysis of output from a computer code. Technometrics **21**, 239–245 (1979)
 8. Saltelli, A., et al.: Global Sensitivity Analysis: The Primer. Wiley, New York (2008)
 9. Au, S., Beck, J.: Estimation of small failure probabilities in high dimensions by subset simulation. Probab. Eng. Mech. **16**(4), 263–277 (2001)
10. Bacharoudis, K., Bakker, O.J., Popov, A., Ratchev, S.: Trade-off study of a variation aware determinate wing assembly against a traditional assembly strategy. In: MATEC Web Conference (2018). https://doi.org/10.1051/matecconf/201823300008
11. Whitney, D.: Mechanical Assemblies: Their Design, Manufacture and Role in Product Development. Oxford University Press, Oxford (2004)
12. MATLAB R (2018b). The MathWOrks, Inc., Natick
13. Desrochers, A., Riviere, A.: A matrix approach to the representation of tolerance zones and clearances. Int. J. Adv. Manuf. Technol. **13**, 630–636 (1997). https://doi.org/10.1007/BF0135 0821
14. Marelli, S., Sudret, B.: UQLab: a framework for uncertainty quantification in MATLAB. In: 2nd International Conference on Vulnerability and Risk Analysis and Management (ICVRAM), pp. 2554–2563 (2014)
15. Metropolis, N., Rosenbluth, A., Rosenbluth, M., Teller, A., Teller, E.: Equation of state calculations by fast computing machines. J. Chem. Phys. **21**(6), 1087–1092 (1953)
16. Hastings, W.: Monte Carlo sampling methods using Markov chains and their application. Biometrica **57**(1), 97–109 (1970)

8

Live Video Assistance Systems for Assembly Processes

Christian Kittl[1][(✉)] and Markus Streibl[2]

[1] Evolaris Next Level GmbH, Graz, Austria
`christian.kittl@evolaris.net`
[2] Know-Center GmbH, Research Center for Data-Driven Business and Big Data Analytics, Graz, Austria
`mstreibl@know-center.at`

Abstract. Work processes and assembly processes are increasingly gaining in complexity in the industrial context and demand a wealth of knowledge from assembly employees, as well as from service and maintenance personnel. The article describes a system developed in order to support assembly workers using a live video assistance system in combination with "wearables" - in particular smart glasses - in complex assembly processes by experts and reports findings from an acceptance analysis study.

Keywords: Assembly processes · Digital assistance system · Wearables · Video support system

1 Introduction and Motivation

Production processes, which significantly contribute to the company's success and the competitiveness of a company, have become more complex and, not least due to digitization in industry, are demanding a change in the training and qualification of employees. Digital assistance systems provide an interface for human-machine interaction and are designed to support employees in complex tasks. The Graz innovation center EVOLARIS is developing, among other things as part of the MMASSIST II research project, a system that supports the shop floor worker in such a way that, when complex installation or maintenance work occurs, experts use live video to monitor and guide the work process, thereby being able to successfully manage high complexity of the task. This on one hand should lead to decreased time that an expert is required to be on site to fix a problem resulting especially in reduced time-to-fix, availability, travel costs, and CO_2 footprint, and on the other hand improve overall process quality. Systems like WhatsApp or Skype can be used on some cases, but often production companies require dedicated solutions, which work with industry grade hardware including smart glasses, have a specialised set of functionalities that are really required by professional workers and easy to use in stress situations, where data can be stored on serviced on premise or in a local data center, and/or the solutions can be personalized/white labelled. Since such systems are still new and there is little experience in practice with regard to their acceptance in the target group and the impact on process efficiency they have, a study was conducted in a survey of users who have already had several months of experience with such a system during a pilot phase.

2 Digital Assistance Systems in Production Processes

Since the eighteenth century, the industry has been undergoing constant change, which has currently reached its peak with the fourth industrial revolution, the networking of intelligent technical systems known as cyber-physical systems (CPS). The basic idea behind networked production was to make it more efficient and flexible by means of forecasts and forecasts. From the data obtained from assembly processes and the associated systems, decision-critical information can be obtained for the company with the appropriate data quality. Digital assistance systems apply this information to assist workers in their actions and their extended use in human-machine interaction, with humans increasingly taking on a supervisory role (Haase et al. 2015). In parallel to the increasing human-machine inter-action, however, the need for rapid knowledge transfer between specialists is also increasing, in order to be able to quickly clarify special questions in the use of increasingly complex machines. The innovation center EVOLARIS is developing such an assistance system, which supports the strategy of "networked" employees via live video remote support.

2.1 Live Video Assistance System EVOCALL

Live Video Assistance Systems enable real-time communication between people in different locations, using cameras in parallel with the audio channel and transmitting their images in real-time to the remote station. Often, smart glasses are used in which information is displayed in the field of view of the user, and a camera is integrated to record and transmit the view range which is currently being focused on to the communication partner (cmp. Fig. 1).

EVOLARIS' live video remote system EVOCALL uses an open source real-time communication technology called Web Real-Time Communication (WebRTC), which is designed to work in conjunction with the most popular consumer devices. The data transfer takes place by means of the DTLS protocol (Datagram Transport Layer Security), which makes a "man in the middle" attack on the open channel, or a manipulation of the data impossible. As can be seen in Fig. 1, the actual WEBRTC server is only needed for the initial connection setup between the individual subscribers. The actual communication, which is additionally secured by SRTP (secure real-time protocol) video and audio encryption, takes place via a separate media server (Fig. 2).

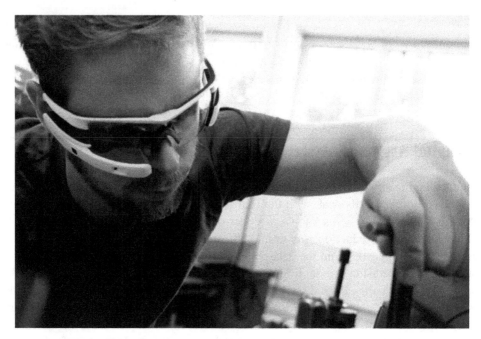

Fig. 1. Smart glasses as part of industrial live video assistance systems

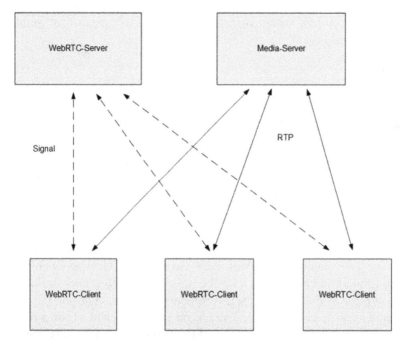

Fig. 2. System architecture of the EVOLARIS live video support system using WebRTC protocol

2.2 Live Video Assistance Systems in Assembly Processes

In the field of production, there is an increasing complexity of the systems working in the collaborative system, as well as their influence on the work to be carried out and the necessary training and qualification of the service/maintenance staff and assembly employees (Spöttl 2017). Streibl (2017) cite the potential application of Live Video Assistance Systems for unscheduled repair with high complexity, thereby restoring system availability in the shortest possible time. The assembly or service or maintenance personnel set up an audio-visual connection with experts with the aid of a smart glasses (cmp. Fig. 1) with the digital system EVOCALL as a basic system. These subject experts receive the live stream of the employees on site from a "first-person view" on the respective terminal. The system now offers the ability to not only describe and guide complex issues using an audio channel, but to capture them in a still image that can be generated from the live video.

2.3 Live Video Assistance Systems for Shadow-Working

In this context, the system can be used by new employees or leasing workers who, for example, have to carry out a complex conversion process for the first time. The machine operator, who is positioned at a different location, has the same machine in his line and now has the possibility, using the Live Video Remote System, to carry out the necessary steps and to transfer these to the data glasses of the employees. The "first-person view" and the additional audio stream enable employees to imitate the activities to be performed. By changing the streaming direction, whereby the video transmitted by the machine expert is no longer displayed in the data glasses of the employees, but now the employees transmit the live video, new possibilities open up in the context of the "shadow-working" process, which is also used in the Field of assembly processes (Frohberg et al. 2009; Pimmer and Pachler 2014).

3 Acceptance of Live Video Remote Support Systems

This section presents the results of an online survey on system acceptance, which was conducted as part of a master thesis accompanying the system development. The survey was aimed at employees in the areas of production, service and maintenance from 15 well-known Austrian, internationally operating companies on their experience with the use of the EVOCALL live video remote support system. The companies were selected according to the criteria of the necessary knowledge transfer, as well as an on-site presence of experts to fulfil the service offered. The participating companies fulfilled both criteria to a high degree and where given access to the EVOCALL system for the duration of 6 months in a trial phase. Of the 200 target people addressed, 50 (25%) participated in the survey. The findings presented here relate in a first step to the dimension of the service in terms of the usefulness and usability of the system, but also in relation to the efficiency and the effectiveness of the processes when using such a digital assistance system. As can be seen in Fig. 3, of more than 70% of the participants, the dimension of perceived usefulness is rated on a five-point scale, where 1 means "applies strongly" and 5 "does not apply at all", to 1 or 2. The points of view of perceived usefulness include a comparison between the experiences made and the expectations (Question 1), the usefulness of the system (Question 2), the simplicity of the system (Question 3), and the usability of the system (Question 4).

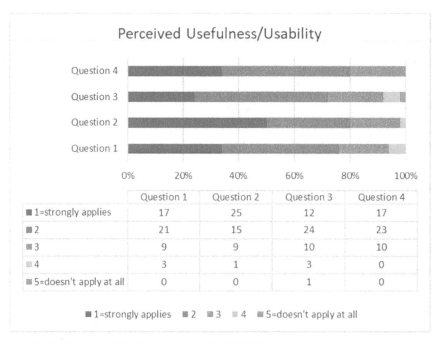

	Question 1	Question 2	Question 3	Question 4
■ 1=strongly applies	17	25	12	17
■ 2	21	15	24	23
■ 3	9	9	10	10
■ 4	3	1	3	0
■ 5=doesn't apply at all	0	0	1	0

■ 1=strongly applies   ■ 2   ■ 3   ■ 4   ■ 5=doesn't apply at all

Fig. 3. Perceived Usefulness of the EVOCALL remote video support system

These results suggest a very high perceived benefit and high acceptance of the live video assistance system by the participants.

The next two questions related to the degree of goal achievement, the result compared to the original goal (effectiveness) and the degree of efficiency, as well as the result versus effort (efficiency) (Fig. 4). More than 90% of respondents believe that using EVOCALL can increase their effectiveness. More than 80% of the respondents that EVOCALL can increase efficiency. The effectiveness in this context refers to problems that exceeded the abilities of the employees and could still be solved through the use of EVOCALL via the assistance of colleagues. The efficiency refers to an accelerated problem-solving cycle and the resulting increase in plant availability.

Further results of the online survey showed that service and maintenance work is characterised by complex and varied activities and that the employees require extensive training. This complexity of the plant requires distinctive communication on different channels when assistance is needed. These channels, however, have limitations with regard to delayed or unclearly assignable responses due to asynchronous communication channels (e-mail or WhatsApp), or more difficult problem identification with regard to problem description due to lack of qualifications by local staff and language barriers (telephone). This results in an increased presence of experts on site, which is reflected in the duration of the repair time and thus in the availability of the system.

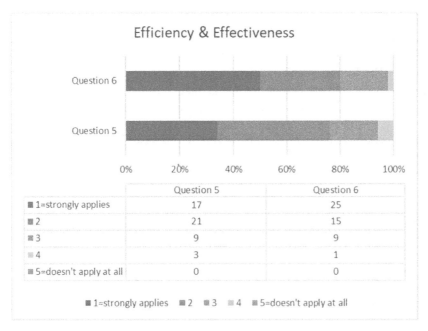

Fig. 4. Efficiency and effectiveness of the EVOCALL remote video support system

As can be seen from the answers reflected in the two figures above, the effectiveness and efficiency of the work processes can be positively influenced by the use of EVO-CALL. Synchronous audio-visual communication enables the employees to carry out more highly qualified work processes under the guidance of experts via EVOCALL, which can lead to a reduced on-site presence of experts according to the results of the surveys.

4 Summary and Conclusion

The change in the industry and its effects on prevailing assembly processes as well as on the changed qualification needs of employees requires the use of new methods and technologies such as digital assistance systems as an interface for a human-machine interaction or as an interface between employees. The analysis of the live video remote support system EVOCALL as such a digital assistance system has shown that the use of production and service processes can be positively influenced. The results from companies that have already tested EVOCALL indicate that live video remote support systems have a high perceived value for users and have a positive impact on the efficiency and effectiveness of task completion. Summarizing the collected results, they clearly indicate that EVOCALL has a positive impact on the current service and maintenance processes, improving communication, reducing the need for on-site presence of experts, and having a positive impact on the problem-solving cycle and the problem-solving skills of service and maintenance personnel. The survey provides new insights by quantifying the extent to which users, who had the opportunity to experience a live video remote support system in practice over a longer period in time (6-monthly trial).

However, due to the relatively small number of cases (n = 50) and the specificity of the tested system, the findings ca not be generalized without further notice. Much depends in practice on the actual implementation of a live video remote support system and how easy it is for the users to use or what features are actually supported and how the integration into the general enterprise IT takes place. Through studies with larger case numbers and through the comparative analysis of various systems, a more general and even better reliable statement about the benefits of such digital assistance systems in production is to be made possible in the future, or the existing findings will be verified.

Acknowledgements. This work was created with support from the 'Production of the Future' program of the Austria Research Promotion Agency (FFG) in the course of the lighthouse project MMASSIST II and the Know-Center within the COMET K2 - Competence Center for Excellent Technologies program of the Austrian Ministry for Transport, Innovation and Technology (bmvit), the Austrian Ministry for Digital and Economic Affairs (bmdw), the Austria Research Promotion Agency and the Styrian Research Promotion Agency (SFG).

References

1. Abicht, L., Spöttl, G.: Qualifikationsentwicklung durch das Internet der Dinge (Development of Qualification through the Internet of Things). W. Bertelsmann Verlag GmbH & Co. KG, Bielefeld (2012)
2. Brandl, P., Aschbacher, H., Husch, S.: Mobiles Wissensmanagement in der Industrie 4.0 (Mobile knowledge management in the Industry 4.0). In: Mensch und Computer 2015 −Workshopband, pp. 225−232. De Gruyter Oldenbourg, Berlin (2015)
3. Frohberg, D., Goth, C., Schwabe, G.: Mobile learning projects: a critical analysis of the state of the art. J. Comput. Assist. Learn. 25, 307−331 (2009)
4. Haase, T., Termath,W., Schumann, M.: Integrierte Lern- und Assistenzsysteme für die Produktion von morgen (Integrated learning and assistance systems for the production of tomorrow). In: Lehren und Lernen fьr die moderne Arbeitswelt, Berlin, pp. 183−207 (2015)
5. Pimmer, C., Pachler, N.: Mobile learning in the workplace: unlocking the value of mobile technology for work-based education. In: Increasing Access through Mobile Learning, pp. 193−203. Athabasca University (2014)
6. Reichel, J., Müller, G., Mandelartz, J.: Betriebliche Instandhaltung (Operational Maintenance). Springer, Heidelberg (2009). https://doi.org/10.1007/978-3-642-00502-2
7. Streibl, M.: Einsatz eines Live-Video-Assistenzsystem im Problemlиsungszyklus von Service- und Instandhaltungspersonal (Application of a live video assistance system in the problem solving cycle of service and maintenance personnel). Master thesis, University of Applied Sciences Campus02, Graz (2017)
8. Spöttl, G.: Industrie 4.0 - Herausforderung für Lehrbetriebe (Industry 4.0 − Challenges for training companies). In: Frenz, M., Schlick, C., Unger, T. (eds.),Wandel der Erwerbsarbeit, pp. 60−75. LIT Verlag Münster (2017)

9

Indirect System Condition Monitoring Using Online Bayesian Changepoint Detection

Emil Tochev$^{(\boxtimes)}$ ⓘD, Harald Pfifer ⓘD, and Svetan Ratchev ⓘD

University of Nottingham, Nottingham, UK
emil.tochev@nottingham.ac.uk

Abstract. This paper presents a method for online vibration analysis and a simple test bench analogue for the solder pumping system in an industrial wave-soldering machine at a Siemens factory. A common machine fault is caused by solder build-up within the pipes of the machine. This leads to a pressure drop in the system, which is replicated in the test bench by restricting the flow of water using a gate valve. The pump's vibrational response is recorded using an accelerometer. The captured data is passed through an online Bayesian Changepoint Detection algorithm, adapted from existing literature, to detect the point at which the change in flow rate affects the pump, and thus the PCB assembly capability of the machine. This information can be used to trigger machine maintenance operations, or to isolate the vibrational response indicative of the machine fault.

Keywords: Predictive maintenance · Bayesian changepoint detection · Industrial application

1 Introduction

This paper is a follow up to an offline fault detection algorithm applied to the presented machine use case [1]. It describes an online, non-disruptive technique to detect a machine fault in a wave-soldering machine in Printed Circuit Board (PCB) manufacturing. This machine works by maintaining a constant flow of solder in the form of a set wave height, over which PCBs are passed in order to connect large numbers of through-hole components efficiently. The fault in question is solder build-up in the machine pipes, which was considered the most common recurring machine fault in the wave-soldering process by Siemens Congleton. As time passes there is a buildup of solder dross in the pipes, which leads to a pressure drop and reduced solder flow rate. Due to the resultant reduced solder wave height, PCBs passing over the wave are left unsoldered, needing repairs and touch ups. The response to these is manual adjustment of the wave height by increasing the pump power. This can be performed a set number of times before full machine maintenance is performed. This process is reactive and repeated on a weekly to monthly basis depending on the solder quality and machine uptime. The project brief set by Siemens requires a non-disruptive and low-cost solution to monitor the machine. The goal is to improve the fault detection rate and reduce the number of unsoldered products.

Awareness of a machine's state at any given time is valuable for making predictive maintenance decisions. Costly maintenance and machine downtime can be minimized effectively by implementing early and accurate fault detection [2]. This is particularly valuable during the current push towards Industry 4.0 (I4.0) [3] and is enabled by the increased prevalence of Industrial Internet of Things (IIoTs) allowing for a greater ability of factories to gather and process machine data [4]. However, the financial and time costs of directly replacing and upgrading machines can dissuade a lot of companies from investing in these technologies. As such, a "wrap and re-use" approach is generally taken instead [5]. This concept of minimal disruption to existing machine setups and production lines, alongside the extraction of new data, without machine downtime is a key motivator for this paper and the proposed methodology.

Due to its age and the hostile internal environment, the wave-soldering machine use case presented in this paper is significantly limited in the usable data that can be collected from it. As such, pump vibrations are used for the vibration analysis in this paper as access to other components is effectively impossible. Pump vibration monitoring is not unique, and many examples can be found in literature [6, 7]. Techniques include comparing recorded pump vibrations against a model of the expected vibrations [8] and using pump vibrations to predict cavitation by training an Artificial Neural Network (ANN) [9]. Similarly, time-frequency analysis of vibrations have been used to diagnose wear in pump valve plates [10]. These analyses can notifying operators when pump maintenance needs to take place.in a timely manner, and are particularly effective at detecting issues such as cavitation, resonance and misaligned or warped components.

However, pump vibration analysis is not (to the author's knowledge) used to monitor general system health and predict faults that occur outside of the pump itself. This is largely assessed using pipe vibrations [11, 12], which can provide insights into general system performance, or be used to locate discrete blockages downstream of pumps [13]. In the motivating scenario, access to the pipes is unavailable, and solder build-up does not form a localized blockage. Any solution needs to have low complexity so that it can be implemented on a low-cost microcontroller. Additionally, there is no pre-existing vibration data with which to establish baseline readings.

This paper uses online sequential Bayesian Changepoint Detection (BCD) based on an existing algorithm [14] and assesses its suitability on a test bench. The use case fault can be presented as an unsupervised segmentation problem as the machine transitions from a functional to a non-functional state. BCD is particularly suitable for this type of problem [15]. It provides a measurement of the probability that, based on the collected information, a change in behaviour has occurred at a certain point [16, 17]. This can then directly notify machine operators of the change in machine state, or be used to isolate the vibrational response of the pump at the point where the solder build-up is affecting the flow rate. In rare cases where the deterioration of the pipe state is instantaneous rather than gradual (such as in the case of seal failure), the change in vibrational response will still be able to inform machine operators of the need for maintenance. Successful applications in literature include the assessment of climate records to locate changepoints in climate regimes [17], detecting faults and failures in valves in an Unmanned Aerial Vehicle (UAV) fuel system [18], and detecting changes in the behaviour of a user of a text-messaging service [16]. Online applications of BCD are used to process live data [19] and

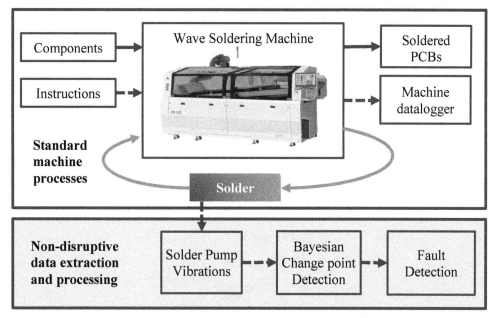

Fig. 1. Wave Soldering Machine process diagram. Dotted arrows represent the movement of data. Solid arrows represent the movement of physical parts. The green box represents the non-disruptive paper contribution. (Color figure online)

predict the likelihood of newly recorded data being part of a "current run" between two changepoints. BCD has also been used for online signal segmentation of epileptic brain activity [20] as well as activity recognition in a home [21]. The variety of applications demonstrates the flexibility of BCD. Alongside the number of changepoints, BCD can also provide an indication of the size of the changes [17], which can highlight significant events. The computational cost of this approach increases as the number of time steps increase, although this can be managed by implementing a maximum length of time for assessment, and storing and reusing previous calculations [14]. Another drawback of this approach is a sensitivity to the prior distribution assigned to the changepoints present in the system.

2   Methodology

The research methodology as illustrated in Fig. 1 aims to use data analytics for improved process control in wave soldering. The data analytics approach is based on non-disruptive data extraction and processing using online sequential Bayesian Changepoint Detection. A test bench setup has been developed to replicate the wave-soldering machine behavior as the industrial machine and environment is not suitable for development. To keep it manageable in a laboratory environment, water is used instead of solder. The difference between the vibrational characteristics of water and solder should not affect the results of the BCD so long as the deterioration of the pipe leads to a change in measured vibrations that the BCD can detect. The experimental set-up and data collection are discussed in Sects. 2.1 and 2.2. As this is virtually identical setup to the setup presented in [1], these sections will largely remain as presented in that earlier work. The BCD formulation is discussed in Sect. 2.3.

2.1 Test Bench Setup

The test bench presented in this paper considers the behaviour of a pump moving water through a closed system. The flow rate is controlled by a gate valve, which is closed in discrete increments and goes from completely open to completely closed. It mimics the effects of solder dross build up in a wave soldering machine, which takes place over several weeks. As such, the steady state behaviour of the pump is the most relevant to this investigation. The schematic for this can be seen in Fig. 2, with a photo of the realised test bench in Fig. 3.

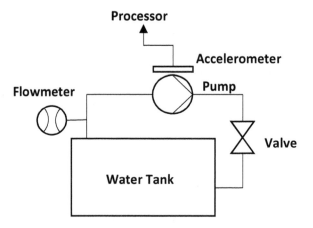

Fig. 2. Test bench schematic

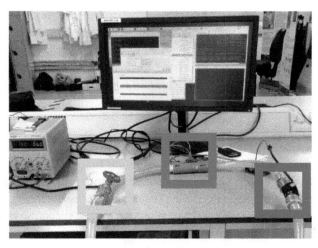

Fig. 3. Test bench photo. Yellow: gate valve; blue: pump and accelerometer; red: flowmeter (Color figure online)

As the valve is closed, the change in the fluid's flow rate is monitored using the flow rate sensor YF-S201, connected to an Arduino. The vibration of the pump is recorded, using an accelerometer (LSM9DS1), at each increment to build up its response profile. This data is then processed at a Raspberry Pi 3B, and the results can be displayed in real time or uploaded to online networks, including any available IIoTs.

2.2 Data Collection from the Test Bench

The change in flowrate as the valve is closed is shown in Fig. 4. There is a small drop in the flow rate until the valve is approximately 70% before a transition period, and an almost linear drop to no flow from approximately 80% closed onwards. The minimal initial change is a result of the low flow rates used in this experiment. Pump vibrations are recorded with a sampling rate of 350 Hz. Each collected sample is 10,000 data points in size. The accelerometer has a range of ± 2 g, a sensitivity of 0.061 mg/LSB, and collects samples in the X, Y and Z axis. This is then converted into the absolute acceleration.

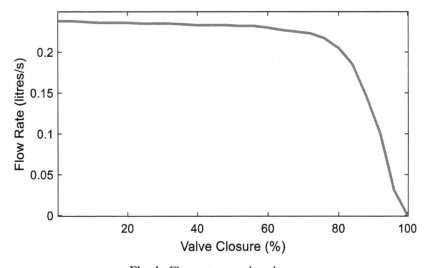

Fig. 4. Flow rate vs. valve closure

A fast Fourier transform (FFT) algorithm is used to extract the frequency and amplitude data from the vibrations [6]. Figures 5 and 6 show the results of the FFT on the vibration data recorded from an open and shut valve respectively. The difference between the two is clearly visible, as the peak frequency shifts to the left. Additionally, it is clear that a lot of noise is present in the system – as would be present in an industrial setting. The solder in the use case might result in different vibrational characteristics. Despite this, the solder blockage should still result in a change in the recorded vibrations over time, which can be detected by the BCD algorithm. This is a significant benefit of the proposed methodology: as long as the input changes in a way that can be detected, the BCD algorithm will be able to assess the probability that a changepoint has occurred at a given point in time. This reduces the need for calibration procedures, which can be expensive and time consuming.

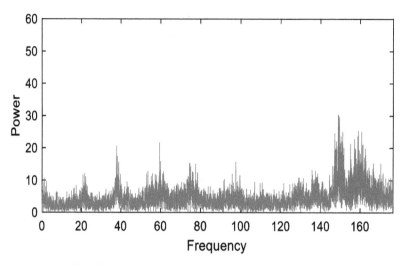

Fig. 5. FFT of pump vibrations while valve is open

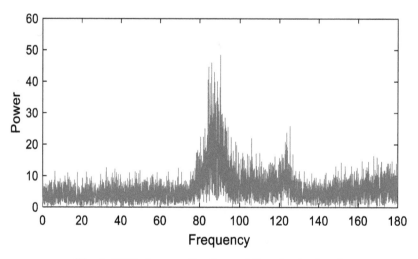

Fig. 6. FFT of pump vibrations while valve is closed

2.3   Online Bayesian Changepoint Detection

Figure 7 presents some of the pump data gathered by the accelerometer. Analysis of the time-domain vibration data has shown that it is not suitable for the analysis – it does not vary significantly enough across the different valve states to be a useful feature for predicting the current state. The mean of the amplitude of the time-domain data is shown to remain roughly constant throughout. However, the plotted features extracted from the FFT (peak frequency and maximum amplitude) can be seen to respond to the change in valve state. As such, these are the features used in the BCD algorithm presented.

The algorithm is based on a simplified version of the sequential BCD algorithm described in [14], modified to detect a single changepoint in the datasets used. The simplified equations are presented below, and [14] should be referenced for additional detail and an extended version of this algorithm. As the algorithm processes the peak

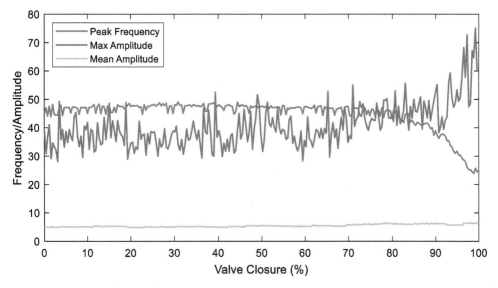

Fig. 7. Data extraction from recorded pump vibrations

frequencies and maximum amplitudes in the same way, the following example will be presented for only the amplitude. An initial assumption is made about the data model: in this case, a linear regression model is used to predict the distribution of the data. Notably, other models can be used, depending on experience with the data.

$$A = \sum\nolimits_{l=1}^{m} \beta_l V_l + \varepsilon \tag{1}$$

Equation (1) presents the linear regression model used to represent the data gathered, where A is the amplitude of the pump vibrations and V_l is the level of valve closure. β_l is the lth regression coefficient and ε is the random error term. The assumptions made about β and ε are the same as in [14], with the same conjugate priors assigned here for both.

$$f\left(A_{i:j}\right) = f\left(A_{i:j}|V\right) \tag{2}$$

Assuming that this regression model applies to the data between the start of the dataset up until the changepoint, and from the changepoint to the end of the dataset, for each possible subset of the data $i:j$, the probability of the data given the regression model is calculated using Eq. (2) and stored.

$$P_1\left(A_{1:j}\right) = \sum\nolimits_{v=1}^{j-1} f(A_{1:v}) f(A_{v+1:j}) \tag{3}$$

In Eq. (3), the probability density of the first j data points containing the changepoint is calculated and stored. Starting at the beginning of the time series, two non-overlapping subsets of data (assumed to be independent as per [22]) are pieced together. By multiplying together the probabilities of the two subsets (calculated in (2)) and summing over all of the placements of the changepoint, the probability density of the data can be calculated.

The final quantity that needs to be specified is the prior distribution of the location of the changepoint. By using an uninformative prior distribution which assumes that the location of the changepoint is equally likely at any datapoint, bias in the algorithm can be avoided. From here, sampling from within the distributions defined above can be performed to ascertain the location of the changepoint and the regression parameters for the subsets of data either side of it.

This is extended in [14] to search for additional changepoints up to a defined maximum number of changepoints k_{max}. This is outside of the scope of this paper, but is achieved by extending Eq. (3) such that the term $f(A_{1:v})$ contains k-1 changepoints when calculating the probability of the location of the kth changepoint. The prior distribution for the number of changepoints is specified, and sampling for changepoints between 0 and k_{max} takes places before sampling for the locations of the change ponts. Additional tuning can be done based on the values of the linear regression model used, as described in [14, 17]. A minimum distance between changepoints can also be specified.

The described algorithm will locate a changepoint in a single set of data of a set length. To expand it efficiently to process incoming data points, the matrices storing the results of Eqs. (2) and (3) are expanded. New rows and columns are added to hold the new probabilities calculated for each newly generated subset of data (by Eq. (2)). A new column is added for the new probability density $P_1(A_{1:N})$ where N is the most recently added datapoint. The full implementation details can be found in [14].

3 Results and Discussion

Figure 4 shows that the flow rate reduction as a result of the valve closure is minimal until the valve is approximately 70% shut. A short transition period can then be seen until the valve is about 80% shut. The flow rate reduction from that point on is nearly linear until it reaches 0 l/s. During the experiment, a total of 260 pump vibration samples were collected as the valve went from completely open to completely closed.

Figure 8 plots the extracted amplitudes at against the resultant posterior probability of the changepoint's location as calculated by the algorithm. It suggests that a changepoint has taken place as the valve is 70% closed and shows a high certainty over a small area. This corresponds with the start of the transitional flow rate period in Fig. 4. A plot of the linear model inferred by the algorithm can also be seen in green in Fig. 8. It follows the collected data quite closely up until the last few readings. Had there been additional samples collected afterwards, the algorithm would have adjusted the inferred model to better match the data.

Performing the same analysis on the peak frequencies gives the results plotted in Fig. 9. In this case, the changepoint is detected later, when the valve is approximated 80% closed, and the posterior probability is lower and spread over a larger area. It corresponds more closely with the end of the transitional period of flow rate noted in Fig. 4. The inferred model follows the extracted frequencies very closely.

Plotting the posterior probabilities of the changepoint as calculated from the amplitude and frequencies extracted from the pump vibrations against the flow rate produced by the pump as the valve is closed produces Fig. 10. By applying this algorithm to the two different sources of data extracted from the pump vibrations, it has been demonstrated

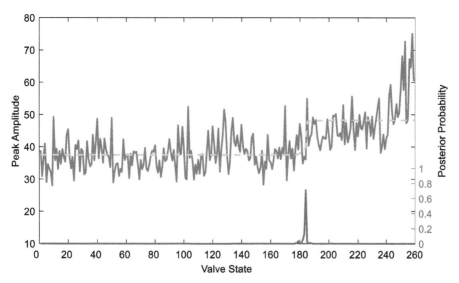

Fig. 8. Predicted changepoint based on extracted amplitudes. The inferred linear model is represented in green. (Color figure online)

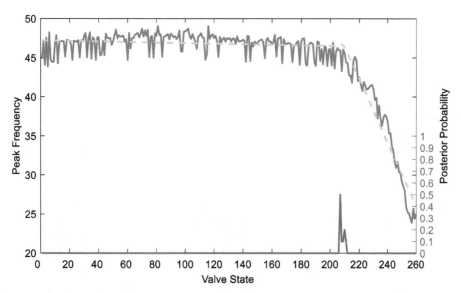

Fig. 9. Predicted changepoint based on extracted frequencies. The inferred linear model is represented in green. (Color figure online)

that the state of this system can be assessed by the vibrational response of the pump. Using the amplitude leads to an earlier detection of a changepoint, which is valuable in processes sensitive to changes in the monitored parameters. The frequency leads to a later detection of the changepoint, more valuable in processes that do not require immediate maintenance or are less sensitive to changes. The wave soldering machine use case presented in this paper falls into the former category and benefits from early detection of a change in flow rate so that maintenance can be performed before faulty products are released.

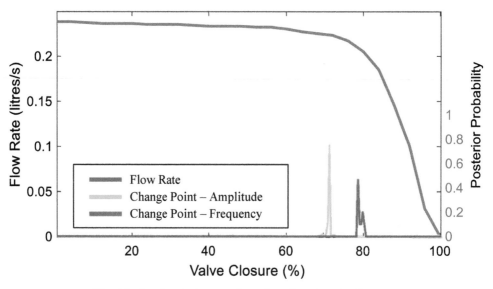

Fig. 10. Predicted changepoints plotted against the flow rate

4 Conclusions

Presented in this paper is an online BCD algorithm adapted from existing literature and applied to an industrial use case. A test bench analogue is used to simulate pipe blockage due to solder build-up in a wave-soldering machine. The pipe state is indirectly monitored using a cheap, non-disruptive device that collects vibration data from the pump feeding the system. The collected data has two features extracted from it, the maximum pump vibrational amplitude and peak frequency as the valve is closed. The BCD algorithm then generates the likelihood of a changepoint having occurred in the flow rate as a result of the pipe blockage. This information is processed online and can be used to identify the current machine state (differentiating between a faulty and non-faulty state) and informs machine operators of the need for maintenance.

This work will be expanded upon in the future with data collected directly from the wave-soldering machine, to assess the suitability of the algorithm and non-disruptive methodology in an industrial environment, as well as the accuracy of the test bench analogue. Additional tests with an accelerometer capable of a faster sampling rate could also be valuable, to ensure that information isn't being lost at higher frequencies the current hardware cannot detect. Integration with local IIoT and cloud platforms is also key to ensuring the data is accessible and useful.

Acknowledgements. The authors would like to thank Siemens Congleton, especially Mr Carl German, for their helpful advice. This work is supported by the ESPRC iCASE entitled "Factory of the Future – Flexible, adaptable and self-optimised manufacturing systems".

References

1. Tochev, E., Rengasamy, D., Pfifer, H., Ratchev, S.: System condition monitoring through Bayesian changepoint detection using pump vibrations. In: IEEE International Conference on Automation Science and Engineering, vol. 2020, pp. 667–672 (2020)
2. Chiang, L.H., Russell, E.L., Braatz, R.D.: Fault Detection and Diagnosis in Industrial Systems, 1st edn. Springer, London (2001). https://doi.org/10.1007/978-1-4471-0347-9
3. Wahlster, W., et al.: Recommendations for implementing the strategic initiative INDUSTRIE 4.0 (2013)
4. Manyika, J., et al.: The Internet of Things: mapping the value beyond the hype. McKinsey Global Institute, p. 144 (2015)
5. Conway, J.: The Industrial Internet of Things: An Evolution to a Smart Manufacturing Enterprise. White Paper. Schneider Electric (2016)
6. Scheffer, C.: Pump condition monitoring through vibration analysis. In: PUMPS Maintenance, Design and Reliability Conference 2008 – IDC Technology, pp. 1–20 (2008)
7. Birajdar, R., Patil, R., Khanzode, K.: Vibration and noise in centrifugal pump - sources and diagnosis methods. In: Proceedings of the 3rd International Conference on Integrity, Reliability and Failure, pp. 20–24 (2009)
8. Rivera, D.L., Scholz, M.R., Fritscher, M., Krauss, M., Schilling, K.: Towards a predictive maintenance system of a hydraulic pump. In: Proceedings of the 16th IFAC Symposium on Information Control in Manufacturing (2018)
9. Siano, D., Panza, M.A.: Diagnostic method by using vibration analysis for pump fault detection. Energy Procedia **148**, 10–17 (2018)
10. Stojek, J.: Application of time-frequency analysis for diagnostics of valve plate wear in axial-piston pump. Arch. Mech. Eng. **57**(3), 309–322 (2010)
11. Kim, Y.I., Simpson, A.R., Lambert, M.F.: Behavior of orifices and blockages in unsteady pipe flows. In: 9th Annual Symposium on Water Distribution Systems Analysis, pp. 15–19 (2007)
12. Collet, Å.S.A., Källman, M.: Pipe Vibrations Measurement. Energiforsk (2017)
13. Lile, N.L.T., Jaafar, M.H.M., Roslan, M.R., Azmi, M.S.M.: Blockage detection in circular pipe using vibration analysis. Int. J. Adv. Sci. Eng. Inf. Technol. **2**(3), 252 (2016)
14. Ruggieri, E., Antonellis, M.: An exact approach to Bayesian sequential changepoint detection. Comput. Stat. Data Anal. **97**, 71–86 (2016)
15. Mohammad-Djafari, A., Féron, O.: A Bayesian approach to changepoints detection in time series. Int. J. Imaging Syst. Technol. **16**(5), 215–221 (2006)
16. Davidson-Pilon, C.: Bayesian Methods for Hackers: Probabilistic Programming and Bayesian Inference (Addison-Wesley Data and Analytics), 1st edn. Addison-Wesley Professional (2015)
17. Ruggieri, E.: A Bayesian approach to detecting changepoints in climatic records. Int. J. Climatol. **33**(2), 520–528 (2013)
18. Niculita, O., Skaf, Z., Jennions, I.K.: The application of Bayesian changepoint detection in UAV fuel systems. Procedia CIRP **22**(1), 115–121 (2014)
19. Adams, R.P., MacKay, D.J.C.: Bayesian online changepoint detection. Technical report, University of Cambridge (2007)
20. Malladi, R., Kalamangalam, G.P., Aazhang, B.: Online Bayesian changepoint detection algorithms for segmentation of epileptic activity. In: Asilomar Conference on Signals, Systems and Computers, pp. 1833–1837 (2013)

21. Aminikhanghahi, S., Cook, D.J.: Using changepoint detection to automate daily activity segmentation. In: 2017 IEEE International Conference on Pervasive Computing and Communications Work in Progress, PerCom WiP 2017, pp. 262–267 (2017)
22. Barry, D., Hartigan, J.A.: A Bayesian analysis for changepoint problems. J. Am. Stat. Assoc. **88**(421), 309 (1993)

10

Orchestration and Situation Awareness in an Assistance System for Assembly Tasks

Wernher Behrendt$^{(\boxtimes)}$ ⓘ and Felix Strohmeier ⓘ

Salzburg Research, Salzburg, Austria
{wernher.behrendt,felix.strohmeier}@salzburgresearch.at

Abstract. We report on the design, specification and implementation of a situation awareness module used for assistive systems in manufacturing, in the context of Industry 4.0. A recent survey of research done in Germany and Europe, concerning assistive technology in industry shows a very high potential for "intelligent assistance" by combining smart sensors, networking and AI. While the state of the art concerning actual technology in industrial use points more towards user-friendly, speech-based interaction with personal assistants for information retrieval (typically of in-house documentation), the research presented here addresses an enterprise-level assistance system that is supported by a number of specialized *Assistance Units* that can be customized to the end users' specifications and that range from tutoring systems to tele-robotics. Key to the approach is situation awareness, which is achieved through a combination of a-priori, task knowledge modelling and dynamic situation assessment on the basis of observation streams coming from sensors, cameras and microphones. The paper describes a working fragment of the industrial task description language and its extensions to cover also the triggering of assistive interventions when the observation modules have sent data that warrants such interventions.

Keywords: Assembly tasks · Situation awareness · Assistance systems · Process language

1 The Concept of Assistance in Industry 4.0

One of the tenets of Industrie 4.0 is the digitization of all processes, assets and artefacts in order to be able to virtualize and simulate production and to achieve maximum flexibility and productivity. While much of the innovation effort is aimed at outright automation, it is also obvious that for the foreseeable future, human-to-machine interaction will remain an important element of any production. With an aging workforce and products that are becoming less standardized (lot-size 1) the notion of assistance has been getting significant attention. In an Austrian "lighthouse-project" the idea of "Assistance-Units" is put forward. This paper presents a taxonomy and internal structure of these units and a proposed formal language to specify their desired interaction with humans when an assistance need arises. It should be noted that the proposed language acts as a mediation layer between higher level business process descriptions (e.g., an order to manufacture a product) and machine-specific programming constructs that are still needed to operate e.g. a welding robot. The purpose of our task description language is to orchestrate human workers, robotic assistance as well as informational assistance, in order to keep the factory IT in sync with progress on the shop-floor.

1.1 Motivation and State of the Art

While there is plenty of research work on collaborative robotics, exoskeletons, and informational assistance through e.g. virtual reality headsets, less work has been done on bringing these diverse forms of assistance under a common roof. A recent study [1] also took a broad view that included assistance systems for both services and industry. There, the authors distinguish three kinds of (cognitive) assistance: (1) Helper systems providing digital representations of e.g. manuals, teaching videos, repair guides, or other elements of knowledge management. (2) Adaptive Assistance systems that are able to take into account some situational context, e.g. through sensors, and that can then provide relevant information that is adapted to the specific situation. (3) Tutoring Assistance systems are also adaptive, but address explicitly, the need for learning in the work context.

The study forecasts a very high market potential for the use of AI in assistive technology and this is of relevance to the category of "machines and networked systems" which gives the closest fit with manufacturing. The study also lists a number of German research projects broadly addressing digital assistance, in the years 2013–2017.

Looking at the current state of the art in industrial use of assistive technology, there is a prevalence of personal digital assistants based on speech recognition engines such as Apple Siri, Microsoft Cortana, Amazon Alexa, or Google's Assistant with its cloud speech tool. These are often combined with VR or AR headsets, or with tablets or smart phones depending on the use case. It should be noted that any user-activated assistance (e.g. by speech recognition) is *reactive*, i.e. it has no option of pro-actively helping the user. A pro-active approach requires the system to somehow know where worker and assistive machinery are, in the overall task. The following example comes from one of our industrial use cases for which a demonstrator is being built.

Motivating Example – Assembly. The use case comes from a manufacturer of electrical equipment for heavy duty power supply units as used for welding at construction sites. There are detailed documents available describing the assembly process and the parts involved. The actual assembly process is done by referring to a paper copy of the assembly manual. There are also CAD drawings available that can be used to derive the physical dimensions of the main parts. There are a number of important steps in the assembly process where the worker has to verify e.g. the correct connection of cables, or where he or she has to hold and insert, a part in a certain way. Furthermore, the assembly steps are associated with typical timings in order to ascertain a certain throughput per hour. The purpose of the associated Assistance Unit (we will use the abbreviation A/U) is to help inexperienced workers learn the process quickly and to remind experienced workers to double-check the critical steps. It should also be possible for the worker to ask for assistance at any point, through speech interaction and the A/U should be able to detect delays in a process step, as well as errors in the order of steps when the order of steps is important for the assembly process.

Further use cases not discussed in this paper address maintenance, repair, re-tooling, working on several machines simultaneously, and physical (robotic) assistance with lifting of heavy parts.

1.2 Structure, Usage and Purpose of Assistance Units

The research into assistance units started with a hypothetical structure that was deemed useful to define a methodology for creating and customizing different kinds of assistance units (Table 1):

Table 1. Initial structure of assistance units.

Characteristic feature	Example
Description of the assistance unit	E.g. Assembly-Assistant
Type of assistance	Cognitive, physical or hybrid
Knowledge resources	E.g. data or media files required
Input format	E.g. speech interface, user interface
Input device(s)	E.g. microphone.
Output format	E.g. video explaining the assembly process
Output device(s)	E.g. tablet and in-built speaker

Looking at the concept from a technical perspective, however, it is difficult to refine this structure sufficiently, in order to use it as a taxonomic discriminator: the *Description* points at a potentially significant set of user requirements that are not covered in the specification. Likewise, distinguishing between *cognitive* and *physical* assistance is a binary decision that can be rewritten as "content management" (for cognitive needs of the user/worker) or "robotics" (addressing physical needs of the end user/worker). Input format and device, and analogously, output format and device are somewhat dependent entities because speech interfaces require microphones and video output requires a screen of some sort. The *"knowledge resources"* are worth a more detailed investigation with two possible technical approaches: firstly, one could think of the resources as media content that is searchable and through appropriate tagging, can be triggered in certain circumstances. The second approach would be to endow the assistance unit with a detailed model of the task and thus, make the unit capable of reasoning over the state of the task in order to assess progress or any deviations. This latter approach involves Artificial Intelligence techniques for knowledge representation and reasoning.

Usage as a Distinguishing Feature? It is clear that in principle, there may be as many kinds of assistance units as there are kinds of manufacturing tasks. So one approach to classification could be high level distinctions of usage. Initially, we classified our use cases as being either assembly or maintenance or re-tooling, but in each of the cases, the distinguishing features only show themselves in the content of the knowledge resources or in the knowledge based model of the actual activity, without having a structural manifestation in the assistance unit itself.

Purpose (of Interaction) to the Rescue? The main reason for wanting a distinction between different kinds of assistance units is to have clearly separable methodologies for their development and deployment. Ideally, one should be able to offer pre-structured assistance "skeletons" that can be parameterized and customized by experts in the application domain, rather than requiring ICT specialists for bespoke programming. Having been dissatisfied with the previous attempts at structuring, we then looked at the way in which human and machine (aka assistance unit) were supposed to interact and this led to a proposed model that distinguishes eight forms of interaction or purpose, for using an assistance unit, with distinctive capabilities specified for each kind of unit (Table 2).

Table 2. Taxonomy of assistance units according to purpose of interaction

Purpose	Capabilities (A/U = Assistance Unit)
Mediator	A/U enables connection to/with a remote expert
Tutor	A/U explains a certain procedure
Trouble-shooter	A/U helps to localize a specific problem
Guard	A/U observes a situation and reports observations
Savior	A/U is called to clear up a known failure condition
Helper	A/U takes over physical sub-tasks in collaboration
Interpreter	A/U finds situation-relevant information from diverse sources, in an ill-defined problem space
Avatar (for tele-presence)	A/U enables an expert to act in a remote location (requires e.g. tele-robotics and situation awareness)

The above taxonomy has the advantage that it requires an increasing set of capabilities going from mediator to avatar. In other words, the distinguishing features allow one to define capabilities on an ordinal scale (Mediator < Tutor < Trouble-shooter < etc.). It is of course questionable whether the *mediator* role qualifies at all, as an assistance unit in its own right, but we may accept that a combination of on-line manuals, plus the ability to call an expert, all packaged in some smart-phone app, is sufficient functionality for a low-hanging fruit w.r.t. assistance units.

1.3 Assistance Units as Actors on the Shop-Floor

One of the defining features of any assistance unit is the ability to recognize when it is needed. This presupposes some form of situational awareness which can be obtained either by explicitly being called by the worker or by some sensory input triggering the A/U. Situational awareness requires explicit knowledge about the environment, knowledge about desirable sequences of actions (e.g. the steps of an assembly task) and it also requires some planning capability unless we can afford the system to learn by trial and error – an unlikely option in a competitive production environment.

Formal and semi-formal production planning methods are already being used in many manufacturing firms. Hagemann [4] gives the example of Event-Process-Chains for planning assembly lines in the automotive sector, but for assistance, one would need a more granular level of description. At the level of robotic task execution, there are examples such as the Canonical Robot Command Language [6] that provides vendor-independent language primitives to describe robotic tasks.

In the field of production optimization, many firms rely on some variety of measurement-time-method (MTM). There are different variants of MTM offering different granularity [3, 5, 7, 9] but the main problem is that the method is not well suited to formally describing purposeful, planned processes with inputs and outputs, but instead, focusses on the description of isolated actions and their time- and effort-related parameters. The method is also propagated rather exclusively, by a community of consultants belonging to the MTM association which keeps control over the intellectual property of practicing the art of MTM analysis.

So, while there are clearly potential connecting points with process planning at large, and with action-based productivity measurement at the more detailed level, one still requires an orchestration formalism that can distinguish between actors, can name inputs and outputs of processes, and can describe the manufacturing process as well as any assistive measure that one may want to add to the manufacturing process. To achieve this goal, we used – as a starting point – the agent model of Russell and Norvig [2] as shown below (Fig. 1).

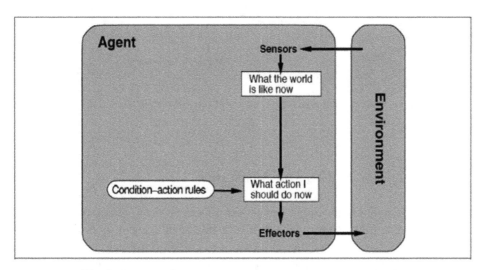

Fig. 1. Simple reflex agent according to Russell and Norvig [2].

The important issue to note is that we distinguish *Environment* and *Agent*, the latter consisting of *sensors* to perceive observations from the environment, *effectors* to manipulate entities in the environment and some form of rationality expressed in a world model and in a rule system that predetermines what actions the agent will take, under certain conditions. For a simple reflex agent as shown above, there is a direct relationship between singular observations and according actions. This is definitely not a sufficient model for what we would call "intelligent" behavior, and so we should extend the basic model, as shown in the next figure.

As can be seen, the second model introduces a *memory* for the agent to store a state of the perceived world, and a *planning mechanism* to reason about the effects of possible actions. This means that the agent can now make decisions concerning its actions, on the basis of some utility function included in the planning mechanism. This agent-model gives us now a better handle on the original structural interpretation of the assistance unit: the input devices are a subset of all sensory input to the A/U and the associated formats are the data structures of those observations (also known as "percepts"). The output devices are a subset of all effectors of the A/U and quite clearly, for these to work in an intelligent way, a reasoning engine of some sort is required between the input and the output mechanisms of the A/U – as illustrated in Fig. 2.

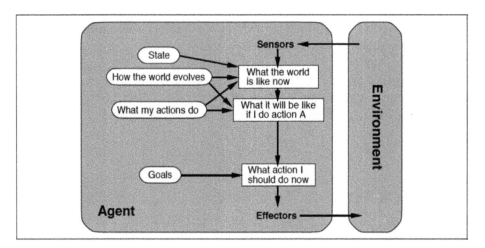

Fig. 2. Agent with explicit goals and reasoning, according to Russell and Norvig [2].

2 Situational Awareness and Assistance

The next step is to apply the agent-based Assistance Units to situations where timely interventions are required by the A/Us that are monitoring the shop-floor processes. We now bring observations, knowledge resources and collaborative activities into play, as proposed in the following conceptual model: in order for the A/U and the worker to be able to collaborate they must be in agreement with respect to the process in which they are involved. They also need to have some mutual understanding what knowledge is relevant for the process at the current step, and at least the A/U should have a basic understanding which knowledge can be assumed as given, for the worker. A concrete assistive intervention would then be to ask the worker whether he/she needs additional information for this step, or the next step, or whether they need any other form of assistance. Figure 3 below illustrates such a situation.

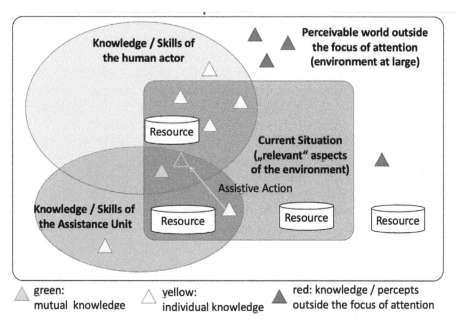

Fig. 3. Establishing a mutual focus of attention between human worker and assistance unit (Color figure online)

The diagram of Fig. 3 shows knowledge items that may come from observations or from prior knowledge, as triangles. The triangles outside the focus of attention (in red) could be any input that is recognized by the sensors of the actors, but which is not having any relevance to the current situation. There could also be red triangles inside the current situation, but outside the mutual focus of attention – these would then represent knowledge items that are not yet, or no longer, of immediate relevance. The arrow going from the yellow triangle of the A/U to the (green) frame of a triangle in the mutual focus of attention, indicates that an assistive intervention is occurring, i.e. the assistance unit is transferring knowledge to the worker, e.g., by reminding him/her to check the polarity of some electrical connection. The objects named "Resource" refer to repositories accessible to the workers and/or the A/Us. In the case of the worker, a printed manual would qualify as a resource, whereas in the case of an A/U we would require digital assets preferably accessible via a URL.

Note that the diagram represents a snapshot at a particular time step in the manufacturing process. The intersection of Assistance Unit, Worker and current overall situation constitutes the mutual focus of attention. It shows one green triangle representing relevant knowledge that the worker has and a green frame of a triangle representing a piece of knowledge that the worker is missing and that the Assistance Unit can bring into play (yellow triangle with arrow to green frame). Going back to the assembly use case introduced earlier, this could be the situation where the worker is reminded to check the polarity of an electrical connection and wants to reassure him-/herself by asking the assistance unit to display the connection diagram.

3 Process Description as Frame for Situational Awareness

Having a model of the overall manufacturing task is necessary for the A/U to be synchronized with the human worker w.r.t. the manufacturing process in which the assistance is supposed to happen. This may look like paying a high price (i.e. heavy modelling) for the sole purpose of getting a reminder to check some quality feature. However, behind the simple example is a more ambitious objective, namely to develop a process modelling methodology that can be used not only for simple assistive interventions, but also for highly synchronized collaborative work, as would be required when a collaborative robot helps a worker to place a truck engine in a chassis frame.

In the use case of the power unit assembly, four sensory inputs are used and related to the manufacturing process in question: (1) a video camera is analyzing the worker's movement in order to recognize certain actions, such as picking a screw and tightening it. (2) a second video stream recognizes artefacts on the work table, such as the side panels of the power unit. (3) A third video stream comes from a Hololens used by the worker, detecting the worker's gaze (direction of viewing) and also recognizing those artefacts that are directly in view of the worker. (4) A microphone picks up utterances of the worker, e.g. when he/she requests additional information, such as the procedure for assembling a specific part of the power unit. The detection systems of these four sensor streams translate the raw data into discrete observations that can then be used by the situational awareness module. In the next section we specify the modelling language that is able to merge process knowledge with observational knowledge, in order to arrive at the required situational awareness.

3.1 Pseudo-Natural Language for Process Steps, Observations and Interventions

The following is an example of the orchestration language for collaboration and assistance on the manufacturing shop floor. It has some syntactic sugar to make it look like a structured natural language, but it has a direct translation into a logic based programming formalism:

```
<Assembly>
Assembling product [PowerUnit-1] involves steps:
  place () material [Base] on equipment [Worktable] with step-
range <10-15s>,
  place () material [Bottom_cover] on top of [Base] with step-
range <10-15s>,
  place (from the right), component [Powersupply] on top of
[Bottom_cover]
     on trigger (show-how) show user (tutorial "Powerunit-1/Pow-
ersupply.mp3");
     on trigger (delay) ask user (need-help-in-task?)
     on trigger (behaviour) ask user (are-you-sure?)
     else do either:
     place (from the left), material [Side_panel_left] on side
of assembly then
place (from the right), material [Side_panel_right];
        or
place (from the right), material [Side_panel_right] then
place (from the left), material [Side_panel_left];
  place () material [Housing] on top of assembly [PowerUnit-1];
  inform about [Bottom_cover]: myfirm/PowerUnit-1/Connect-
ors_bottom_cover.jpg;
  inform about [Powersupply]: ]: myfirm/PowerUnit-1/Powersup-
ply.mp3;
  inform about [PowerUnit-1]: myfirm/PowerUnit-1/Assembly.mp3;
  assist on demand [PowerUnit-1]: Lifting_robot_Lifty;
  in_panic_do [PowerUnit-1]: emergency_plan_call_the_doc-
tor.help
</Assembly>
```

A similar description is conceivable for another task, e.g. the packaging of the power supply unit after assembly[1] :

```
<Packaging>
Packing product [PowerUnit-1] involves steps:
  Pick () material [cardboard-VPK1] and place it¹ on equipment
[worktable],
  Transform [cardboard-VPK1] through [make-PU1-box] into mate-
rial [PU1-box],
  Place (bottom down) product [PowerUnit-1] into [PU1-box],
  [...]
</Packaging>
```

Here, the construct transform [X] through [P] allows us to declare a subtask make-PU1-box which needs to be further specified elsewhere.

At this stage, our task description language is not complete yet, but the fragment above has been formalized and used for the demonstration of the assembly use case. In

---

[1] We allow simple anaphoric references: "and place **it**" refers to the cardboard.

the research implementation, we have focused on the formal constructs and it would be the task of productization, to add a compiler/interpreter that transforms the structured natural language into the respective formal constructs.

The following table summarizes our current set of constructs. The middle column shows the language construct, on the right we give examples or comments and on the left we explain the function of the construct for the purpose of expressing either manufacturing task steps or interventions by the assistance unit (Table 3).

Table 3. Constructs of the task description language for assistance units

Meta-language explanation	Language construct	Examples/Comments
Assistance trigger	**trigger** (show-how | delay | behavior | panic)	Show-how is initiated by the worker; delay gets triggered when the time is used up; behavior is used when a deviation is observed; panic triggers a defined emergency procedure
A/U Intervention control	On trigger T <action> ... else	If trigger T is raised then do [...], else do [...]
Object	**product** [ID]	We associate assembly tasks with products, e.g. PowerUnit-1 with some catalogue-ID
Object	**equipment** [ID]	Instrumental objects such as tools, e.g. a screwdriver or a workbench, or an info-screen
Object	**material** [ID]	A part made of homogeneous material, e.g. a metal base of some product
Object	**component** [ID]	A specific functional part of a product that may itself be a subassembly or product
Object	**assembly** [ID]	A non-functional intermediate state of a product during the manufacturing process
Object	**user** [ID]	A human worker involved in the task
Action	**place** (+ qualifiers)	E.g. place (from the left) ...
(More actions will need to be defined)	**pick X from Y**	E.g. taking a screw from a container
	(do) show X [to user]	What the A/U should display to the user
	(do) ask [user]	What the A/U should ask the user
	(do) help [user]	Refers to physical or reasoning help
A high-level action pointing to another task specification	**Transform** [X] through [P] into <object> newX	References a sub-process P, which transforms X into a new shape or form "NewX" e.g. creating a box out of some sheet of cardboard
Spatial qualifiers	**on top of**	These are qualifiers that have a local interpretation from the worker's point of view
	from the right **from the left below, from below**	They must be used carefully because they are relative to the worker's assumed position
Domain-specific terms	[Dom-Spec-Term]	E.g. material [Bottom-cover] – the referenced objects must be recognizable for the assistance system through some identification mechanism (e.g. RFID, image recognition)

At present, the domain-specific language only uses the action constructs "pick", "place" and "insert" for assembly tasks. This corresponds to the fact that the observational modules cannot distinguish any further activities, e.g. "gluing" or "screwing" etc. As soon as we extend the scope of manufacturing activities to e.g. machine re-tooling or to machine maintenance, we will have to extend the vocabulary, e.g. to express that some machine part may have to be disassembled. However, such distinctions only make sense if they can be detected by the observational modules. One simple "fallback"-detection mechanism is of course, to require the worker to confirm that step X has been done. What should become clear though is, that we already have a sufficient set of language constructs to combine actors' task specifications, observations and triggered interventions, as the minimally required vocabulary.

4   Summary, Work in Progress and Beyond

We have presented a conceptual model and an orchestration language for specifying tasks on a manufacturing shop floor. The language allows the user to also specify assistive interventions in relation to observations that come as information streams from different sensory channels. At the time of writing, a software demonstrator for the described assembly use case is being implemented by the research partners and will be validated by the industrial use case partner.

The implementation of the situation awareness module is inspired by the Situation Calculus, a modelling approach for cognitive robotics pioneered in the works of Reiter [14], Levesque, Lesperance et al. [13]. We use the word "inspired" because at present, we do not make full use of e.g. the IndiGolog programming environment developed by that group at the University of Toronto [15]. Instead, we remain with the more straightforward task specification and use the unification algorithm of Prolog to activate the assistance triggers when certain conditions in the observation streams are met. In a future project, we plan to map our task specifications to equivalent actions and preconditions/post conditions as required by the Situation Calculus.

Acknowledgement. This work has been co-funded by the Austrian Research Promotion Agency (FFG) and by the Austrian Ministry for Transport, Innovation and Technology (bmvit), through the project "MMAssist II" (FFG No.: 858623) within the research program "Production of the Future". We are grateful to the anonymous reviewers for pointing out weaknesses and giving advice on related work.

References

1. Apt, W., Schubert, M., Wischmann, S.: Digitale Assistenzsysteme - Perspektiven und Herausforderungen für den Einsatz in Industrie und Dienstleistungen. In: Hrsg.: Institut für Innovation und Technik (iit)in der VDI/VDE Innovation + Technik GmbH, WeApWi 2018, p. 80 (2018)
2. Russell, S., Norvig, P.: Artificial Intelligence – A Modern Approach, 3rd edn. Prentice Hall, Upper Saddle River (2012)
3. Hold, P., Ranz, F., Sihn, W.: Konzeption eines MTM-basierten Bewertungsmodells für digitalen Assistenzbedarf in der cyber-physischen Montage (2016)
4. Hagemann, S: Optimierung des Fertigungsplanungsprozesses im Karosseriebau durch die Entwicklung eines Konzepts zur automatisierten Generierung von Fertigungsanlagen mithilfe eines wissensbasierten Systems, p. 202. Master-Arbeit, Otto von Guericke Univ. Magdeburg (2016)
5. Bokranz, R., Landau, K.: Handbuch Industrial Engineering: Produktivitätsmanagement mit MTM. Schäfer-Peschel (2012)

6. Proctor, F.M., Balakirsky, S.B., Kootbally, Z., Kramer, T.R., Schlenoff, C.I., Shackleford, W.P.: The canonical robot command language (CRCL). Ind. Robot. **43**(5), 495–502 (2016). https://doi.org/10.1108/IR-01-2016-0037

7. Kelterborn, D.: Erweiterung eines Systems vorbestimmter Zeiten zur Bewertung der körperlichen Belastung in der Produktionslogistik. Dissertation, TU München (2016). http://www.fml.mw.tum.de/fml/images/Publikationen/Kelterborn.pdf

8. Mertens, A., Schlick, C.: Vorlesungsfolien 2016/17. RWTH Aachen, IAW. https://www.iaw-aachen.de/files/iaw/vorlesungen/Winter/2017/IEE/IEE_LE05_WiSe17_Slides.pdf

9. Benter, M.: Analyse von Arbeitsabläufen mit 3D-Kameras. Dissertation (2018). https://tore.tuhh.de/bitstream/11420/1920/1/Dissertation_BenterMartin.pdf

10. Hengstebeck, A., Weisner, K., Klöckner, M., Deuse, J., Kuhlenkötter, B., Roßmann, J.: Formal modelling of manual work processes for the application of industrial service robotics. In: 48th CIRP Conference on MANUFACTURING SYSTEMS - CIRP CMS 2015, Procedia CIRP, vol. 41, pp. 364–369 (2016)

11. Bauer, S.: Prozesssprachenbasiertes System zur Ansteuerung digitaler Menschmodelle als Teilkomponente einer Software zur Planung und Visualisierung menschlicher Arbeit in der Digitalen Fabrik. Dissertation (2015). https://monarch.qucosa.de/api/qucosa%3A20388/attachment/ATT-0/

12. Korn, O.: Context-aware assistive systems for augmented work - a framework using gamification and projection (2014). http://www.oliver-korn.de/wp-content/uploads/2014/05/Context-Aware-Assistive-Systems-for-Augmented-Work.-A-Framework-Using-Gamification-and-Projection_WEB.pdf

13. Levesque, H., Reiter, R., Lespérance, Y., Lin, F., Scherl, R.: GOLOG: a logic programming language for dynamic domains. J. Logic Program. **31**, 59–84 (1997)

14. Reiter, R.: Knowledge in Action. Logical Foundations for Specifying and Implementing Dynamical Systems. MIT Press, Cambridge (2001)

15. De Giacomo, G., Lespérance, Y., Levesque, H.J., Sardina, S.: IndiGolog: a high-level programming language for embedded reasoning agents. In: El Fallah Seghrouchni, A., Dix, J., Dastani, M., Bordini, R.H. (eds.) Multi-Agent Programming, pp. 31–72. Springer, Boston, MA (2009). https://doi.org/10.1007/978-0-387-89299-3_2

11

Strategies for Dealing with Problems in Robotised Unscrewing Operations

Jun Huang$^{(\boxtimes)}$ ⓘ, Duc Truong Pham ⓘ, Ruiya Li ⓘ, Kaiwen Jiang ⓘ, Dalong Lyu, and Chunqian Ji ⓘ

Department of Mechanical Engineering, School of Engineering, University of Birmingham, Birmingham B15 2TT, UK
{j.huang.1,d.t.pham,C.Ji}@bham.ac.uk, {rxl721,xj797, dxl887}@student.bham.ac.uk

Abstract. Disassembly is the first step in a remanufacturing process chain with unscrewing being usually the most frequent task. In previously reported research in the authors' laboratory, a new method has been developed for using robots to unfasten screws. Uncertainties and variability in the physical condition of screws induced by dirt, rust, or mechanical damage pose difficulties for such robotised unscrewing systems. There are three common failure modes: screwdriver missing screw head, screwdriver slipping on screw head and screw too tight to remove. This paper presents strategies to handle these failure modes, making the developed robotised method more robust and reliable. The strategies include conducting a second search and second unfastening trial as well as involving collaboration with a human operator. Tests were carried out to validate the proposed strategies. The results show that the strategies could deal with the failure modes, enabling 100% successful operation.

Keywords: Remanufacturing · Robotic disassembly · Automated unscrewing

1 Introduction

Remanufacturing is an increasingly significant part of a circular economy, delivering economic, environmental and social benefits [1, 2]. In remanufacturing, disassembly of end-of-life (EoL) products is a critical first step [3]. Disassembly is labour intensive and skill intensive and disassembly costs usually represent a substantial proportion of the cost of the remanufactured product. Robotic technology has been proposed for disassembly [4, 5], with a range of approaches having been explored for robotic disassembly applications [6–8]. For example, robot-assisted disassembly was used for dismantling electronic products as early as 1994 [9]. Robots have many advantages including high accuracy, speed and repeatability and the ability to handle repetitive and tedious disassembly operations such as unscrewing [10]. Screws are very common mechanical fasteners as they can be dismantled non-destructively for future maintenance, repair, remanufacturing and recycling [11]. However, unscrewing is difficult to be automated. This is due to uncertainties and variability in the location and the physical condition of screws in EoL products caused by corrosion, contaminants (grease and dirt), deformation and other forms of mechanical damage [12].

A robotic system was prototyped for automated screw removal from e-waste products such as laptops [13]. Computer vision and force sensing were employed to locate screws automatically. An accelerometer mounted on a screwdriver was used to detect when a screw had been completely detached from a mating threaded hole. A screw removal success rate of 96.5% was achieved, which was affected by the lighting conditions of the computer vision system. A robotic workstation fitted with Kinect cameras was developed for autonomous disassembly of electric vehicle motors [14]. A detection algorithm was proposed to locate the position and determine the type of the screws to be removed by the robot. A hybrid workstation with a collaborative robot was presented for performing unscrewing in EoL electric vehicles (EV) batteries which contained substances hazardous to human health [15, 16]. A bit holder was designed to allow the robot to change different socket wrench bits. An electric screwdriver and a camera-based location detection system were also proposed for automatic unscrewing tasks [17]. A spiral search strategy was designed for a robot to locate and engage a screw head, ensuring that no position was scanned twice [18]. In addition, a robotised screwing and unscrewing technique was developed for dismantling electronic devices [19]. A robot was released by Apple in 2016 for removing screws on EoL iPhones to disassemble them for remanufacturing and recycling to reduce e-waste [20].

The above research has mainly focused on methods and devices for automated unscrewing. Few studies have considered the uncertain physical conditions of screws in EoL products. Four common conditions have been identified in automated unscrewing operations [21]. They include three failure modes: (1) screwdriver missing screw head, (2) screwdriver slipping on screw head and (3) screw too tight to remove. In previously reported research in the authors' laboratory, a new method was developed for using a collaborative robot to unfasten screws [22]. This paper presents strategies for handling the above failure modes in robotised unscrewing operations, making the developed method more robust and reliable.

The remainder of this paper is organised as follows. Section 2 briefly introduces a human-robot collaborative disassembly cell built in the authors' laboratory and the automated unscrewing method implemented in that cell. Section 3 describes the proposed failure handling strategies. Section 4 reports on tests carried out to validate the proposed strategies. Section 5 concludes the paper and provides suggestions for future work.

2   Automated Unscrewing Method

2.1   A Human-Robot Collaborative Disassembly Cell

Figure 1 shows a human-robot collaborative disassembly cell for unfastening screws built in the authors' laboratory. The cell mainly composes a collaborative robot (KUKA LBR iiwa 14 R800), an electrical nutrunner (torque spindle, Georges Renault SAS MC51-10) and a geared offset attachment (LUBBERING basic line 4-22-15). The nutrunner was installed on the flange of robot. A spindle controller (Georges Renault SAS, 8216-CVIC H-4) was used to control and programme the nutrunner. The geared offset attachment mounted on the nutrunner could unfasten Hexagonal head bolts with flanges, as shown in Fig. 1. When connected, the robot could trigger and stop the nutrunner.

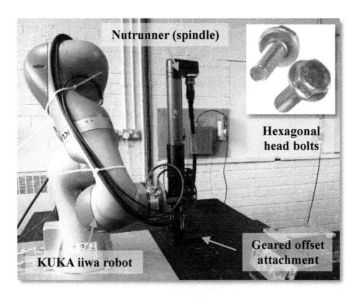

Fig. 1. A robotic cell for automated unscrewing.

The robot has active compliance control using a Cartesian impedance controller. This facilitates human-robot collaboration for complex disassembly operations in the cell. A human operator can work alongside the robot directly without safety guarding, providing the cell with higher flexibility and adaptability and thus a better ability to handle disassembly uncertainties.

2.2 Automated Unscrewing Process

Figure 2 shows the developed automated unscrewing process, which involves four stages: approach, search and engage, unfasten, and assess and leave. The control strategies of torque, position and active compliance are adopted during the process. The corresponding control method of each stage is briefly introduced below. More details about the automated unscrewing method could be found in [22].

1) Approach. The robot with a nutrunner moves to an estimated position above screw head. The nutrunner rotates in the fastening direction at a low speed to ensure that any loose screw will be tightened up before unfastening, making the following stage easier to control. Then, the robot turns on its compliant mode. The compliant behaviour of the robot is achieved by impedance control, which is modelled on a virtual spring-damper system with configurable stiffness and damping [23]. Thanks to compliance, the robot can avoid hard collisions with humans operating in its workspace.
2) Search and engage. Due to factors such as the uncertain mechanical condition of screws and the limited accuracy of robot motion, there is a position error between

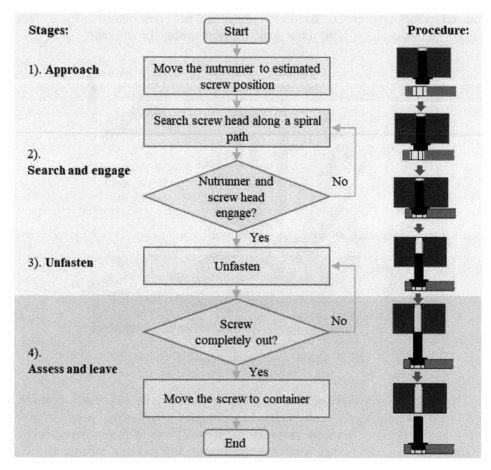

Fig. 2. Automated unscrewing process.

the hexagonal hole in the geared offset attachment and the hexagonal screw head. A spiral motion is designed for the robot to search for and engage the screw head. The equations of the spiral path employed are [22]:

$$
\begin{cases}
x = \frac{f_s}{\pi} \sqrt{\frac{2\pi n_s}{5} t} \cos\left(\sqrt{\frac{2\pi n_s}{5} t}\right) \\
y = \frac{f_s}{\pi} \sqrt{\frac{2\pi n_s}{5} t} \sin\left(\sqrt{\frac{2\pi n_s}{5} t}\right)
\end{cases}
\tag{1}
$$

where x and y are the coordinates along the X and Y axes, respectively. f_s is the size of the hexagonal screw head chamfer. n_s is the rotating speed of the tool and t is search time.

3) Unfasten. Once the tool and screw head have engaged, the robot stops its search motion and the nutrunner rotates in the unfastening direction. Under the compliant mode, the robot can follow the movement of the screw during run-out.

4) Assess and leave. When the screw has been separated from the screw hole, the screw oscillates slightly along its axis due to the chamfer at the end of the screw threads and continuous rotation of the tool. The position information of the robot along the

direction of the screw axis is employed to determine when the screw is completely out. Finally, the separated screw is moved away.

3 Mitigating Strategies for Failure Modes

3.1 Strategies for Dealing with Failure Modes

Three common failure modes are identified in automated unscrewing operations, which are: (1) screwdriver missing screw head, (2) screwdriver slipping on screw head and (3) screw too tight to remove [21]. Figure 3 illustrates the flow chat of the proposed strategies to deal with these problems.

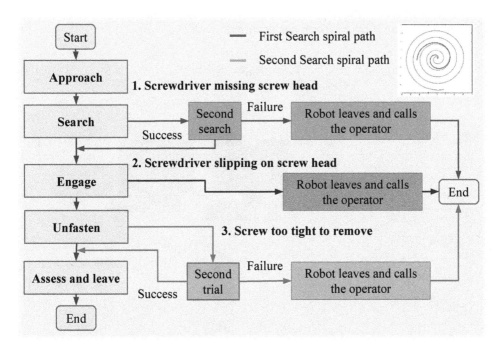

Fig. 3. The flow chart of the proposed strategies.

If the position error were without the spiral search range, the tool would miss the screw head in its search motion (failure mode 1). Conducting a second spiral search along a path with a larger range and higher density is proposed as a strategy to handle this problem, as shown in Fig. 3. If the second search succeeds, subsequent unscrewing steps will proceed. Otherwise, human-robot collaboration will be implemented to cope with this screw in the human-robot collaborative disassembly cell. The robot will leave its search position and call a human operator to come to dismantle the screw.

Due to rust, corrosion or mechanical damage to a screw, the tool may slip on the screw head (failure mode 2). It is difficult for the robot to disassemble screws in such a situation. Once the situation is detected by the robot, the operator will again be called to handle it. If a screw is too tightly fixed, the tool is unable to disassemble it because the required loosening torque exceeds the maximum capability of the tool (failure mode 3). Although the screw has not been successfully removed in the unfastening operation, the impact force exerted by the tool might have loosened it. A second unfastening attempt is made to apply another impact force to try and release the screw. If this fails again, the robot will leave the current position and call the operator.

3.2 Detection Methods for Failure Modes

Before adopting the above strategies, it is critical for the robot to detect these failure modes during automated unscrewing. Information regarding the position and torque of the robot is employed for this detection. Figure 4 shows how information on the position of the robot tool is used to determine a search failure. Once the tool fits in the screw head, its position along the Z axis will increase from P_{z0} to P_{z1}. The following equation is used to determine if engagement has occurred:

$$P_{z1} - P_{z0} > \Delta P \tag{2}$$

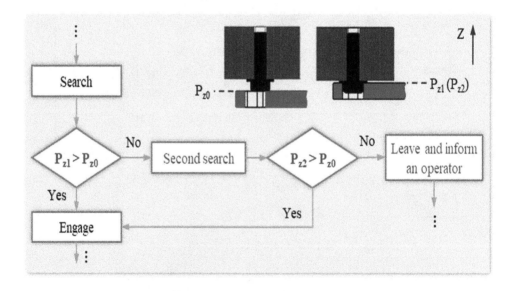

Fig. 4. Detection of failure mode 1.

where P_{z0} and P_{z1} are the initial and end positions of the tool during search along the Z axis, respectively. ΔP is a set threshold value for position change and is related to the size of the screw head. In the second search motion, the same way could be employed to determine whether the tool fits in the screw head or not, as shown in Fig. 4.

Robot's torque information is employed to detect failure modes 2 and 3, as shown in Fig. 5. A target torque value (T_{t0}) is set to stop the search, once the tool engages the screw head during a searching process. As shown in Eq. (3), the applied torque on the tool (T_e) will increase once the tool engages the screw head due to its slow rotation in fastening direction. However, if the tool slips on screw head, torque on the tool could not increase to the target value.

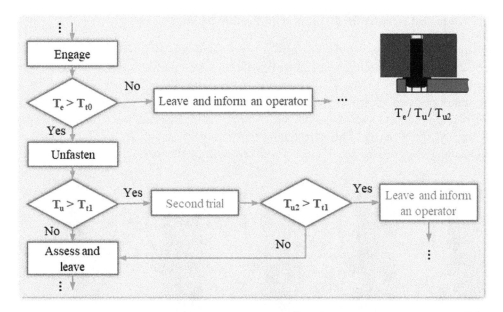

Fig. 5. Detections of failure modes 2 and 3.

$$T_e > T_{t0} \tag{3}$$

If the screw is too tight to be removed, the applied torque on robot tool (T_u) will increase and exceed the maximum safe torque value (T_{t1}), as expressed in Eq. (4). Therefore, the torque on robot tool during unfastening process could be used to detect the failure mode 3.

$$T_u > T_{t1} \tag{4}$$

4   Experimental Tests and Results

The robot cell in Fig. 1 was implemented for experimental tests to validate the above strategies. Hexagon headed screws (M6 × 16 mm) with flange were installed on a metal plate. Table 1 lists the set speed and torque values of the nutrunner in stages 2 and 3. A flashing LED strobe light connected to robot controller was adopted to inform a human operator to handle the screws when the robot was unable to do that.

Table 1. Parameters of the nutrunner.

Search and engage		Unfasten	
Rotating speed of the tool	25 r/min	Rotating speed of the tool	100 r/min
Target fastening torque	14 Nm	Maximum unfastening torque	25 Nm

4.1 Tests and Results for Dealing with Failure Mode 1

The proposed strategy of second search worked and successfully engaged the screw head after the first search failed. Figure 6 presents selected image frames captured from the testing process. Figure 6(a) shows the robot with the nutrunner approaching an estimated position of the screw head. The failure of the first search can be seen in Fig. 6(b). Figure 6(c) shows that the tool capturing and engaging the screw head within the second spiral search. The unfastening of the screw is shown in Fig. 6(d). Once the unfastening stage finished, the screw was taken away by the robot, as shown in Fig. 6(e).

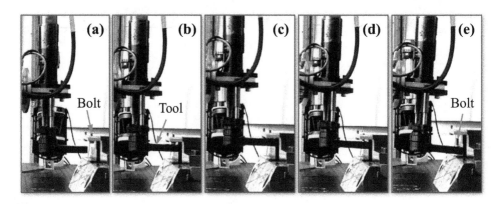

Fig. 6. Strategy of conducting a second search: (a) approach, (b) the first search fails, (c) the second search succeeds, (d) unfasten, and (e) assess and leave.

Figure 7 shows the torque and position information measured by the robot during the unscrewing process. Four stages are illustrated clearly. The torque value of -2.5 Nm was set as a threshold value to stop the search once the tool engaged the screw head. Position information was used to determine whether the first search was successful and when the screw was completely out during unfastening.

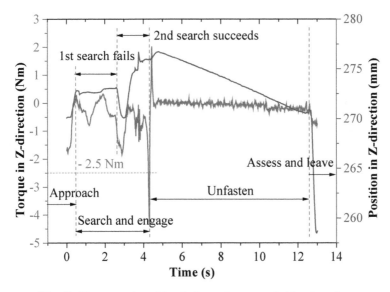

Fig. 7. Torque and position information recorded by the robot.

The strategy for dealing with the failure of both searches was tested. Figure 8 illustrates the selected image frames captured from the unscrewing process. After the tool approached the screw head (Fig. 8(a)), both the first and second searches failed, as shown in Fig. 8(b) and (c), respectively. Then, the robot left its current position and turned on the strobe light to inform an operator (Fig. 8(d)). Figure 8(e) shows the operator unfastening the screw with a spanner. Figure 9 shows the measured torque and position information by the robot during the unscrewing process. The maximum torque of the robot did not reach the threshold value of −2.5 or 2.5 Nm, which was used to stop the search once the tool engaged with the screw head.

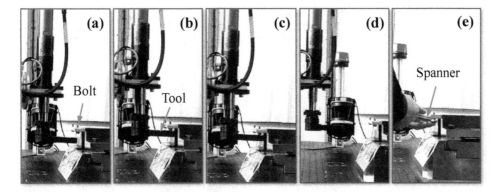

Fig. 8. Strategy for dealing with the failure of both searches, (a) approach, (b) the first search fails, (c) the second search fails, (d) leave and inform an operator, and (e) handle the screw by the operator.

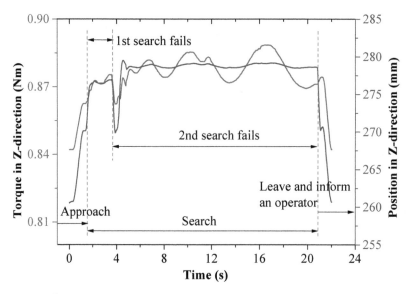

Fig. 9. Torque and position information recorded by the robot.

4.2 Tests and Results for Dealing with Failure Mode 2

Figure 10 shows selected image frames captured from the testing of the strategy proposed for handling the failure mode associated with the tool slipping on the screw head. Figure 10(c) shows the tool slipped on the head of screw after the nutrunner approached the screw (Fig. 10(a)) and fitted in the screw head (Fig. 10(b)). Once slipping was detected, the robot left its current position and called the operator using the strobe light (Fig. 10(d)) to handle the screw with a special tool (Fig. 10(e)). Figure 11 depicts the recorded position and torque information by the robot. During slipping, the tool stayed nearly in a fixed position with small fluctuations.

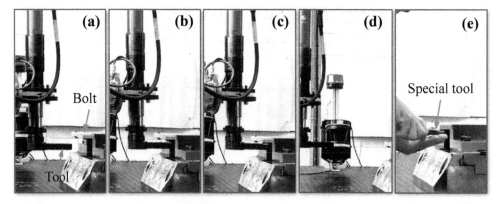

Fig. 10. Strategy for dealing with slipping, (a) approach, (b) search and fit in, (c) slip, (d) leave and inform an operator, and (e) handle the screw by the operator.

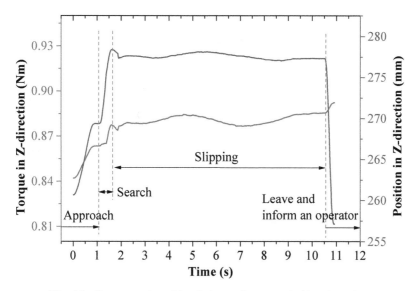

Fig. 11. Torque and position information recorded by the robot.

4.3 Tests and Results for Dealing with Failure Mode 3

Figure 12 shows image frames captured in the test of the strategy to handle a screw that is too tight to remove. Figure 12(a) depicts the tool approaching the screw head. Then, the tool searched for and engaged with the screw head, as shown in Fig. 12(b). However, the tool was unable to unfasten the screw because it was too tight (Fig. 12(c)). The tool left its current position and turned on the strobe light (Fig. 12(d)). Finally, an operator came to disassemble the screw with a hammer and a spanner (Fig. 12(e)). Figure 13 shows the recorded torque and position of the robot. Before the robot left, the position of the tool almost did not change after engaging with the screw head.

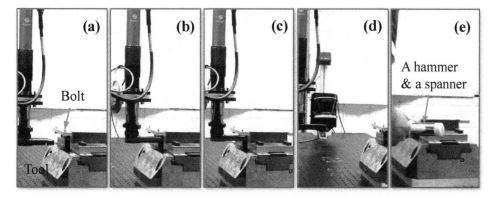

Fig. 12. Strategy for dealing with a screw that is too tight to remove, (a) approach, (b) search and engage, (c) the screw too tight to remove, (d) leave and inform an operator, and (e) handle the screw by the operator.

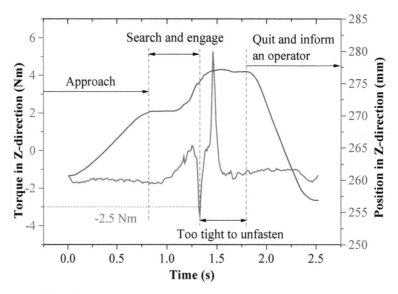

Fig. 13. Torque and position information recorded by the robot.

The proposed strategy involving a second unfastening attempt was tested. Figure 14 illustrates the selected image frames captured during the test. After approaching the screw (Fig. 14(a)), the robot searched for and engaged with the screw head (Fig. 14 (b)). Figure 14(c) shows the first unfastening failed because the screw was too tight. The second unfastening trial succeeded as shown in Fig. 14(d). After the screw was separated from the screw hole, the robot moved the screw away (Fig. 14(e)). The large torque fluctuations during the two unfastening trials are clearly captured, as shown in Fig. 15.

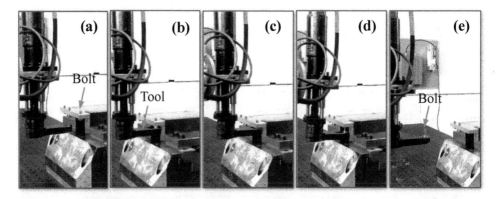

Fig. 14. Strategy of conducting a second unfastening attempt, (a) approach, (b) search and engage, (c) the first attempt fails, (d) the second attempt succeeds, and (e) assess and leave.

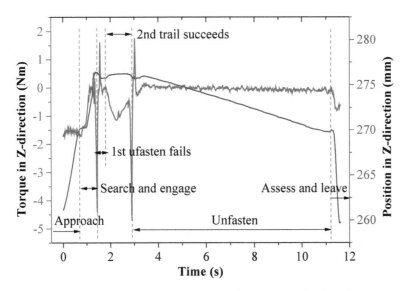

Fig. 15. Torque and position information recorded by the robot.

5 Conclusion

Unscrewing is one of the most common disassembly operations. Automating unscrewing can release people from tedious and repetitive work. Unlike the case of screwing in assembling a new product, unscrewing is difficult to automate due to the poor physical conditions of screws in EoL products. This paper has presented strategies for handling the three main failure modes in automated unscrewing operations, namely, screwdriver missing screw head, screwdriver slipping on screw head and screw too tight to remove. The strategies involve conducting a second search and second unfastening trial or collaborating with a human operator. The paper has briefly introduced a robotic unscrewing method implemented in a human-robot collaborative disassembly cell. The unscrewing process has four stages: approach, search and engage, unfasten, and assess and leave. Experiments have been conducted to test and validate the proposed strategies. The results obtained have demonstrated the feasibility of the strategies which can be adopted to enhance the robustness and reliability of the robotised unscrewing method developed.

In the future, the proposed strategies will be integrated and further tests will be conducted to improve the robustness and efficiency of the robotised unscrewing method. The unscrewing system will also be adapted to make it suitable for different types of screws and bolts.

Acknowledgments. This research was supported by the Engineering and Physical Sciences Research Council (EPSRC) (Grant. No. EP/N018524/1).

Appendix

The automated unscrewing method presented in Sect. 2 was implemented in a turbocharger disassembly demonstration which can be viewed on YouTube at https://www.youtube.com/watch?v=kOwGe_LbLzs.

References

1. Kerin, M., Pham, D.T.: A review of emerging industry 4.0 technologies in remanufacturing. J. Cleaner Prod. **237**, 117805 (2019)
2. Stahel, W.R.: The circular economy. Nat. News **531**(7595), 435 (2016)
3. Vongbunyong, S., Chen, W.H.: Disassembly Automation. Disassembly Automation. SPLCEM, pp. 25–54. Springer, Cham (2015). https://doi.org/10.1007/978-3-319-15183-0_3
4. AUTOREMAN project. http://autoreman.altervista.org/index.html. Accessed 03 Oct 2019
5. Huang, J., Pham, D.T., Wang, Y., Ji, C., Xu, W., Liu, Q.: A strategy for human-robot collaboration in taking products apart for remanufacture. FME Trans. **47**, 731–738 (2019)
6. Li, J., Barwood, M., Rahimifard, S.: Robotic disassembly for increased recovery of strategically important materials from electrical vehicles. Robot. Comput. Integr. Manuf. **50**, 203–212 (2018)
7. Palmieri, G., Marconi, M., Corinaldi, D., Germani, M., Callegari, M.: Automated disassembly of electronic components: feasibility and technical implementation. In: ASME 2018 International Design Engineering Technical Conferences and Computers and Information in Engineering Conference. American Society of Mechanical Engineers (2018)
8. Kristensen, C.B., Sørensen, F.A., Nielsen, H.B.D.B., Andersen, M.S., Bendtsen, S.P., Bøgh, S.: Towards a robot simulation framework for E-waste disassembly using reinforcement learning. In: 29th International Conference on Flexible Automation and Intelligent Manufacturing (2019)
9. Weigl, A.: Requirements for robot assisted disassembly of not appropriately designed electronic products: lessons from first studies. In: Proceedings of 1994 IEEE International Symposium on Electronics and the Environment, pp. 337–342 (1994)
10. Huang, J., et al.: A screw unfastening method for robotic disassembly. In: the International Conference on Sustainable Smart Manufacturing (S2M 2019) (2019)
11. Jia, Z., Bhatia, A., Aronson, R.M., Bourne, D., Mason, M.T.: A survey of automated threaded fastening. IEEE Trans. Autom. Sci. Eng. **16**(1), 298–310 (2019)
12. Gao, Y., Feng, Y., Wang, Q., Zheng, H., Tan, J.: A multi-objective decision making approach for dealing with uncertainty in EOL product recovery. J. Cleaner Prod. **204**, 712–725 (2018)
13. DiFilippo, N.M., Jouaneh, M.K.: A system combining force and vision sensing for automated screw removal on laptops. IEEE Trans. Autom. Sci. Eng. **15**(2), 887–895 (2018)
14. Bdiwi, M., Rashid, A., Putz, M.: Autonomous disassembly of electric vehicle motors based on robot cognition. In: Proceedings of the IEEE International Conference on Robotics and Automation (ICRA 2016), pp. 2500–2505 (2016)
15. Chen, W.H., Wegener, K., Dietrich, F.: A robot assistant for unscrewing in hybrid human-robot disassembly. In: Proceedings of the IEEE International Conference on Robotics and Biomimetics (ROBIO 2014), pp. 536–541 (2014)
16. Gerbers, R., Wegener, K., Dietrich, F., Dröder, K.: Safe, flexible and productive human-robot-collaboration for disassembly of lithium-ion batteries. In: Kwade, A., Diekmann, J. (eds.) Recycling of Lithium-Ion Batteries. SPLCEM, pp. 99–126. Springer, Cham (2018). https://doi.org/10.1007/978-3-319-70572-9_6

17. Wegener, K., Chen, W.H., Dietrich, F., Dröder, K., Kara, S.: Robot assisted disassembly for the recycling of electric vehicle batteries. Procedia CIRP **29**, 716–721 (2015)
18. Gerbers, R., Mücke, M., Dietrich, F., Dröder, K.: Simplifying robot tools by taking advantage of sensor integration in human collaboration robots. Procedia CIRP **44**, 287–292 (2016)
19. Mironov, D., Altamirano, M., Zabihifar, H., Liviniuk, A., Liviniuk, V., Tsetserukou, D.: Haptics of screwing and unscrewing for its application in smart factories for disassembly. Haptics Sci. Technol. Appl. **10894**, 428–439 (2018)
20. How and why Apple's robot Liam disassembles iPhones. https://www.zdnet.com/article/how-and-why-apples-robot-liam-disassembles-iphones/. Accessed 2019
21. Apley, D.W., Seliger, G., Voit, L., Shi, J.: Diagnostics in disassembly unscrewing operations. Int. J. Flex. Manuf. Syst. **10**(2), 111–128 (1998)
22. Li, R., et al.: Unfastening of hexagonal headed screws by a collaborative robot. IEEE Trans. Autom. Sci. Eng. **17**, 1–14 (2020)
23. KUKA Sunrise.OS 1.11. http://www.oir.caltech.edu/twiki_oir/pub/Palomar/ZTF/KUKARo boticArmMaterial/KUKA_SunriseOS_111_SI_en.pdf. Accessed 03 Oct 2019

12

High-Load Titanium Drilling Using an Accurate Robotic Machining System

Robert Brownbill[1]([⊠]) [iD], Philip Silk[2] [iD], Peter Whiteside[1] [iD], Windo Hutabarat[3] [iD], and Harry Burroughes[2] [iD]

[1] Electroimpact UK Ltd., Manor Lane, Hawarden, Deeside CH5 3ST, UK
{robertb,peterw}@electroimpact.com
[2] The Advanced Manufacturing Research Centre - The AMRC, University of Sheffield, Factory 2050, Sheffield S9 1ZA, UK
{p.silk,h.burroughes}@amrc.co.uk
[3] Department of Automatic Control and System Engineering, University of Sheffield, Portobello Street, Sheffield S1 3JD, UK
w.hutabarat@sheffield.ac.uk

Abstract. Robotic drilling systems have been used in the manufacture of large aerospace components for a number of years. Systems have been developed by several systems integrators in order to accurately drill materials from CFRP to Titanium. These systems, however, have been unable to achieve large diameter holes in Titanium due to reduced structural stiffness and end effector capabilities. Typically, large holes are either drilled using large cartesian CNC-controlled machines or drilled using automated drilling units (ADU). However, there is a pull from aerospace OEMS to move away from large monolithic machines, in favour of flexible robotic system. Flexible robotic systems provide a number of benefits for large structure assembly. The following report primarily outlines drilling trials conducted on the Accurate Robotic Machining System, during which holes from 25 mm to 32 mm ID were drilled in titanium implementing an empirical test schedule. Additionally, a discussion on the benefits of drilling large diameter holes using flexible robotic platforms.

Keywords: Robotic drilling · Titanium drilling · Robotic drilling systems · Large hole titanium drilling · Heavy Duty Robot · Accurate robotics

1 Introduction

Robotic drilling systems have been used in the manufacture of aerospace components for a number of years. There have been systems developed to accurately drill materials such as Aluminium, CFRP and Titanium.

To the best of the authors' knowledge, the largest hole drilled by a robotic drilling system in titanium was $1.0''$ (25.4 mm) in diameter, although this was also carried out under research conditions. Aerospace production holes drilled through Aluminium with robotic drilling systems currently don't typically exceed $5/8^{th}{}''$ (15.88 mm).

To achieve the hole quality demanded by the aerospace industry, it has been typical that all 'large diameter' holes are either drilled using CNC-controlled machines, expensive bespoke Cartesian drilling machines or drilled manually using automated drilling units (ADUs).

There are huge benefits to using a robotic drilling system over a typical machining centre. The current industry move to 'flexible' and 'elastic' automation cells means that re-tasking or repurposing the automation is essential to ensuring the overall equipment effectiveness (OEE) is maximized through the simple change of the end-effector. This, in most cases, can easily be an automated process requiring no human interaction.

Robotic systems require much simpler civil engineering works and have a much smaller 'footprint' for the same working volume than that of a traditional gantry machine. These benefits coupled with much shorter lead time and reduced overall cost provide a strong business case for investment into this technology.

These systems, however, have been unable to achieve large diameter holes due to the inherent reduced structural stiffness of the robot arm coupled with the limited robot payload. This has meant that end-effector capabilities are typically not up to the same standard as Cartesian CNC Milling Machines.

Large diameter drilling using robots is also challenging due to the positional accuracy of 'off-the-shelf' robot arm being in excess of ± 0.5 mm. One way to resolve these problems is by improvements to the feedback system, such as the Electroimpact Accurate package. This Accurate package enable the system to achieve a positional accuracy of ± 0.25 mm or better across the robot's working volume. The increase in accuracy also does not require external metrology equipment feedback. Additionally, this also ensure the robotic system remains accurate for multiple processes, without the requirement for localised datum feature relocation or re-teaching of positions.

Further complications are seen during drilling, whereby the thrust force causes the robot arm to flex, especially when the loads are close to the limits of the robot system. The robot's rigidity is not enough to prevent 'skidding' of the tool tip across the workpiece, which subsequently leads to damage, poor quality parts and hole being drilled far outside of positional tolerances.

Skidding can also be prevalent of the robot nosepiece during clamp up process. As the load is increased through the robot arm - a typical system with no secondary feedback are unable to compensate for the arm flex resulting in the nose-piece skidding on the structure causing damage and requiring expensive rework. The additional scales and enhanced kinematic model guarantee the "anti-skid" technology.

The pressure foot allows the system to remain clamped to the component throughout the drilling cycle and even when full retract pecks are used, there is no danger of movement of the system.

Titanium is used in aircraft structures for high-strength applications in high-stress areas such as around the Engine Pylons and Landing Gear attachment points. Fastener sizes of up to $1.25''$ (31.75 mm) are commonly seen in long-haul aircraft wing structures in these areas. During the manufacture of these wing structures there is the requirement to drill a large number of different holes in multiple stack assemblies. Stack assemblies can consist of multiple layers or 'stacks' of different materials including CFRP, Aluminium and Titanium. This assembly process ensures the drilled holes are concentric on final assembly of the components (Fig. 1).

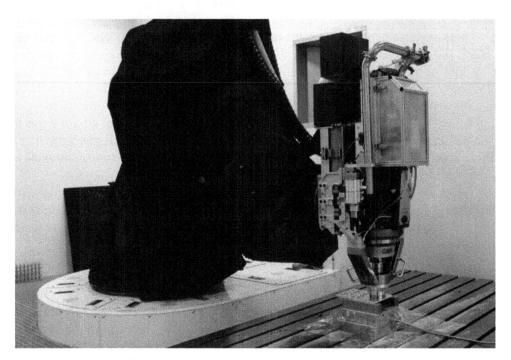

Fig. 1. AMRC accurate robotic machining system

The following report outlines drilling trials conducted using empirical methods on the Accurate Robotic Machining System, during which holes from 25 mm to 32 mm diameter were drilled in titanium.

2 Related Works

As the size of the assemblies grows, the cost of a traditional gantry-style machine becomes less economical compared to that of a robotic system with the same capabilities [1]. Industry demand for the drilling of large-scale aerospace components, which contain titanium, has increased. Robotic drilling of titanium using serial robots has been attempted but high compliance is a major challenge [2]. Ways to improve the accuracy of robots using auxiliary devices such as external feedback sensors have been proposed [3], but the use of such robots to drill high-load large-diameter holes is not found in literature.

No such works have been found exploring the use of articulated robots for large hole drilling, without the use of external thrust-reducing mechanisms (such as vibration assistance). No internal research was carried out within Electroimpact as there was, until now, no direct request from a potential Customer for that requirement. This paper takes that Customer request and directly addresses their requirements, filling in the knowledge gap of all parties involves into the large-hole pure drilling capability of the robotic system.

3   Accurate Robot Architecture

With the addition of secondary feedback, high-order kinematic model, and a fully inte-grated conventional CNC control, robotic technology can now compete on a performance level with customized high precision motion platforms. As a result, the articulated arm can be applied to a much broader range of assembly applications that were once limited to custom machines [4].

Although Electroimpact's accurate upgrade is not the only way to increase robot accuracy, it provides multiple advantages over systems such as real-time metrology feedback. As part of the upgrade process from 'off-the-shelf' robot to Accurate Robot, Electroimpact fits high accuracy external scales to every axis of the robot structure (Fig. 3). The Accurate Robot system is controlled via industry standard Siemens 840Dsl CNC which handles all controls requirements and offers a familiar interface to program-mers and operators. Drawing from common axis configuration in machine tool design, the robot arm is integrated by Electroimpact with patented secondary position sensors at the output of each axis.

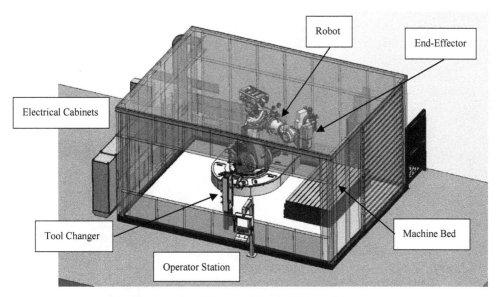

Fig. 2. AMRC factory 2050, ARMS cell layout

The upgrade significantly improves the system enabling calibrated to accuracies to be below ±0.25 mm over a large global volume. This patented solution has broadened the range of applications for unguided industrial robots in the aerospace industry to include high-precision single and dual-sided drilling and fastening, accurate material removal (trimming, milling), and accurate robotic fibre placement [5] (Fig. 2).

The system implemented at the AMRC utilizes a KUKA Titan as the base architecture before the electronics were upgraded with the Accurate Package.

The end-effector in this application is a fixed spindle with small quill axis (~60 mm) allowing for milling and drilling operations.

Although globally, Electroimpact will guarantee accuracies of ±0.25 mm over the robot's working envelope, the compensation routine was optimized for use in the machining volume over the fixed bed, this has seen the accuracy (for this application) improve to around ±0.17 mm.

ARMS is unique as it is currently, the only one to utilize the Accurate Robot architecture. The robot used has a large working volume and medium load (750 kg). Other models are available, with shorter reach, increasing the maximum payload but reducing the working volume. Below, details are provided on the modifications carried out to create ARMS.

3.1   Kinematic Model

The Electroimpact kinematic model utilizes the secondary feedback of external encoders as well as the robot-specific data to greatly improve accuracy. The kinematic model is able to compensate the robots commanded position for the full working envelope and full working payload of the robot, ensuring that the actual position of the tool-point is always accurate even during high load process.

The patented kinematic model uses the dual feedback of the motor encoder positions and high accuracy secondary scales to adjust the robots commanded position and compensate for structural flex and deflections in the system due to loading.

The compensation routine carried out during installation, is also taken into account in the kinematic model to ensure that the robot is not only highly repeatable but, more importantly, highly accurate within the global reference system.

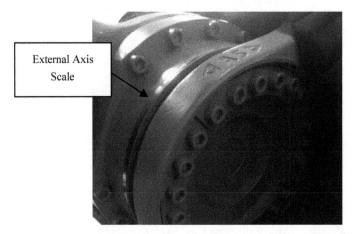

Fig. 3. External axis scale (secondary feedback) showing the encoder strip to gain an accurate position of each joint.

The enhanced kinematic model takes into account the moments of inertia, gravity loads of the arm sections, payload droop and applied (clamp) force deflections to update the Siemens built-in robot kernel for motion. This enables accuracy across the entire working volume. If required, the 'working volume' can be reduced and more data taken over a smaller volume to optimise and improve the accuracy of the system to suit a specific application. For ARMS, the accuracy package was optimised over the machine bed working volume.

The deflection model, measured by the scales, allows for real-time compensation from external forces. This uses the control system to effectively remove the backlash effects and gives an (almost) infinitely stiff axis. This will also mean that accuracy and repeatability is greatly improves through an omni-directional routine, rather than approaching a datum point from the same approach direction. Figure 4 shows a real-time snapshot of the commanded versus actual/measured position for the robot system.

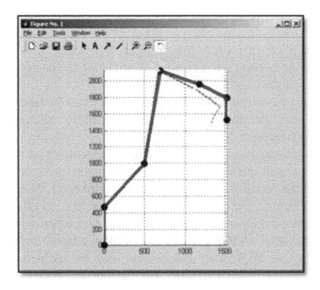

Fig. 4. Kinematic model deflections

3.2 Spindle

The spindle chosen by the AMRC was GMN HCS 280 – 18000/60. This was the largest spindle available at the time from GMN allowing for the widest range of capabilities from this system. For a Research Technology Organization (RTO), testing on this system will allow research partners and companies to monitor different parameters (such as spindle torque and thrust load) and enable them to size their own systems appropriately.

3.3 Pressure Foot

A removable pressure foot was included in the system to allow for advanced drilling operations. Although the accuracy and effective rigidity of the robot is greatly increased due to the accurate package, it is not sufficient to cope with drilling/peck loading. Therefore, a pressure foot is used to apply pre-load to the workpiece. This preload should be greater than the peak drilling thrust load to prevent movement of the end-effector mid-cycle. Load cells within the pressure foot allow the robot to clamp to a user-defined preload.

Drill thrust load is also monitored and should the thrust load exceed a certain percentage of the preload, the CNC will display an alarm – stopping the cycle and preventing damage to the workpiece.

Although active normality correction is common on specific drilling system, there is no such feedback on ARMS. There is only passive normality correction of the pressure foot by means of a swivel nose piece of "cup and cone" type design.

A proximity switch ensures that the controller is aware of the fitment of the pressure foot to prevent collisions and damage to the system.

3.4 Additional Sensors/Data Sources/Systems

The system uses additional sensors to ensure better part quality. There are load cells that allow the controller to measure the pressure foot applied force (clamp force). This force can be adjusted as per the user requirements.

There is a laser distance measurement that measures the distance travelled by the pressure foot and controller uses this data to adjust point the drilling tool centre point for the top of stock measurement.

Built into the spindle is a high-accuracy displacement sensor. This is vital and required for the best part quality. As the spindle heats up, the thermal expansion of the components results in a Z shift that must be accounted for in the controller.

There are also thru-bit and flood coolant system on the end-effector. These were required for the titanium drilling processes. These provide a superior finish on advanced material compared to MQL. Although, the system may be adapted through minor design alterations to accept an MQL unit. The coolant may be disabled, and compressed air diverted to enable an air-blast cooling. The flexibility to choose the coolant technique allows the AMRC and ARMS to tailor their research to suit each clients desired application.

3.5 Programmable Drilling Parameters

Up to 16 separate parameters can be adjusted during a drilling procedure in order to optimise the process. The parameters fall under one of the following categories.

- Feeds and speeds: RPM, mm/rev, mm/min
- Peck cycle: distance and number of pecks
- Allowable spindle thrust force: max/min
- Auxiliary services: Coolant, air blast
- Pressure foot load

4 Industrial Applications

As previously mentioned, robotic drilling solutions have been used in the aerospace industry for a number of years. The robotic system designed and integrated into aerospace production facilities up to date have only had the capability to drill hole which do not exceed 5/8th (15.88 mm) in diameter. However, across aerospace facilities there are requirements to drill large holes.

Electroimpact have previously commissioned systems such as Gear Rib Automated Wing Drilling Equipment (GRAWDE), which have been designed to drill holes up to 1.25 inch (31.75 mm) diameter in the A380 gear rib. This system however, is a Cartesian machine and as such as limited flexibilities and a fix role. A similar Cartesian system produced by Electroimpact, the Horizontal Automated Wing Drilling Equipment (HAWDE), allows for the drilling of wing assemblies with working envelopes of 42 m × 8 m × 2 m [6]. The system is able to accurately position a drilling tool with 5 degrees of freedom. These cartesian systems highlight the need for large volume drilling systems capable of drilling larger holes. Other such cartesian systems have been utilized on other wing-box assembly lines for the latest generation aircraft programs from multiple global manufacturers.

Although, both systems (GRAWDE, HAWDE) are able to meet the drilling requirements of Airbus, they have been specifically designed for their roles. As such the reutilisation of such machinery is difficult and now that the production of the A380 has stop the machinery is likely to be decommissioned, with no further use. Robotic systems are able to provide an alternative to this issue, as reutilisation a capable with the change/redesign of an end effector.

Developmental robotic systems such as ARMS at the AMRC demonstrate how such robotic architecture can achieve comparable large-hole drilling capability to the more expensive and constrained cartesian-machine counterparts.

5 Experimental Methods

ARMS was used to assess the feasibility of using an Electroimpact Accurate Robot to drill aerospace production holes in high-load areas of the aircraft structure. Although metric drills were used, sizes were chosen to best match the equivalent imperial sizes that would be typical of a production system.

Coupons of 45 mm thick 6Al4V Titanium were prepared to fit in a machinist vice. The test schedule was created to evaluate the system's capabilities with increasing hole diameter through the following sizes:

a) 27.5 mm One Shot
b) 28.5 mm Ream (from 27.5 mm Downsize Hole)
c) 29.5 mm One Shot
d) 32.0 mm One Shot

Tests (a) & (b) are representative of a 1⅛"production hole. It was noted that reaming thrust loads and drill torques were much less than the one-shot pre-ream drill cycle. Therefore, tests (c) & (d) were not reamed. Capability to drill 32.0 mm one-shot hole is representative of a 1¼" production hole.

Although in most industrial applications a solid carbide twist drill would be used to drill these holes, for the purposes of these drill trials, a Guehring RT800 3D tipped drill was used as a cost-effective, representative example. The benefit of being able to quickly change the RT800WP (carbide, FireEX coated) drill tip meant the tool didn't need to be reset in the holder and length re-measured for each size change – drastically speeding up the testing process. The use of this tipped drill will provide a good baseline for feasibility studies for industrial applications, typically, tipped drills require more torque and more thrust loading than their solid carbide counterparts.

Furthers trials, around 12 months later, were carried out using a 27.54 mm diameter solid carbide twist drill, provided by an Industrial partner to prove process capability. It was observed that the drill thrust loads were approximately 10–20% lower using the solid carbide twist drill over the tipped cutter.

Successful cycles were run with spindle speed ranges of 100–250 RPM and feed rates of 0.09 – 0.17 mm/rev. Clamp load was close to the robot's maximum. A peck-drilling cycle was used with flood and thru-bit coolant active.

A 3-axis Dynamometer was used to measure drilling forces and monitor the process for excessive vibrations. The vice was mounted to the dynamometer interface plate and forces in three dimensions measured.

Hole quality inspected using a CMM at Electroimpact's facility along with a surface roughness indicator.

As ARMS doesn't have local normality correction (as a production drilling robot would have) and the titanium coupons were not perfectly flat, perpendicularity to the top surface of the coupon was not as important as the hole-vector parallelism between all holes on the coupon. This was measured to assess if the drill had a tendency to 'wander' away from the thrust axis.

The edge of the coupon was water cut from a larger titanium plate. With no datum feature, hole position was measured relative to the first hole given the programmed hole spacing.

6   Results and Discussion

The Accurate Robotic Machining System was capable of drilling all the holes as detailed in the testing schedule to a very high standard, suitable to meet a typical aerospace manufacturers machine specification (Fig. 5).

The tipped drill has 'h7' tolerance and was used as the reaming tool. Although not indicative of an industrial process, all drilling parameters were observed to be well within the capabilities of the system. It was, however, observed that carrying out a 'rapid retract' once the reaming cycle was completed left a spiral score mark within the hole – this could be solved by feeding the tipped drill back out of the hole or using a specific machine reamer.

Testing was repeated during a second session using a tipped machine reamer at the 28.5 mm diameter (reaming from 27.5 mm downsize diameter) along with drilling using a full-length solid carbide production cutter. Limited cycles were run using these cutters to reduce unnecessary wear. Eight holes were drilled 27.5 mm one shot, three were reamed thru and one was partially reamed (to measure concentricity – the systems ability to return to the same hole). The scoring that can be seen in hole #1 (top right) was due to a rapid retract command as part of the ream cycle – this was then changed to a feed retract on the subsequent two and a half holes and excellent surface finish results were seen (Fig. 6).

Fig. 5. 32.0 mm test coupon a (guehring tipped drill)

Fig. 6. Production cutter coupon drill and ream holes (holes 1,2,3: One-shot drill 27.5 mm & Ream 28.5 mm, hole 4: Partial ream, holes 5,6,7,8: One-shot drill 27.5 mm)

6.1 Dynamometer Results

Good, consistent results were seen during the drilling process with no unwanted vibration observed (Fig. 7).

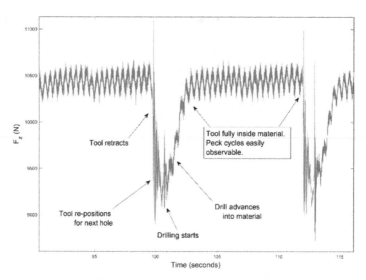

Fig. 7. Dynamometer force results

6.2 Hole Quality

Results were collated from 48 holes (in six coupons) as detailed in the test schedule. The above table of results is the range observed across all coupons and would meet a typical Aerospace Industry specification for holes of this diameter (Table 1).

Table 1. Collated results of the trial using tipped cutters.

Quality metric	Result
Hole position	±0.25 mm
Diameter (drill)	+0/+46 μm
Diameter (ream)	−23/−18 μm*
Hole cylindricity	47 μm
Hole vector parallelism (to Hole 1)	0.15 mm
Hole surface finish quality (drill)	<1.4 μm Ra
Hole surface finish quality (ream)	<0.8 μm Ra

*Measurements fall within the tolerance band of the 'h7' cutter.

In all cases, ARMS was able to achieve the 32.0 mm (1.260″) diameter holes, drilled one-shot through Titanium. Spindle torque loading was not observed to exceed 50% throughout drilling cycles, with no greater than 25% torque observed for the reaming cycles (Table 2).

The results from the limited trial of the production cutters and reamers show the improvements in cylindricity, surface finish quality and vector parallelism as expected

Table 2. Collated results of the trial using production cutters (27.5 mm/28.5 mm diameters only).

Quality metric	Result
Hole position	±0.25 mm
Diameter (drill)	−3/ +10 μm
Diameter (Ream)	0/−+3 μm
Hole cylindricity (Ream)	16 μm
Hole vector parallelism (to Hole 1)	0.019 mm
Hole#4 Concentricity (Drill/ream) Hole surface finish quality (drill)	0.026 mm <1.3 μm Ra
Hole surface finish quality (ream)	<0.45 μm Ra

from the use of a solid carbide cutter. The increased stiffness of the tools and use of a reaming cutter far exceeded the production requirements that were being assessed.

Spindle torque values were observed to be comparable to that of the tipped cutters with a minor increase for the first drilled holes, as this was a brand-new cutter. Torque values were observed to return to those observed previously after the second hole.

The limiting factor throughout these trials was the pre-load clamp force available to counter the drill thrust loading. This was close to the Robot's maximum for the largest holes drilled.

7 Conclusions

Confidence has been proven that the Electroimpact Accurate Robot architecture is capable of meeting aerospace production requirements for high-load fastener holes of up to 1¼″ diameter. However, this has been conducted, both in a favourable Robot pose and under research condition.

ARMS is reaching the limits of its advanced material drilling capability due to the limits of the clamping pre-load available. Should the drilling of larger holes be required, additional measures to reduce drill thrust load would be necessary.

The Electroimpact Accurate Robot package providing the controls-based stiffness has enabled this system to do something previously thought not possible.

The focus of future work will be to reduce the clamp up and thrust force required to produce a large diameter hole in Titanium, primarily through process optimisation. This will allow large diameter holes to be drilled where fixturing, orientation and access are not optimum or vary in the case of production setups.

Acknowledgements. We gratefully acknowledge the support of Royal Academy of Engineering, Advanced Manufacturing Research Centre, Electroimpact UK Ltd, The University of Sheffield, HVM Catapult and Aerospace Technology Institute.

References

1. Verl, A., Valente, A., Melkote, S., Brecher, C., Ozturk, E., Tunc, L.T.: Robots in machining. CIRP Ann. **68**(2), 799–822 (2019)
2. Kim, S.H., et al.: Robotic machining: a review of recent progress. Int. J. Precis. Eng. Manuf. **20**(9), 1629–1642 (2019)
3. Bi, S., Liang, J.: Robotic drilling system for titanium structures. Int. J. Adv. Manuf. Technol. **54**(5), 767–774 (2011)
4. Saund, B., DeVlieg, R.: High accuracy articulated robots with CNC control systems. SAE Int. J. Aerosp. **6**(2), 780–784 (2013)
5. DeVlieg, R.: Accurate robot technology (2019). https://electroimpact.com/Products/Robots/Overview.aspx. Accessed on 19 Dec 2019
6. Calawa, R., et al.: HAWDE Five Axis Wing Surface Drilling Machine (2004). https://www.electroimpact.com/WhitePapers/2004-01-2806.pdf. Accessed on 29 July 2020

13

Investigation on the Convergence of the Genetic Algorithm of an Aerodynamic Feeding System Due to the Enlargement of the Solution Space

Torge Kolditz$^{(\boxtimes)}$ (iD), Caner-Veli Ince (iD), and Annika Raatz (iD)

Institute of Assembly Technology, Leibniz Universitaet Hannover, 30823 Garbsen, Germany
kolditz@match.uni-hannover.de

Abstract. To meet the demands for flexible assembly technology, an aerodynamic feeding system has been developed. The system autonomously finds the optimal configuration of four parameters – two angles of inclination, nozzle pressure and component speed – using a genetic algorithm, which has been presented in earlier work. To increase the flexibility of the feeding system, an actuator was implemented, that enables the variation of the nozzle position orthogonally to the moving direction of the components. This paper investigates the effects of the more flexible flow against the components on their behavior when passing the nozzle. Additionally, the nozzle position was implemented into the genetic algorithm as a fifth parameter. Therefore, the impact of the enlargement of the solution space of the genetic algorithm due to the implementation of a fifth parameter is investigated in this paper as well.

Keywords: Assembly · Genetic algorithm · Aerodynamic feeding

1 Introduction

The buyer's market is changing, which places new demands on products. These demands include individual design, a high standard of quality and a minimum price. Added to this is the shortening of the product's lifespan [1]. Production must adapt to these demands while the industry is pursuing cost reduction in order to maximize profits. Secondary processes that do not make a direct contribution to assembly must therefore be kept lean, reliable and inexpensive. Apart from organizational and constructive measures, automation is one way to rationalize assembly processes [2].

The costs of an automated production line are largely generated by feeding and transport systems. The actual assembly process is responsible for about 20% of the costs [3]. Feeding plays an important role, as the objects are transported as bulk material for cost reasons. Bulk material is cheaper and easier to handle [4]. For the following process, however, the objects are required in a defined position. For this reason, a targeted orientation from the bulk material must take place so that the next process can be performed [5]. The feeding process can be divided into four subtasks [3].

- Separation: The objects are sorted from the bulk material.
- Transport: The ordered objects must now be transported to the next process.
- Orientation: After the ordering of the objects, each part has an arbitrary orientation. The orientation process aligns the objects into a defined orientation.
- Positioning: The objects are now designed for the next process so that direct processing is possible.

Often, a vibratory bowl feeder is used to perform these tasks. It has a simple design, can be used for a wide range of geometries and is robust in operation [2, 6]. Objects that are not oriented correctly are returned to the process [7]. The configuration of the vibratory bowl feeder depends on the geometry of the objects and takes place experimentally, which is time intensive [8]. One reason for the high amount of time required is that it is not possible to make general statements about the behavior of objects in a vibratory bowl feeder [9]. Therefore, feeding technology has a high potential for optimization.

To meet the demands for a highly flexible and simultaneously efficient feeding technology, an aerodynamic feeding system has been developed at the Leibniz University of Hanover [10–13]. The system uses a constant air jet to exert a force on the components passing the nozzle. Using a genetic algorithm, the system is designed to parameterize itself for an optimal output rate. The principle of aerodynamic orientation as well as the genetic algorithm will be elucidated in the following.

2 The Aerodynamic Feeding System

Basic Principle. The aerodynamic feeding system presented and used in this work operates with only one air jet, which every component passes. In other work, systems have been presented that use multiple nozzles or air cushions to orient and transport parts [14, 15]. Figure 1 shows the process of aerodynamic orientation in the described feeding system. It becomes clear that the component behaves differently depending on the orientation it has when arriving at the nozzle. If the workpiece arrives in the wrong orientation, it is turned over by the air jet, as can be seen in Fig. 1a), whereas it keeps its orientation, if it already arrives in the correct orientation (Fig. 1b)). The reason for the different behaviors of the component depending on the initial orientation lies in the shape and the mass distribution of the workpiece. The exemplary workpiece in Fig. 1 has a varying projected area against the airflow. Therefore, the wider part of the component experiences a higher drag force than the thinner part, which results in a momentum generating the rotation of the component. In the example, the angle of inclination α promotes clockwise rotation and hinders counterclockwise rotation, resulting in the same output orientation regardless of the input orientation.

Apart from the angle of inclination α, the orientation process is primarily influenced by three additional parameters, seen in Fig. 1:

- Angle of inclination β
- Nozzle pressure p
- Component speed v

The angle β influences the force of gravity acting on the component on the one hand and determines the impact of the friction between the component and the guiding plane. The nozzle pressure p directly affects the magnitude of drag force acting on the workpiece. If it is set too low, the component might not rotate at all, whereas a higher pressure can lead to multiple and unpredictable rotations. Lastly, the component speed v determines, how fast a workpiece passes the air jet and therefore how long it is affected by the drag forces. The parameter can be controlled by adjusting the speed of a conveyor located ahead of the nozzle.

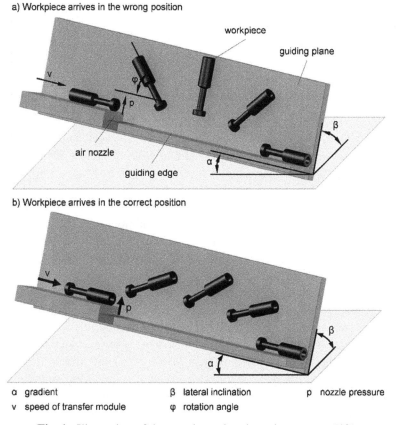

a) Workpiece arrives in the wrong position

b) Workpiece arrives in the correct position

| α gradient | β lateral inclination | p nozzle pressure |
| v speed of transfer module | φ rotation angle | |

Fig. 1. Illustration of the aerodynamic orientation process [10]

After the orientation process, each component's orientation is determined using a line scan camera. By dividing the number of components in the right orientation by the number of all components measured, an orientation rate between 0 and 100% is calculated. In various experiments, it was shown that the nozzle pressure p has the highest impact on the orientation rate, followed by the interaction between p and v as well as p and β [16]. The identified main effects and interactions are shown in Fig. 2. Even though the effects of parameter changes on the orientation process are known, the parametrization of the feeding system for new components takes a lot of time and expertise with the equipment. To tackle this disadvantage, a genetic algorithm has been implemented in the systems control, which will be presented in the following section.

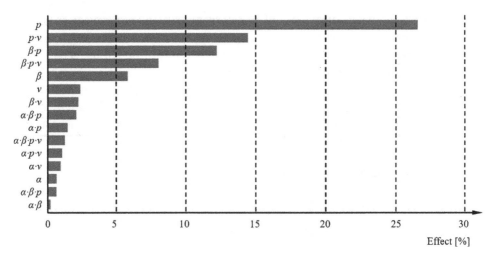

Fig. 2. Values of the main effects and interactions between parameters on the orientation rate [16]

Genetic Algorithm. Finding a set of parameters inducing a satisfactory orientation rate (e.g. >95%) constitutes a non-linear optimization problem. Additionally, the interrelation between input (the parameters) and the output (orientation rate) is not necessarily a continuous function. Therefore, a genetic algorithm (GA) is used as an optimizer [10, 11, 16]. The structure of the genetic algorithm is shown in Fig. 3. One generation contains 4 individuals whose fitness is evaluated by the orientation rate. The parameters of the GA were optimized in previous studies carried out by BUSCH [16]. The best individual is automatically taken over as parent individual in the next generation, the second parent individual is determined by roulette selection. Recombination is done via uniform crossover and the mutation rate is 55%.

With the range and increments of the four "old" parameters, as shown in Table 1, a large solution space with up to 14,214,771 possible configurations is spanned. Nevertheless, the genetic algorithm has proven to be a very effective and time-saving regarding the adjustment of the feeding system to new workpieces [16]. Taking into account the fifth parameter, the solution space would grow to up to 440,657,901 possible configurations. This shows, why it is important to investigate the effect of a fifth parameter to the system and the algorithm on the convergence of the very same.

Table 1. Range and Increments of the aerodynamic feeding systems parameters

Parameter	Minimum value	Maximum value	Increment
α	20°	25°	0.1°
β	39°	50°	0.1°
p	0.1 bar	0.9 bar	0.01 bar
v	50 m/min	80 m/min	1 m/min
z	0 mm	30 mm	1 mm

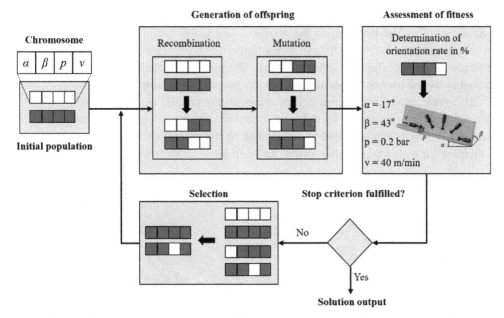

Fig. 3. Structure of the genetic algorithm of the aerodynamic feeding system [10]

3 Implementation of the Nozzle Position as Fifth Parameter

Previously, a fixed nozzle position had to be manually selected for each component, which could be set via a manual positioning table. In the case of rotationally symmetrical components, positioning the center of the nozzle half the diameter of the component away from the guiding plane seems reasonable. This way, the workpiece should receive the maximum amount of drag force, which would lead to a minimal pressure needed. In practice, experiments show that, depending on the dimensions and geometry of the part, a centered air jet can cause an inflow paradox, where the component is aspirated and in consequence slowed down by the air jet. The reason for this lies in Bernoulli's principle, which states that increasing the speed of a flowing fluid is accompanied by a decrease of the pressure [17]. This effect can occur in the gap between the nozzle and the component passing it. Preliminary experiments show, that this effect can be significantly reduced by moving the nozzle orthogonally to the moving direction of the components.

Another problem occurs, when adapting the feeding system to more complex components that have irregular shapes. Manually adjusting the nozzle position can easily become an optimization problem of its own.

In order to expand the spectrum of components the feeding system can handle and reduce the effects of the inflow paradox a linear actor that can vary the position of the nozzle orthogonally to the moving direction of the components was implemented in the feeding system. This parameter, called z, is shown in Fig. 4. The magnitude of z (Table 1) is defined as the distance between the center of the nozzle and the guiding plane.

To automatically control parameter z, a motorized linear positioning table with a preloaded spindle drive was chosen. With this hardware, a positioning accuracy of 0.01 mm can be reached. The stroke is 75 mm. The high precision and stroke are chosen to ensure that the actuator can continue to be used even in future modifications of the feeding system. The position of the nozzle is controlled using an analog output with an output range of 0–10 V DC and a resolution of 16 bit. The trim range of the linear actuator can be specified via setup software. The position of the nozzle can be set either manually by the user or autonomously by the genetic algorithm.

The implementation of the nozzle position into the genetic algorithm was achieved by expanding the chromosomes from four to five alleles. The processes of selection, recombination and mutation also had to be adapted to the extended chromosomes while the principles – e.g. one-point-, two-point- and uniform-crossover – remained unchanged.

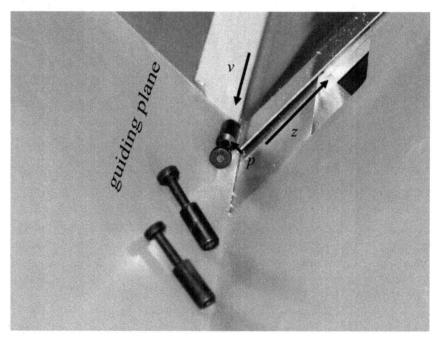

Fig. 4. Orientation process of exemplary workpieces with the parameters v (conveyor), p (nozzle) and z (linear positioning)

4   Effect of the Nozzle Position on the Orientation Process

To assess the effect of the variation of the nozzle position on the orientation process, the behavior of the workpieces at a varying inflow is evaluated. The entire orientation process of one workpiece, from the first contact with the air jet to the impact on the chute, takes about 0.2 s. To allow for the analysis of the orientation process, it is filmed with a frame rate of 240 fps. This way, the behavior of the workpieces can be reviewed properly. In the following, two exemplary components are examined for their behavior under different inflow conditions.

Pneumatic Plug. As first exemplary part, a plug for pneumatic pipes is used. The part can be seen in Fig. 4. The workpiece is well suited for first experiments, as it has a simple geometry due to the rotational symmetry. In addition, due to the strongly varying projected area, it is a component that is generally very well suited for aerodynamic orientation. The measurements of the component are shown in Fig. 5.

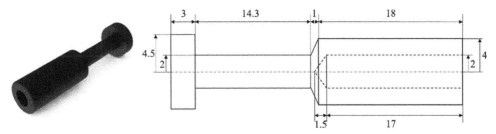

Fig. 5. Measurements of pneumatic plug

Since the nozzle pressure has the strongest influence on the orientation process, to reduce the testing effort, only the parameters p and z are varied. The step size of the pressure p is chosen relatively high, with 0.05 bar to reduce the testing effort. Usually the system controls p with a resolution of 0.01 bar, because the workpieces have a low weight and the orientation process is sensitive to pressure changes. The resulting experimental plan is shown in Table 2. For each measurement, five workpieces were delivered to the nozzle in the wrong orientation and five workpieces were delivered in the right orientation. The orientation process of each workpiece is then evaluated to determine the orientation rate presented in Table 2. Entries with a dash indicate, that no orientation process takes place, which means, that neither the workpieces arriving at the nozzle in the right orientation nor those arriving in the wrong orientation are rotated by the air stream. A value of 0.9 means, for example, that 9 of 10 workpieces leave the orientation process in the right orientation.

Table 2. Orientation rate of pneumatic plug depending on nozzle pressure and nozzle position with $\alpha = 22°$, $\beta = 45°$ and $v = 70$ m/min

	0 mm	2 mm	4 mm	6 mm	8 mm	10 mm
0.10 bar	–	–	–	–	–	–
0.15 bar	–	–	0.9	0.8	0.8	–
0.20 bar	–	0.9	0.6	0.5	0.5	–
0.25 bar	–	0.9	0.1	0.5	0.5	–
0.30 bar	–	0.6	0.0	0.2	0.2	0.1

The examination of the results in Table 2 shows that good orientation rates can be achieved even with the nozzle not aligned to the centerline of the workpiece. The variation of the nozzle position allows for high orientation rates even at nozzle pressures that would normally lead to poor orientation rates. This can be seen when comparing the second column of Table 2 ($z = 2$ mm) to the third column ($z = 4$ mm): While the orientation rate rapidly drops with pressures above 0.15 bar with $z = 4$ mm, a high orientation rate can be achieved at pressures of 0.2 and 0.25 bar, when the nozzle is at $z = 2$ mm. This leads to the conclusion that although the solution space becomes larger due to the addition of a fifth parameter, new parameter combinations with a high orientation rate arise.

In addition to the evaluation of the orientation process via the orientation rate, a qualitative evaluation of the process is also carried out in the following by considering the trajectory of the components. Figure 6 shows the trajectories of four components during the orientation process. They differ by the set of system parameters and the incoming orientation as described in the subframes.

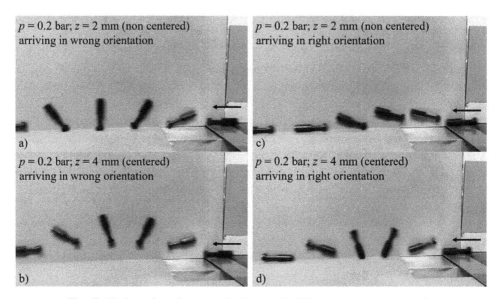

Fig. 6. Trajectories of pneumatic plugs with different parameters p and z

It becomes clear, that the position of the nozzle has decisive influence on the trajectory of the workpieces. The comparison of Fig. 6a) and b) shows that a very stable reorientation of the component can be achieved even with a non-centered nozzle position. The fact that the component in Fig. 6a) does not lift off the chute is to be seen as a major advantage. When the component hits the chute out of flight as seen in Fig. 6b), the impact impulse can lead to uncontrolled jumping of the component on the chute, thus preventing optimal exploitation of the orientation process.

Particularly noteworthy is the stable behavior of those components, which already arrive at the nozzle in the correct orientation. It was observed in all tests, for which Fig. 6c) and d) are exemplary, that the components exhibit a much more predictable and reproducible behavior when the nozzle position is not centered. With a centered nozzle position, a small pressure range must be found in which the incorrectly arriving components are still reoriented but the correctly arriving components are not reoriented yet. With the non-centered nozzle position, on the other hand, the varying projected area of the component against the inflow can be utilized much better. Therefore, a higher range of nozzle pressure can be harnessed, which has a positive effect on the convergence of the genetic algorithm.

Printed Sleeve. In addition to the pneumatic plugs, the effect of a flexible inflow was also investigated on plastic sleeves. The sleeves are rotationally symmetrical parts as well. However, in contrast to the pneumatic plugs, the sleeves have a completely homogenous projected inflow surface. Because of these characteristics and the higher diameter, it was expected that the inflow paradox caused by Bernoulli's principle would have an impact on the orientation process. This assumption was confirmed during the evaluation of the tests. The dimensions of the sleeves are shown in Fig. 7. The sleeves were manufactured using a 3D printer and the eccentricity is 10%.

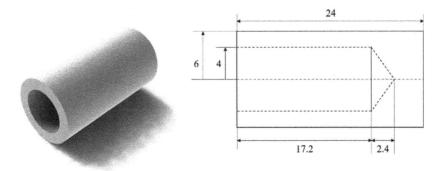

Fig. 7. Measurements of plastic sleeve

The trajectories of the components during the orientation processes with different parameter settings are shown in Fig. 8. To better illustrate the orientation of the cylindrical sleeves, the end with the center of mass has been digitally marked with a $+$ symbol. Considering Fig. 8a), it becomes clear, that a nozzle pressure of 0.2 bar is enough to reorient the plastic sleeve with $z = 2$ mm. Nevertheless, with $z = 6$ mm (centered) no reorientation takes place (Fig. 8b). The different amounts of uplift on the components also becomes clear by comparing Fig. 8c) and d): When the sleeve arrives at the nozzle positioned 2 mm from the guiding plane, it is slightly lifted but does not rotate more than a few degrees. The component arriving with the nozzle centered ($z = 6$ mm) passes about half of its length over the nozzle without getting any lift. This circumstance is attributed to the Bernoulli Effect. When the sleeve passes over the nozzle, it creates a gap between itself and the nozzle carrier. Therefore, the flow path of the air jet is narrowed with results in a higher velocity of the fluid. This, according to Bernoulli's principle, leads to a decrease of pressure between the sleeve and the carrier and results in the part being dragged down.

This is contrasted by the behavior of the component when the nozzle position is not centered. On the one hand, this increases the distance between the nozzle and the workpiece. On the other hand, the air jet does not hit the workpiece inside the narrow gap between workpiece and nozzle carrier, which prevents the acceleration of the air flow and therefore a decrease of pressure.

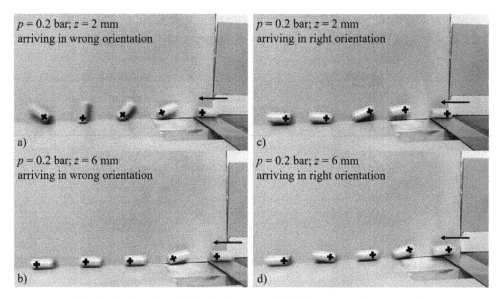

Fig. 8. Trajectories of plastic sleeves with different parameters p and z

Analysis of all trajectories of the experiments with the pneumatic plugs and the plastic sleeves shows the advantages of the variable nozzle position even with geometrically simple components. Essentially, four findings can be derived:

1. Even at higher pressures, the trajectory of the workpiece is lower when the nozzle position is not centered. This is an advantage, because the impulse at the impact on the slide is lower. This in turn leads to less jumping of the components on the slide and thus, finally, to a more stable and reliable feeding process.
2. Components that already arrive at the nozzle in the right orientation are reoriented easily, when the nozzle position is aligned to their centerline. When the nozzle position is not centered, components arriving in the right orientation have a much lower risk of being inadvertently reoriented. The reason for that is, that the varying projected area of the component can be exploited much better, when the core of the air jet is not aligned with the centerline of the component. This way, during the passing of the thicker part, much more momentum is generated than during the passing of the thinner part.
3. With the nozzle position at extreme values ($z = 0$ mm or $z = 10$ mm) very little lift is generated. Therefore, it is concluded that the nozzle bore must be positioned in the range of the measurements of the fed component.
4. The unwanted effect of Bernoulli's principle can be significantly reduced by varying the nozzle position. Reducing this effect leads to a more stable orientation process that can be achieved with lower nozzle pressures.

5   Convergence of the Genetic Algorithm

In order to investigate and evaluate the impact of the fifth parameter on the convergence and setting time of the genetic algorithm, additional trials needed to be carried out. To do so, the genetic algorithm was run five times with and five times without a variable nozzle position. The tests were carried out alternately to compensate for the influence of environmental influences like changes in ambient pressure or non-measurable variables like pollution of the slide by dust or abrasion of the components. To determine the orientation rate of one individual, the orientation of 100 components is measured. With a feeding rate of about 200 parts per minute for the experimental feeding system (limited by the centrifugal feeder) two individuals can be tested per minute. As exemplary component, the pneumatic plug from previous testing was chosen. The range of the parameters α, β and ν was chosen according to Table 1. Based on the preliminary tests in Sect. 4 the minimum and maximum values of p were set to 0.1 and 0.3 bar respectively. Also, the range of the nozzle position was set from 1 to 9 mm in accordance with the aforementioned preliminary testing.

Figure 9 shows the distribution of the number of individuals needed by the GA to reach an orientation rate of 95% or higher. It becomes clear, that with a variable nozzle position, the genetic algorithm needs far fewer individuals to find a satisfying solution. The longest setting time with the variable nozzle position is about as long as the shortest setting time with fixed nozzle position. Additionally, the deviation of the maximum and minimum setting time from the average setting time is much smaller with a variable nozzle position.

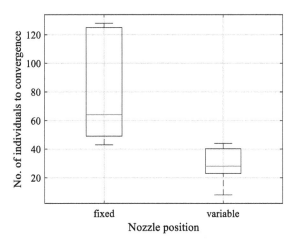

Fig. 9. Distribution of number of individuals needed by the GA to reach an orientation rate of 95% or higher with fixed and variable nozzle position.

The advantages of the variable nozzle position as fifth parameter also become clear when looking at Table 3. The average number of individuals, which correspond directly to the setting time is reduced by 64% with a variable nozzle position compared to a fixed nozzle position. Also, the maximum number of individuals of five runs with variable nozzle position corresponds approximately to a third of the maximum number of individuals of five runs with fixed nozzle position. This is a huge advantage considering that the setting time is directly dependent on the number of individuals and that during the setting process the system is not productive. All in all the experiments clearly show, that adding the fifth setting parameter does not impair the convergence of the GA and therefore the setting time of the feeding system. On the contrary, the average setting time is significantly reduced.

Table 3. Minimum, maximum and average number of individuals to convergence, Standard deviation and average orientation rate (OR)

	Minimum	Maximum	Average	Std. dev.	Av. OR
Fixed	43	128	82	36.6	0.958
Variable	8	44	29.4	12.4	0.970

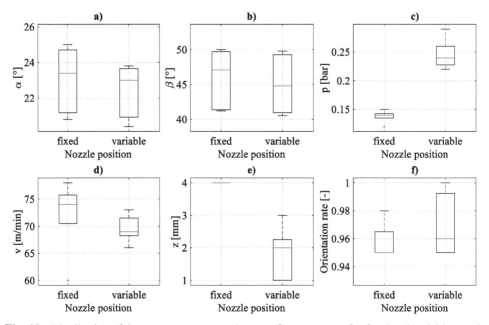

Fig. 10. Distribution of the system parameters in case of convergence for fixed and variable nozzle position.

Figure 10 shows the distribution of the system parameters at the end of each test run, when convergence (orientation rate $\geq 95\%$) was reached. In each plot, the left box shows the distribution for a fixed nozzle position, whereas the right box shows the distribution for a variable nozzle position. While α and β show no significant differences, the nozzle pressure p (Fig. 10c)) is generally higher with a variable nozzle position. At the same time, the range of p is also wider with the variable nozzle position. Considering that for a system configuration with only four parameters, the nozzle pressure p has the highest effect on the orientation rate (c.f. Fig. 2), it is assumed, that the higher acceptable range of the pressure p significantly contributes to the shorter setting time.

Figure 10e) shows that all values for z are between 1 mm and 3 mm with a median of 2 mm. This shows that the fixed nozzle position of 4 mm was not the optimal position and that – using the fifth parameter – the system is now able to determine the optimal nozzle position autonomously, which in turn reduces the setting time. The higher median and range of the orientation rate at convergence (Fig. 10f)) is an indication for a higher process stability that can be achieved with a non-centered nozzle position.

6   Conclusion and Outlook

In this work, the extension of an aerodynamic feeding system was presented. In order to increase the flexibility of the system, the position of the nozzle perpendicular to the direction of movement of the components was introduced as fifth adjustment parameter in addition to two angles, the nozzle pressure and the feeding speed. As a result of the new parameter, the number of possible configurations of the system increased significantly. In order to investigate the effects of the nozzle position on the autonomous adjustment algorithm (GA) of the aerodynamic feeding system, the behaviour of the components in the orientation process was examined in detail. It was found that even with simple components, a flexible inflow can lead to an increased resilience against variation of nozzle and ambient pressure. Since the pressure has been identified as main factor determining the orientation rate, this higher resilience induces an elevated process reliability. In addition, the disturbing influence of Bernoulli's effect could be reduced by means of a displaced inflow.

Subsequently, it was investigated how the setting time of the aerodynamic feeding system changes due to the enlarged solution space of the genetic algorithm. It was found that the adjustment time with a variable nozzle position can be reduced by more than 60% on average compared to a fixed nozzle position, despite the larger solution space. The reason for this is the higher range of possible nozzle pressures, generating a high orientation rate and the higher process stability mentioned above.

Further experiments on the convergence of the GA are to be carried out in future work. The component spectrum and complexity will be varied, expecting to show further advantages of the variable nozzle position. In addition, the analysis of the parameter sets at convergence (Fig. 10) shows that the effects of the parameters on the orientation rate have shifted. For example, the system's sensitivity to pressure changes seems to be lower, while the nozzle position seems to have a high impact on the orientation process. It is therefore necessary to determine the effects of the system parameters on the orientation rate again, using Design of Experiments methods.

Acknowledgement. The authors would like to thank the German Research Foundation (DFG) for their financial support of the research project RA 1736/19-2.

References

1. Hsuan Mikkol, J., Skjøtt-Larsen, T.: Supply-chain integration. Implications for mass customization, modularization and postponement strategies. Prod. Planning Control **15**(4), 352–361 (2007). https://doi.org/10.1080/0953728042000238845

2. Lotter, B., Wiendahl, H.-P.: Montage in der industriellen Produktion. Springer, Belin Heidelberg (2006)

3. Krüger, J., Lien, T.K., Verl, A.: Cooperation of human and machines in assembly lines. CIRP Ann. **58**(2), 628–646 (2009). https://doi.org/10.1016/j.cirp.2009.09.009

4. Bohringer, K.-F., Bhatt, V., Goldberg, K.Y.: Sensorless manipulation using transverse vibrations of a plate. In: Proceedings of 1995 IEEE International Conference on Robotics and Automation, Nagoya, Japan, pp. 1989–1996 (1995)

5. Warnecke, H.-J.: Die Fraktale Fabrik. Revolution der Unternehmenskultur. Springer, Berlin (1992). https://doi.org/10.1007/978-3-662-06647-8

6. Klocke, F., Pritschow, G.: Autonome Produktion. Springer, Berlin (2004). https://doi.org/10.1007/978-3-642-18523-6

7. Schroer, B.J.: Electronic parts presentation using vibratory bowl feeders. Robotics **3**(3–4), 409–419 (1987). https://doi.org/10.1016/0167-8493(87)90057-X

8. van der Stappen, A.Frank., Berretty, R.-P., Goldberg, K., Overmars, Mark H.: Geometry and part feeding. In: Hager, Gregory D., Christensen, H.I., Bunke, H., Klein, R. (eds.) Sensor Based Intelligent Robots. LNCS, vol. 2238, pp. 259–281. Springer, Heidelberg (2002). https://doi.org/10.1007/3-540-45993-6_15

9. Ngoi, B.K.A., Lim, L.E.N., Ee, J.T.: Analysis of natural resting aspects of parts in a vibratory bowl feeder – validation of "drop test". Int. J. Adv. Manufact. Technol. **13**(4), 300–310 (1997). https://doi.org/10.1007/BF01179612

10. Busch, J., Blankemeyer, S., Raatz, A., Nyhuis, P.: Implementation and testing of a genetic algorithm for a self-learning and automated parameterisation of an aerodynamic feeding system. Procedia CIRP **44**, 79–84 (2016). https://doi.org/10.1016/j.procir.2016.02.081

11. Busch, J., Knüppel, K.: Development of a self-learning, automatic parameterisation of an aerodynamic part feeding system. AMR **769**, 34–41 (2013). https://doi.org/10.4028/www.scientific.net/AMR.769.34

12. Fleischer, J., Herder, S., Leberle, U.: Automated supply of micro parts based on the micro slide conveying principle. CIRP Ann. **60**(1), 13–16 (2011). https://doi.org/10.1016/j.cirp.2011.03.004

13. Frädrich, T., Pachow Frauenhofer, J., Torsten, F., Nyhuis, P.: Aerodynamic feeding systems. An example for changeable technology. Assembly Autom. **31**(1), 47–52 (2011). https://doi.org/10.1108/01445151111104164

14. Lorenz, B.-M.: Aerodynamische Zuführtechnik. In: Fortschritt-Berichte VDI; Reihe 2, Fertigungstechnik, vol. 524. VDI-Verlag, Düsseldorf (1999)

15. Rybarczyk, A.: Auslegung aerodynamischer Zuführverfahren. In: Berichte aus dem IFA 1, pp. 1–124. Produktionstechnisches Zentrum Hannover, Garbsen (2004)

16. Busch, J.: Entwicklung einer intelligenten aerodynamischen Zuführanlage für die Hochleistungsmontage. In: Berichte aus dem IFA 7/2016. PZH Verlag, Garbsen (2016)

17. Chattot, J.J., Hafez, M.M.: Theoretical and Applied Aerodynamics. Springer, Dodrecht (2015). https://doi.org/10.1007/978-94-017-9825-9

14

Attention Analysis for Assistance in Assembly Processes

Lucas Paletta$^{(\boxtimes)}$

DIGITAL – Institute for Information and Communication Technologies, JOANNEUM
RESEARCH Forschungsgesellschaft MbH, 8010 Graz, Austria
lucas.paletta@joanneum.at

Abstract. Human attention processes play a major role in the optimization of human-machine interaction (HMI) systems. This work describes a suite of innovative components within a novel framework in order to assess the human factors state of the human operator primarily by gaze and in real-time. The objective is to derive parameters that determine information about situation awareness of the human collaborator that represents a central concept in the evaluation of interaction strategies in collaboration. The human control of attention provides measures of executive functions that enable to characterize key features in the domain of human-machine collaboration. This work presents a suite of human factors analysis components (the Human Factors Toolbox) and its application in the assembly processes of a future production line. Comprehensive experiments on HMI are described which were conducted with typical tasks including collaborative pick-and-place in a lab based prototypical manufacturing environment.

Keywords: Human factors analysis · Intuitive assistance · Dynamic attention

1 Introduction

Human-machine interaction in manufacturing has recently experienced an emergence of innovative technologies for intelligent assistance [1]. Human factors are crucial in Industry 4.0 enabling human and machine to work side by side as collaborators. Human-related variables are essential for the evaluation of human-interaction metrics [2]. To work seamlessly and efficiently with their human counterparts, complex manufacturing work cells, such as for assembly, must similarly rely on measurements to predict the human worker's behavior, cognitive and affective state, task specific actions and intent to plan their actions. A typical, currently available application is anticipatory control with human-in-the-loop architecture [3] to enable robots to perform task actions that are specifically based on recently observed gaze patterns to anticipate actions of their human partners according to its predictions.

In order to characterize the human state by means of quantitative measurement technologies we expect that these should refer to performance measures that represent psychologically relevant parameters. Executive functions [18] were scientifically investigated to represent activities of cognitive control, such as, (i) inhibition in selective attention, (ii) task switching capabilities, or (iii) task planning. These functions are dependent on dynamic attention and are relevant too many capability requirements in assembly. (i) appropriate focus at the right time to manual interaction, (ii) switching attention between multiple tasks at the same time, and (iii) action planning in short time periods for optimized task performance. Consequently, measuring and modeling of the state of cognition relevant human factors as well as the current human situation awareness are mandatory for the understanding of immediate and delayed action planning. However, the state-of-the-art does not yet sufficiently address these central human cognitive functions to an appropriate degree. This work intends to contribute to fill this gap by presenting a novel framework for estimating important parameters of executive functions in assembly processes by means of attention analysis. On the basis of mobile eye tracking that has been made available for real-time interpretation of gaze we developed software for fast estimation of executive function parameters solely on the basis of eye tracking data. In summary, this work describes a review of novel methodologies developed at the Human Factors Lab of JOANNEUM RESEARCH to measure the human factors states of the operator in real-time with the purpose to derive fundamental parameters that determine situation awareness, concentration, task switching and cognitive arousal as central for the interaction strategies of collaborative teams. The suite of gaze based analysis software is referred as Human Factors Toolbox (Fig. 1).

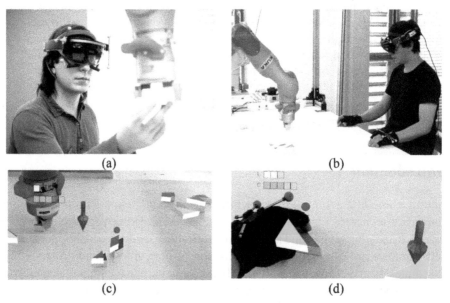

Fig. 1. Human-robot collaboration and intuitive interface (HoloLens, eye tracking, markers for OptiTrack localization) for the assessment of human factors state to characterize key features in the collaboration domain. HRC within a tangram puzzle assembly task. (a) The operator collaborates with the robot in the assembly (only robot can treat 'dangerous' pieces). (b) Egocentric operator view with augmented reality based navigation (arrow), piece localization, gaze (blue sphere), current state of mental load (L) and concentration (C) in the HoloLens display. (c) Recommended piece (arrow) and gaze on currently grabbed puzzle piece.

Human situation awareness is determined on the basis of concrete measures of eye movements towards production relevant processes that need to be observed and evaluated by the human. Motivated by the theoretical work of [4] on situation awareness the presented work specifically aims at dynamically estimating (i) distribution of attentional resources with respect to task relevant 'areas of interaction' over time, determined by features of 3D gaze analysis and a precise optical tracking system, and (ii) derive from this human factors in real-time, such as, (a) human concentration on a given task, (b) human mental workload, (c) situation awareness and (d) executive functions related measure, i.e., task switching rate. Gaze in the context of collaboration is analyzed in terms of - primarily, visual - affordances for collaboration. In this work we demonstrate the relevance of considering eye movement features for a profound characterization of the state of human factors in manufacturing assembly cells by means of gaze behavior, with the purpose to optimize the overall human-machine collaboration performance.

In the following, Sect. 2 provides an overview on emerging attention analyses technologies in the context of manufacturing human-machine interaction. Section 3 provides insight into the application of a learning scenario in an assembly working cell. Section 4 provides conclusions and proposals for future work,

2 Human Factors Measurement Technologies for Human-Machine Interaction

2.1 Intuitive Multimodal Assistive Interface and Gaze

In the conceptual work on intuitive multimodal assistive interfaces, the interaction design is fully aligned with the user requirements on intuitive understanding of technology [5]. For intuitive interaction, one opts for a human-centered approach and starts from inter-human interactions and the collaborative process itself. The intuitive interaction system is based on the following principles:

- **Natural interaction**: Mimicking human interaction mechanisms a fast and intuitive interaction processes has to be guaranteed.
- **Multimodal interaction**: Implementation of gaze, speech, gestural, and Mixed-Reality interaction offers as much interaction freedom as possible to the user.
- **Tied modalities**: Linking the different interaction modalities to emphasize the intuitive interaction mechanisms.
- **Context-aware feedback**: Feedback channels deliver information regarding task, environment to the user. One has to pay attention at what is delivered when and where.

A central component entitled 'Interaction Model' (IM) acts as interaction control and undertakes the communication with the periphery system. The IM also links the four interaction modalities and ensures information exchange between the components. It triggers any form of interaction process, both direct and indirect, and controls the context-sensitivity of the feedback. It is further responsible for dialog management and information dispatching.

In human factors and ergonomics research, the analysis of eye movements enables to develop methods for investigating human operators' cognitive strategies and for reasoning about individual cognitive states [6]. Situation awareness (SA) is a measure of an individual's knowledge and understanding of the current and expected future states of a situation. Eye tracking provides an unobtrusive method to measure SA in environments where multiple tasks need to be controlled. [7] provided first evidence that fixation duration on relevant objects and balanced allocation of attention increases SA. However, for the assessment of executive functions, the extension of situation analysis towards concrete measures of distribution of attention is necessary and described as follows.

2.2 Recovery of 3D Gaze in Human-Robot Interaction

Localization of human gaze is essential for the localization of situation awareness with reference to relevant processes in the working cell [8]. Firstly proposed 3D information recovery of human gaze with monocular eye tracking and triangulation of 2D gaze positions of subsequent key frames within the scene video of the eye tracking system. Santner et al. [9] proposed gaze estimation in 3D space and achieved accuracies ≈ 1 cm with RGB-D based position tracking within a predefined 3D model of the environment. In order to achieve the highest level of gaze estimation accuracy in a research study, it is crucial to track user's frustum/gaze behavior with respect to the worker's relevant environment. Solutions that realize this include vision-based motion capturing systems: OptiTrack[1] can achieve high gaze estimation accuracy (≈ 0.06 mm).

2.3 Situation Awareness

Based on the cognitive ability, flexibility and knowledge of human beings on the one hand and the power, efficiency and persistence of industrial robots on the other hand, collaboration between both elements is absolutely essential for flexible and dynamic systems like manufacturing [10]. Efficient human-robot collaboration requires a comprehensive perception of essential parts of the working environment of both sides. Human decision making is a substantial component of collaborative robotics under dynamic environment conditions, such as, within a working cell. Situation awareness and human factors are crucial, in particular, to identify decisive parts of task execution.

In human factors, situation awareness is principally evaluated through questionnaires, such as, the Situational Awareness Rating Technique (SART [11]). Psychological studies on situation awareness are drawn in several application areas, such as, in air traffic control, driver attention analysis, or military operations. Due to the disadvantages of the questionnaire technologies of SART and SAGAT, more reliable and less invasive technologies were required, however, eye tracking as a psycho-physiologically based, quantifiable and objective measurement technology has been proven to be effective [7, 12]. In several studies in the frame of situation awareness, eye movement features, such as dwell and fixation time, were found to be correlated with various measures of performance. [13, 14] have developed measurement/prediction of Situation Awareness in Human-Robot Interaction based on a Framework of Probabilistic Attention, and real-time eye tracking parameters.

---

[1] http://www.naturalpoint.com/optitrack.

2.4 Cognitive Arousal and Concentration Estimation

For quantifying stress we used cognitive arousal estimation based on biosensor data. In the context of eye movement analysis, arousal is defined by a specific parametrization of fixations and saccadic events within a time window of five seconds so that there is good correlation ($r = .493$) between the mean level of electro-dermal activity (EDA) and the outcome of the stress level estimator [15] (Fig. 2).

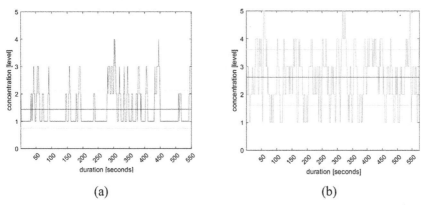

(a)   (b)

Fig. 2. Measure of attentional concentration on tasks. (a) Concentration level during a session without assistance (red line is the mean; red is standard deviation), and (b) concentration level during the session with assistance. On average, the concentration increased when using the intuitive assistance. (Color figure online)

For the estimation of concentration or sustained attention, we refer to the areas of interaction (AOI) in the environment as representing the spatial reference for the task under investigation. Maintaining the attention on task related AOI is interpreted as the concentration on a specific task [16], or on session related tasks in general. Various densities of the fixation rate enable the definition of a classification of levels of actual concentration within a specific period of time, i.e., within a time window of five seconds.

2.5 Estimation of Task Switching Rate

Task switching, or set-shifting, is an executive function that involves the ability to unconsciously shift attention between one task and another. In contrast, cognitive shifting is a very similar executive function, but it involves conscious (not unconscious) change in attention. Together, these two functions are subcategories of the broader cognitive flexibility concept. Task switching allows a person to rapidly and efficiently adapt to different situations [17].

In a multi-tasking environment, cognitive resources must be shared or shifted between the multiple tasks. Task switching, or set-shifting, is an executive function that involves the ability to unconsciously shift attention between one task and another. Task switching allows a person to rapidly and efficiently adapt to different situations. The task-switching rate is defined by the frequency by which different tasks are actually operated. The difference between tasks is defined by the differences in the mental model which is necessary to represent an object or a process in the mind of the human operator. Mental models are subjective functional models; a task switch requires the change of the current mental model in consciousness and from this requires specific cognitive resources and a load.

In the presented work, processing of a task is determined by the concentration of the operator on a task related area of interaction (AOI). Interaction is defined by areas in the operating environment where the operator is manipulating the location of puzzle objects, i.e., grabbing puzzle pieces from a heap of pieces, or putting pieces onto a final position in order to form a tangram shape. Whenever the gaze of the operator intersects with an AOI that belongs to a specific task, then it is associated with an on-going task. The task switch rate is then the number of switches between tasks per period of time, typically the time of a whole session (see Fig. 3 for a visualization). Task switching has been proposed as a candidate executive function along with inhibition, the maintenance and updating of information in working memory, and the ability to perform two tasks at the same time. There is some evidence not only that the efficiency of executive functions improves with practice and guidance, but also that this improvement can transfer to novel contexts. There are demonstrable practice-related improvements in switching performance [18–20].

2.6 Cognitive Arousal and Attention in Multitasking

Stress is defined in terms of psychological and physical reactions of animate beings in response to external stimuli, i.e., by means of stressors. These reactions empower the animate to cope with specific challenges, and at the same time there is the impact of physical and mental workload. [21, 22] defined stress in terms of a physical state of load which is characterized as tension and resistance against external stimuli, i.e., stressors which refers to the general adaptation syndrome. Studies confirm that the selectivity of human attention is performing better when impacted by stress [35] which represents the 'narrowing attention' effect. According to this principle, attention processes would perform in general better with increasing stress impact.

Executive functions are related to the dynamic control of attention which refers to a fundamental component in human-robot collaboration [36]. Executive functions refer to mechanisms of cognitive control which enable a goal oriented, flexible and efficient behavior and cognition [37, 38], and from this the relevance for human everyday functioning is deduced. Following the definition of [23], executive functions above all include attention and inhibition, task management or control of the distribution of attention, planning or sequencing of attention, monitoring or permanent attribution of attention, and codification or functions of attention. Attention and inhibition require directional aspects of attention in the context of relevant information whereas irrelevant information and likewise actions are ignored. Executive functions are known to be impacted by stress once the requirements for regulatory capacity of the organism are surpassed [24, 40]. An early stress reaction is known to trigger a saliency network that mobilizes exceptional resources for the immediate recognition and reactions to given and in particular surprising threats. At the same time, this network is down-weighted for the purpose of executive control which should enable the use of higher level cognitive processes [41].

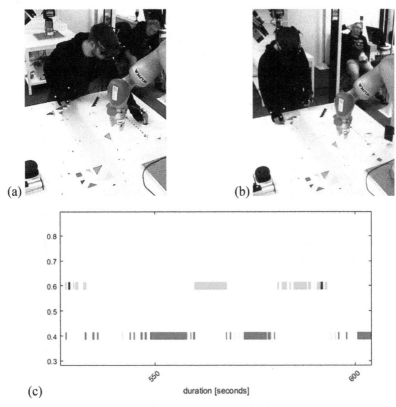

Fig. 3. Task switching between collaborative and the single task. (a) Placing a puzzle piece to goal area in the collaborative task. (b) The operator places a puzzle piece to the goal area of single task. (c) Switch between collaborative task (S1, above, green) and single task (S2, below, red). Task duration is determined by the human gaze being focused within an AOI related to the specific task. (Color figure online)

This executive control network is particularly important for long-term strategies and it is the first that is impacted by stress [25].

In summary, impact of stress can support to focus the selective attention processes under single task conditions, however, in case of multiple task conditions it is known that stress impacts in a negative way the systematic distribution of attention onto several processes and from this negatively affects the performance of executive functions. Evaluation and prevention of long-term stress in a production work cell is a specific application objective. Stress free work environments are more productive, provide more motivated co-workers and error rates are known to be lower than for stressed workers. The minimisation of interruption by insufficient coordination of subtasks is an important objective function which has executive functions analysis as well as impact by stress as important input variables.

Multi-tasking, Executive Functions and Attention. Multi-tasking activities are in indirect relation with executive functions. Following Baddeley's model of a central executive in the working memory [38] there is an inhibitor control and cognitive flexibility directly impacting the (i) multi-tasking, (ii) the change between task and memory functions, (iii) selective attention and inhibition functions. The performance in relation to an activity becomes interrupted once there is a shift between one to the other ("task switch"). The difference between a task shift which particularly requires more cognitive resources, and a task repetition is referred to as 'switch cost' [26] and in particular of relevance if the task switch is more frequently, and also referring to the frequency of interruptions after which the operator has to continue the activity from a memorized point where the switch started. Task switches in any case involve numerous executive function processes, including shift of focus of attention, goal setting and tracking, resources for task set reconfiguration actions, and inhibition of previous task groups. Multi-Tasking and the related switch costs define and reflect the requirements for executive functions and from this the cognitive control of attention processes, which provides highly relevant human factors parameters for the evaluation of human-robot collaboration systems.

The impact of executive functions on decision processes was investigated in detail by [27]. Specifically they researched on aspects of applying decision rules based on inhibition and the consistency in the perception of risk in the context of 'task shifting'. The results verify that the capacity to focus and therefore to inhibit irrelevant stimuli represents a fundamental prerequisite for successful decision processes. At the same time, the change between different contexts of evaluation is essential for consistent estimation of risk (Fig. 4).

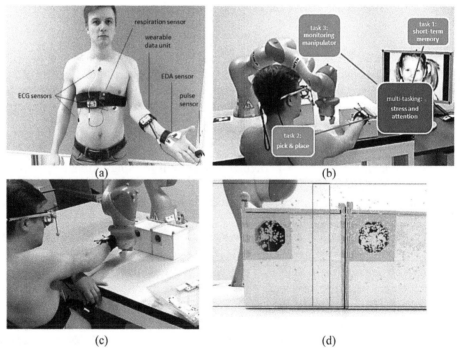

Fig. 4. Bio-sensor and eye tracking glasses setup in the Human Factors Lab at JOANNEUM RESEARCH. (a) Bio-sensor setup with EDA sensor, HRV and breathing rate sensors. (b, c) Eye-hand coordination task interrupted by a robot arm movement. (d) Target areas with holes and gaze intersections centered around the center as landing point of eye-coordination task.

Measurements of Emotional and Cognitive Stress. Stress or activity leads to psychophysiological changes, as described by [28]. The body provides more energy to handle the situation; therefore the hypothalamic-pituitary-adrenal (HPA) axis and the sympathetic nervous system are involved. Sympathetic activity can be measured from recordings of, for example, electro-dermal activity (EDA) and electrocardiogram (ECG). Acute stress leads to a higher skin conductance level (SCL) and also to more spontaneous skin conductance reactions (NS.SCR). [29] showed in his summary of EDA research that these two parameters are sensitive to stress reactions. In a further step, [30] examined the reaction of stress by measuring EDA with a wearable device, during cognitive load, cognitive and emotional stress, and eventually classified the data with a Support Vector Machine (SVM) whether the person received stress. The authors conclude that the peak high and the instantaneous peak rate are sensitive predictors for the stress level of a person. The SVM was capable to classify this level correctly with an accuracy larger than 80%. The electrocardiogram shows a higher heart rate (HR) during stress conditions meanwhile the heart rate variability (HRV) is low [31], and the heart rate was found to be significantly higher during cognitive stress than in rest. [32] found in their survey that the HRV and the EDA are the most predictive parameters to classify stress. [33] used a cognitive task in combination with a mathematical task to induce stress. Eye activity can be a good indicator for stressful situations as well. Some studies report more fixations and saccades guided by shorter dwell time in stress, other studies reported fewer fixations and saccades but longer dwell time. Many studies use in addition the pupil diameter for classification of stress, such as reported. In the survey from [32], the pupil diameter achieved good results for detecting stress. A larger pupil diameter indicates more stress. In the study of [34], blink duration, fixations frequency and pupil diameter were the best predictors for work load classification (Fig. 5).

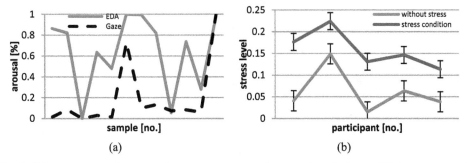

(a)   (b)

Fig. 5. Measurement of stress using eye movement features in relation to EDA measures. (a) The relative increase and decrease of EDA and 'stress level' method based output are correlated with Pearson r = .493 and from this the gaze based method provides an indication of arousal as measured by EDA. (b) The stress level measured with higher and lower cognitive stress (NC and SC condition) very well reflects the required cardinal ranking.

Stress Level Estimation. Eye movement based classification method, i.e., the 'stress level' estimation method, very well estimates the EDA arousal level, as well as the cardinal ranking for different levels of stress impact. The stress level estimation is computed by thresholds on the number of saccades and the mean dwell time during an observation window of 5000 ms. For level 2 the number of saccades should be between 15 and 25, and mean dwell time below 500 ms, For level 3, more than 25 saccades and mean dwell time below 250 ms is requested.

Sample Study on Stress and Attention in Multitasking Human-Robot Interaction. The presented work aimed to investigate how the impact of cognitive stress would affect the attentional processes, in particular, the performance of the executive functions that are involved in the coordination of multi-tasking processes. The study setup for the proof-of-concept involved a cognitive task as well as a visuomotor task, concretely, an eye-hand coordination task, in combination with an obstacle avoidance task that is characteristic in human-robot collaboration. The results provide the proof that increased stress conditions can actually be measured in a significantly correlated increase of an error distribution as consequence of the precision of the eye-hand coordination. The decrease of performance is a proof that the attentional processes are a product of executive function processes. The results confirm the dependency of executive functions and decision processes on stress conditions and will enable quantitative measurements of attention effects in multi-tasking configurations.

3   Use Case for Real-Time Human Factors Measurements in Assembly Work Cells

The use case for an assembly work cell is depicted in Fig. 6. The worker learns about to assemble a transformer with its individual components, interacting with various areas in its environment, e.g., to pick up a component from one area of a table and to place it to another part of a table.

The learning scenario demonstrates the feasibility of the concentration measurement technology. (1a) View on the worker with focus on work (1a, 3a) and being interrupted by a chat with a colleague (2a). Accordingly, the level of concentration measured drops down during the chat (2c) but is high during focused work (1c, 3c). (1b, 2b, 3b) demonstrates the egocentric view of the worker by means of the HoloLens headset with gaze cursor (blue) and concentration (orange) and stress (yellow) measurement bars.

The development of the demonstrator about the learning scenario is in progress. It is overall based on the human factors measurement technologies described above. Upon completion, a supervisor worker will be capable to select specific tasks from a novel assembly work and investigate how well a rooky worker is performing in comparison to expert data which are matched towards the novel data from the rooky. A distance function will finally provide insight into parts of the interaction since with substantial distance to the expert profile and from this enable to put the focus on parts of the sequence that most need training. Furthermore, the pattern of interaction, i.e., gaze on objects and following interactions, is further investigated for additional optimisations if applicable.

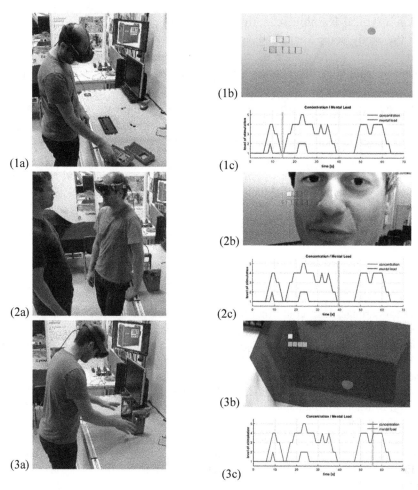

Fig. 6. Learning scenario demonstrating the feasibility of the concentration measurement technology. (1a) View on the worker with focus on work (1a, 3a) and being interrupted by a chat with a colleague (2a). Accordingly, the level of concentration measured drops down during the chat (2c) but is high during focused work (1c, 3c). (1b, 2b, 3b) demonstrates the egocentric view of the worker by means of the HoloLens headset with gaze cursor (blue) and concentration (orange) and stress (yellow) measurement bars. (Color figure online)

4   Conclusions and Future Work

This work presented innovative methodologies for the assessment of executive functions to represent psychologically motivated quantitative estimations of human operator performance in assembly processes. We estimated dynamic human attention from mobile gaze analysis with the potential to measure, such as, attention selection and inhibition, as well as task switching ability, in real-time. We presented a suite of different components with gaze based human factors analysis that is relevant for the measurement of cognitive and psychophysiological parameters. In this manner, this work intends to provide a novel view on human operator state estimation as a means for the global optimization of human-machine collaboration.

Within a typical learning scenario of a human operator within an assembly work cell and the study setup including application of state-of-the-art intuitive assistance technology for the performance of collaborative tasks, we illustrated the potential of interpretation from gaze based human factors data in order to evaluate a collaborative system.

In future work we will study the potential of more complex eye movement features, such as, for planning processes, to enable a more detailed analysis of the dynamic distribution of attentional resources during the tasks.

Acknowledgments. This work has been supported by the Austrian Federal Ministry for Climate Action, Environment, Energy, Mobility, Innovation and Technology (BMK) within projects MMASSIST (no. 858623) and FLEXIFF (no. 861264).

References

1. Saucedo-Martínez, J.A., et al.: Industry 4.0 framework for management and operations: a review. J. Ambient Intell. Humaniz. Comput. **9**, 1–13 (2017)
2. Steinfeld, A., et al.: Common metrics for human-robot interaction. In: Proceedings of the ACM SIGCHI/SIGART Human-Robot Interaction (2006)
3. Huang, C.-M., Mutlu, B.: Anticipatory robot control for efficient human-robot collaboration. In: Proceedings of the ACM/IEEE HRI 2016 (2016)
4. Endsley, M.R.: Toward a theory of situation awareness in dynamic systems. Hum. Factors **37**(1), 32–64 (1995)
5. Paletta, L., et al.: Gaze based human factors measurements for the evaluation of intuitive human-robot collaboration in real-time. In: Proceedings of the 24th IEEE Conference on Emerging Technologies and Factory Automation, ETFA 2019, Zaragoza, Spain, 10–13 September 2019 (2019)
6. Holmqvist, K., Nyström, M., Andersson, R., Dewhusrt, R., Jarodzka, H., van de Weijler, J.: Eye Tracking – A Comprehensive Guide to Methods and Measures, p. 187. Oxford University Press, Oxford (2011)
7. Moore, K., Gugerty, L.: Development of a novel measure of situation awareness: the case for eye movement analysis. Hum. Factors Ergon. Soc. Ann. Meet. **54**(19), 1650–1654 (2010)
8. Munn, S.M., Pelz, J.B.: 3D point-of-regard, position and head orientation from a portable monocular video-based eye tracker. In: Proceedings of the ETRA 2008, pp. 181–188 (2008)
9. Santner, K., Fritz, G., Paletta, L., Mayer, H.: Visual recovery of saliency maps from human attention in 3D environments. In: Proceedings of the ICRA 2013, pp. 4297–4303 (2013)
10. Heyer, C.: Human-robot interaction and future industrial robotics applications. In: Proceedings of the IEEE/RSJ IROS, pp. 4749–4754 (2010)
11. Taylor, R.M.: Situational awareness rating technique (SART): the development of a tool for aircrew systems design. In: Situational Awareness in Aerospace Operations, pp. 3/1–3/17 (1990)
12. Stanton, N.A., Salmon, P.M., Walker, G.H., Jenkins, D.P.: Genotype and phenotype schemata and their role in distributed situation awareness in collaborative systems. Theoret. Issues Ergon. Sci. **10**, 43–68 (2009)
13. Dini, A., Murko, C., Paletta, L., Yahyanejad, S., Augsdörfer, U., Hofbaur, M.: Measurement and prediction of situation awareness in human-robot interaction based on a framework of probabilistic attention. In: Proceedings of the IEEE/RSJ IROS 2017 (2017)

14. Paletta, L., Pittino, N., Schwarz, M., Wagner, V., Kallus, W.: Human factors analysis using wearable sensors in the context of cognitive and emotional arousal. In: Proceedings of the 4th International Conference on Applied Digital Human Modeling, AHFE 2015, July 2015 (2015)
15. Paletta, L., Pszeida, M., Nauschnegg, B., Haspl, T., Marton, R.: Stress measurement in multitasking decision processes using executive functions analysis. In: Ayaz, H. (ed.) AHFE 2019. AISC, vol. 953, pp. 344–356. Springer, Cham (2020). https://doi.org/10.1007/978-3-030-20473-0_33
16. Bailey, B.P., Konstan, J.A.: On the need for attention-aware systems: Measuring effects of interruption on task performance, error rate, and affective state. Comput. Hum. Behav. **22**(4), 685–708 (2006)
17. Monsell, S.: Task switching. Trends Cogn. Sci. **7**(3), 134–140 (2003)
18. Miyake, A., Friedman, N.P., Emerson, M.J., Witzki, A., Howerter, A., Wager, T.D.: The unity and diversity of executive functions and their contributions to complex 'frontal lobe' tasks: a latent variable analysis. Cogn. Psychol. **41**, 49–100 (2000)
19. Jersild, A.T.: Mental set and shift. Arch. Psychol. **89** (1927)
20. Kramer, A.F., Hahn, S., Gopher, D.: Task coordination and aging: explorations of executive control processes in the task switching paradigm. Acta Psychol. **101**, 339–378 (1999)
21. Selye, H.: A syndrome produced by diverse nocuous agents. Nature **138**(32) (1936)
22. Folkman, S.: Stress: Appraisal and Coping. Springer, New York (1984). https://doi.org/10.1007/978-1-4419-1005-9_215
23. Smith, E., Jonides, J.: Storage and executive processes in the frontal lobes. Science **283**, 1657–1661 (1999)
24. Dickerson, S., Kemeny, M.: Acute stressors and cortisol responses: a theoretical integration and synthesis of laboratory research. Psychol. Bull. **130**, 355–391 (2004). https://doi.org/10.1037/0033-2909.130.3.355
25. Diamond, A.: Executive functions. Annu. Rev. Psychol. **64**, 135–168 (2013). https://doi.org/10.1146/annurev-psych-113011-143750
26. Meyer, D.E., et al.: The role of dorsolateral prefrontal cortex for executive cognitive processes in task switching. J. Cogn. Neurosci. **10** (1998)
27. Del Missier, F., Mäntyla, T., Bruine de Bruin, W.: Executive functions in decision making: an individual differences approach. Think. Reason. **16**(2), 69–97 (2010)
28. Cannon, W.B.: The Wisdom of the Body. Norton, New York (1932)
29. Boucsein, W.: Electrodermal Acivity. Plenum, New York (1992)
30. Setz, C., Arnrich, B., Schumm, J., La Marca, R., Tröster, G., Ehlert, U.: Discriminating stress from cognitive load using a wearable EDA device. IEEE Trans. Inf Technol. Biomed. **14**(2), 410–417 (2010)
31. Taelman, J., Vandeput, S., Spaepen, A., Van Huffel, S.: Influence of mental stress on heart rate and heart rate variability. In: Vander Sloten, J., Verdonck, P., Nyssen, M., Haueisen, J. (eds.) 4th European Conference of the International Federation for Medical and Biological Engineering, vol. 22, pp. 1366–1369. Springer, Heidelberg (2009). https://doi.org/10.1007/978-3-540-89208-3_324
32. Sharma, N., Gedeon, T.: Objective measures, sensors and computational techniques for stress recognition and classification: a survey. Comput. Methods Program. Biomed. **108**, 1287–1301 (2012)
33. Sun, F.-T., Kuo, C., Cheng, H.-T., Buthpitiya, S., Collins, P., Griss, M.: Activity-aware mental stress detection using physiological sensors. In: Gris, M., Yang, G. (eds.) MobiCASE 2010. LNICST, vol. 76, pp. 211–230. Springer, Heidelberg (2012). https://doi.org/10.1007/978-3-642-29336-8_12
34. Van Orden, K.F., Limbert, W., Makeig, S.: Eye Activity Correlates of Workload during a Visuospatial Memory Task. Hum. Factors: J. Hum. Factors Ergon. Soc. **43**, 111–121 (2001)

35. Chajut, E., Algom, D.: Selective attention improves under stress: implications for theories of social cognition. J. Pers. Soc. Psych. **85**, 231–248 (2003)
36. Bütepage, J., Kragic, D.: Human-robot collaboration: from psychology to social robotics (2017). arXiv:1705.10146
37. Baddeley, A.D., Hitch, G.: Working memory. In: Bower, G.A. (ed.) The Psychology of Learning and Motivation: Advances in Research and Theory, vol. 8, pp. 47–89 (1974)
38. Lezak, M.D.: Neuropsychological Assessment. Oxford University Press, New York (1995)
39. Koolhaas, J.M., Bartolomucci, A., Buwalda, B., De Boer, S.F., Flügge, G., Korte, S.M., et al.: Stress revisited: a critical evaluation of the stress concept. Neurosci. Biobehav. Rev. **35**, 1291–1301 (2011)
40. Hermans, E.J., Henckens, M.J.A.G., Joels, M., Fernandez, G.: Dynamic adaptation of large-scale brain networks in response to acute stressors. Trends Neurosci. **37**, 304–314 (2014)

15

Plenoptic Inspection System for Automatic Quality Control of MEMS and Microsystems

Moritz A. Kirschmann[1]([✉]), Jörg Pierer[1], Alexander Steinecker[1], Philipp Schmid[1], and Arne Erdmann[2]

[1] CSEM SA, Gründlistrasse 1, 6055 Alpnach Dorf, Switzerland
moritz.kirschmann@csem.ch
[2] Raytrix GmbH, Schauenburgerstr. 116, 24118 Kiel, Germany

Abstract. Optical quality control of MEMS and microsystems is challenging as these structures are micro-scale and three dimensional. Here we lay out different optical systems that can be used for 3D optical quality control in general and for such structures in particular. We further investigate one of these technologies – plenoptic cameras and characterize them for the described task, showing advantages and disadvantages. Key advantages are a huge increase in depth of field compared to conventional microscope camera systems allowing for fast acquisition of non-flat systems and secondly the resulting total focus images and depth maps. Finally we conclude that these advantages render plenoptic cameras a valuable technology for the application of quality control.

Keywords: Optical inspection · Lightfield camera · Plenoptic camera · Automatic defect recognition · 3D inspection

1 Introduction

1.1 MEMS and Typical Defects

Advancements in manufacturing techniques of micro-electro-mechanical systems (MEMS) and microsystems such as deep reactive ion-etching further increased the range of possible applications of these systems. Bridging the world of electronics and mechanics, MEMS are used for applications as micro actuators, generating sound, vibration and liquid flow in microfluidic pumps, while micro sensors turn acceleration, gyroscopic forces, inertia, pressure, sound waves et cetera into electric signals. These actuators and sensor are used in many industries such as mobile computing, automotive, VR/AR, electronic entertainment, pharma and medical. To achieve high production yield and quality of the final products quality control is key. Functional testing of MEMS is often only possible in a further integrated assembly. Yet it is desirable to assess product quality as early as possible to avoid assembly of defect components into integrated systems rendering a whole assembly worthless. To assess quality in an early stage avoiding further assembly, optical quality control is one possibility. However, MEMS have a key property that makes optical quality control specially challenging: functional structures of MEMS are intrinsically extended in depth (see Fig. 1, Fig. 2 and Fig. 3).

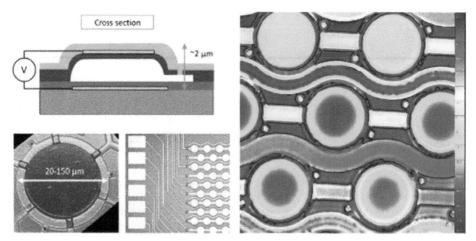

Fig. 1. Schematic cross-section of a Capacitive Micromachined Ultrasonic Transducer (CMUT) device (top-left), optical microphotographs of CMUT devices in top view (lower-left) and (right) a col-or-coded depth map acquired by holographic microscopy (image curtesy of Philips Electronics Nederland B.V.).

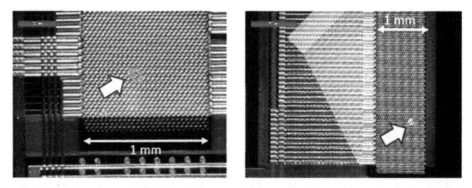

Fig. 2. Microphotograph of CMUTs with typical defects highlighted by white arrows: Missing CMUT disks (left) and dust, resist or other particles (right); (image curtesy of Philips Electronics Nederland B.V.).

An optical quality control system for MEMS must therefore fulfill three require-ments: (1) Micrometer-scale features must be resolved in all three spatial dimensions. Production defects such as a displaced transducer bridge or wire bond may only be detectable by utilizing height data captured by the optical system. (2) The relevant depth of the product must be acquired at sufficient resolution. (3) The system's throughput must be high enough to allow for real-time inspection of produced units.

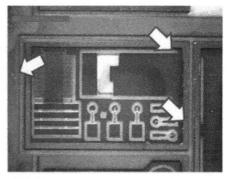

Not removed and now delaminating pieces of side wall passivation

Particles (various nature)

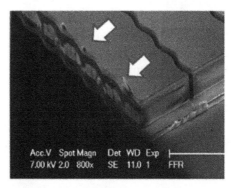

Crack in silicon island

Polymer / oxide residues at the edge of the island

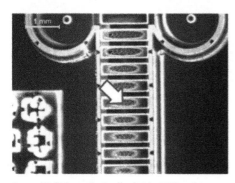

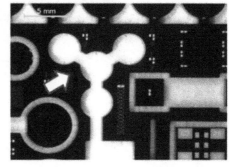

Loss of BOX layer during backside DRIE etching resulting in local thinning of Si islands even to the extend that CMUTs become visible from backside

Missing structures removed during processing

Fig. 3. A selection of failures and defects that can occur during the fabrication of the Flex-to-Rigid structures (image curtesy of Philips Electronics Nederland B.V.).

1.2   State of the Art (3D) Inspection Technology

Different optical acquisition systems can be used for quality control in general but only a few are suitable for MEMS inspection. The straightforward approach is the application of conventional wide field microscopy. Considering a typical microscope objective with sub-micrometer resolution a Field of View (FoV) in the range of 0.3 mm^2 might be captured with one image. Capturing the area of an eight-inch wafer (30'000 mm^2) would already require 100'000 images. The typical Depth of Field (DoF) of the same lens covers maximally 2 in height [1]. For MEMS with 3D structures covering a thickness ranging from sub-micrometer up to several 100 μm, a technique called "focus stacking" may be used to expand the DoF and acquire depth data [2]. For very common structures 100 μm in height the eight-inch wafer required an amount of 5 million images. Even with a fast camera enabling 100 fps (frames per second) and a manipulation system matching this speed for repositioning the wafer it would take 14 h to capture the 3D data, not yet considering any kind of image analysis. While 2D inspection is a very common technique, 3D by focus stacking is not employed in industry for MEMS inspection.

Another possibility to obtain 3D depth information are stereo camera images by analyzing shift of parallax of image features. However, parts of an image that are occluded from one view lack parallax information. This renders inference of the depth impossible at these places. Systems with more cameras mitigate this issue as the chance of occluding parts of the image for all but one camera decreases with the number of cameras [3]. However, the complexity and bulkiness of the system also increases with the number of cameras. The need for two lenses and cameras imaging the same FoV limits the application to macroscopic lenses. Thus the limited achievable resolution, laterally as well as in height, so far prohibits the application of stereo camera systems for MEMS inspection (Fig. 4).

Fig. 4. Stereo camera system offered by Ensenso GmbH [4].

Laser Line Triangulation (LLT) illuminates the sample by swiping a projected laser line from an angle to the viewing direction [5]. Depth displacement in the imaged sample shifts the apparent laser line position. On uniform samples such systems deliver precise depth maps quickly [6] but samples with strong differences in reflectivity and absorption can cause artefacts. The lateral resolution of such systems is mostly limited by diffraction properties of the projected laser beam (several μm) while the depth resolution is a function of incidence angle, sensor pixel size and lens magnification. Common systems range from μm to several 10 μm. LLT systems do not generate photo-like images and therefore need to be combined with microscope cameras in order to deliver image and depth map.

A very similar technology probably in direct competition to plenoptic cameras is structured illumination microscopy. It probably also is the most versatile technology ranging from moiré fringe exploitation [7] to various kind of pattern projection and 3D information extraction [8]. In the first case the superposition of a well-defined illumination pattern with the structure of the object generates a beat pattern otherwise known as moiré fringes. The scene has to be captured several times with slightly re-oriented or phase shifted pattern. The simpler pattern projection relies on known geometric relations between camera and projector with the advantage to need only one image per scene, depending on the actual pattern. In both cases subsequent processing of the image(s) enables the generation of 3D data. With proper computational hardware and a fast camera several 3D images might be obtained per second. In terms of DoF, FoV and resolution the same constraints as for any other optical system apply (Fig. 5).

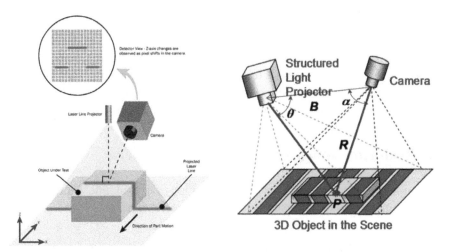

Fig. 5. Schematics of (left) laser line triangulation [5] and (right) structured light illumination [8].

Imaging based on holography employing laser interference (DHM Digital Holographic Microscopy) offers outstanding depth resolution around 20 nm and simultaneously a considerable DoF of up to a few $100 \mu m$ [9–11]. The latter one, however, is only true for rather continuous structures. As soon as steps and sharp edges are involved those numbers get down to sub-um up to a few um. The lateral resolution as well as the FoV are limited by laws of physics just as for the other optical imaging technologies as well. Even so this technology has some drawbacks, it offers very high performance in terms of 3D imaging. Unfortunately, this comes literally at costs at least an order of magnitude higher than any of the other systems (Fig. 6).

OCT (Optical Coherence Tomography) as a 3D imaging technology shall be mentioned as well. Although an interferometric principle as holography it relies on a short coherence length of broadband light sources such as superluminescent LEDs [12]. Typical depth resolution achieved goes down to the sub-micrometer range. The DoF of an OCT system depends on either a mechanical movement of a mirror in the reference arm (Time Domain OCT) or the wavelength sweeping of the source (Frequency Domain

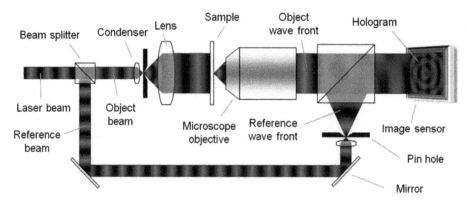

Fig. 6. Typical outline of a Digital Holographic Microscopy system [11].

OCT) and is for TD-OCT at least in theory only limited by size constraints. Lateral resolution again is limited by physics, depending on the lens used. Besides the need for depth scanning which increases the acquisitions time the small number of pixels of available cameras with smart pixels (e.g. 280×292 [13]) limits the FoV and therewith further increases the acquisition time. It shall be mentioned that standard cameras may be used as well but demand a way more complex setup [14].

2 3D Real-Time Imaging with Plenoptic Camera

In the following the hard- and software technology of plenoptic cameras and their applications in our context of inspection systems are described.

2.1 Principle of Plenoptic Camera Technology

The general principle of a plenoptic, also known as light field camera dates back to Leonardo Da Vinci and he even described the principle of a pinhole camera to capture the light field [15]. The first multi-lens concept and actual camera was described and developed by physicist Gabriel Lippmann in 1908 [16] although the term "light field" was not used at this time. In 1992 Edward Adelson and John Wang published an article describing the plenoptic camera concept as, in its basic principle, is used until today [17].

Conventional 2D digital cameras use objectives which images an object onto a 2-dimensional array of photosensitive elements. In a plenoptic camera, as Adelson and Wang described, a microlens array is placed between main lens and the photosensitive camera chip. Hereby the main lens generates an intermediate image which subsequently is imaged by the microlenses onto subsegments of the photosensitive part of the chip [18] (see Fig. 7).

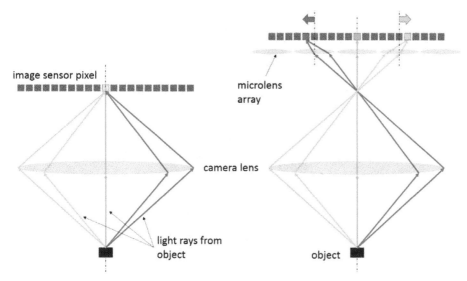

Fig. 7. Schematic representation of imaging with standard (left) and plenoptic camera (right). (Color figure online)

As depicted by the small red respectively yellow arrow on the right side of Fig. 7, the object point will be imaged on a different camera pixel with respect to the optical axis of the corresponding microlens. Based on that not only the position of the object point in space can be determined but as well the direction wherefrom the light rays originated. Adjacent microlenses are producing sub-images with are partially overlapping FoVs. Knowing the configuration of main lens, microlens array and camera chip it is possible to computationally reconstruct a 2D image and a depth map [19] (Fig. 8) which together are used to form the 3D image as depicted in Fig. 9.

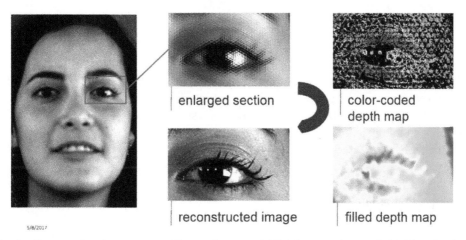

Fig. 8. Computational reconstructed image (bottom middle) from raw image (left). The microlens sub-images are visible in the enlarged image (top middle). The image on the top right shows the color-coded depth map for high contrast areas while below the same map is filled.

Fig. 9. Real-time 3D image as obtained by Raytrix light field camera.

2.2 Application of Plenoptic Cameras for MEMS and Microsystems Inspection

As summarized above many 3D imaging technologies exist, each having its strengths and weaknesses. The same is true for plenoptic cameras. Due to redundant imaging of object points on several microlens sub-images the reconstructed 2D image loses planar resolution by a factor of 2-times in every direction. This may be countered by use of large pixel count camera chips. However, this increases the amount of data to be handled by the camera interface, the computational hardware and finally by means of storage. Actually these are the main reasons why plenoptic cameras became available for real world applications only during the last decade. Modern GPU hardware made real-time reconstruction of high pixel count light field camera images manageable.

Plenoptic cameras of Raytrix offer unique advantages for industrial applications. As only one camera with a standard main lens is needed, the entire setup becomes rather lean and consumes little space. Assuming a fast interface, e.g. Camera Link, acquisition of full 3D images at 80 frames per second is feasible. As a side effect of the special Raytrix technology using microlenses with different focal lengths on each of the arrays [19], the DoF is increased by a factor of 6 compared to a standard cameras. The probably biggest advantage compared to many of the other 3D imaging technologies is the almost total lack of occlusion. As can be seen in Fig. 10 this enables inspection of devises with high aspect ratios and steep edges.

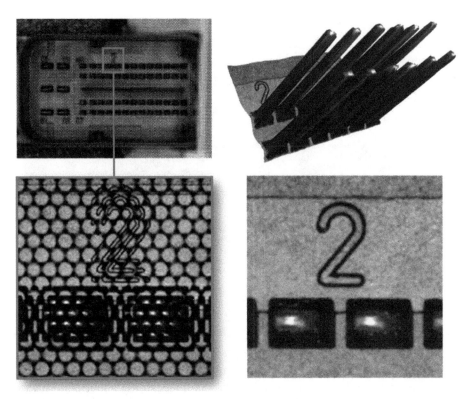

Fig. 10. Upper left: raw image from a plenoptic camera, Lower left: detail crop from the area marked by the red rectangle. Round sub-images created by the microlenses are visible. Note the duplication of features in neighboring sub-images. Lower right: algorithmically reconstructed sharp image. Right: 3D rendering of the image. (Color figure online)

Within a European project "CITCOM"[1] we are investigating in detail the 3D MEMS inspection using light field cameras. We used and assessed two different plenoptic camera-main lens combinations during development of an automatic optical quality-control system. Specs of those are provided in Table 1. Shown in Fig. 11 is the test setup

Table 1. Main specifications of used plenoptic cameras

	Raytrix R26	Raytrix R12
Working distance	48 mm	20 mm
Field of View	7.8×7.8 mm^2	0.65×0.44 mm^2
Lateral resolution	3 μm	0.7 μm
Depth of Field	1.1 mm	60 μm
Depth resolution	2.5 μm	0.4 μm
Frame rate (max)	81 fps	30 fps

[1] www.citcom.eu; This project has received funding from the European Union's HORIZON 2020 research and innovation program under Grant Agreement no. 768883.

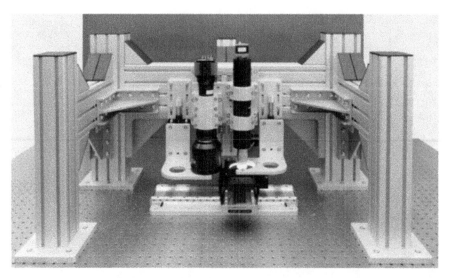

Fig. 11. Development setup with two plenoptic cameras Raytrix R26 (left) and R12 (right).

(no cabling) with a Raytrix R26 camera and $3\times$ telecentric lens on the left side and a R12 in microscope configuration employing a $20\times$ main lens.

The R26 setup enables very fast capturing of an entire eight-inch wafer. Considering an overlap of 10% to enable stitching of the images only about 600 images are needed which might be acquired in less than 10 s. In practice, however, not the speed of the camera is limiting the acquisition time but the movement of the stages. While the 3D reconstruction of a single image can be obtained at the maximal frame rate on PCs employing 4 GPUs (Graphic Processing Units), image stitching and automated recognition of defects and anomalies have to be considered as well.

While most of the typical defects and anomalies might be found with this setup, some demand for higher resolution in both, lateral as well as vertical direction. For those cases a second camera, an R12 in combination with a microscope objective, are used on specific areas of interest. Scanning the entire wafer with this camera is neither useful considering the necessary 130'000 images at 30 fps (frames per second) taking more than one hour at best, nor is it needed. With a FoV covering less than 0.3 mm^2, most of the wafer or substrate area appears as a plain, feature-less surface, while in specific areas a closer look might be highly appreciated.

Images taken with the setup described above are presented in Fig. 12 allowing for metrology in all spatial dimensions on a sub-micrometer scale.

An actual disadvantage that accounts for other techniques as well is the inability to computationally reconstruct the depth map at locations with missing contrast. However this can be mitigated by illuminating with a light patterned as depicted in Fig. 13. Those images were generated within a Bachelor thesis [20] initiated and supervised by CSEM. This structured illumination reveals the surface topology and allows a 3D reconstruction even if contrast is lacking.

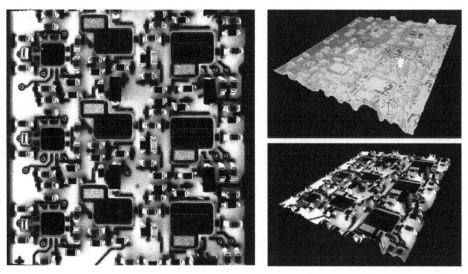

Fig. 12. Left: total focus image of PCB captured with Raytrix R26 and a 3x tele-centric lens. Right: 3D rendered image (bottom) with color coded depth map overly (top).

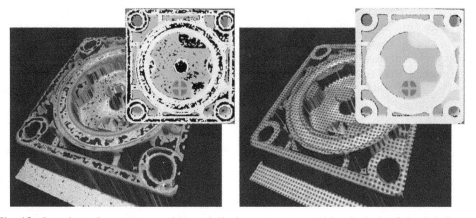

Fig. 13. Imaging of component with partially low contrast resulting in lack of depth information (left). Patterned illumination projection mitigates the effect of contrast-arm surfaces (right). Colored images depict the color-coded depth maps of the 3D objects. Images by [20].

As the reconstructed total focus images and depth maps can be exported as 2D image data, existing software for quality control, fault detection and anomaly detection can directly process and analyze these images. In order to achieve a proper performance of the system, parameters for reconstruction of total focus and depth maps need to be adapted for different inspection scenarios.

3 Conclusion

Real-time 3D inspection is not needed for every application. However, where it is the case multiple technologies might be considered ranging from simple stacking of 2D images over stereo camera configuration all the way to interferometric systems. As usual complexity and cost are increasing with more demanding needs. Plenoptic cameras might not be perfect and certainly will not replace every other inspection technology. However, as is the case for MEMS and other microsystems in general, plenoptic cameras have a huge potential whenever the following criteria seem to be advantageous:

- 6-times larger Depth of Field compared to standard camera
- occlusion-free 3D imaging
- real-time 3D image acquisition up to 80 frames per second
- simple implementation due to single camera/lens configuration
- cost efficient compared to competing technologies with similar performance
- simple combination with other means of inspection, e.g. electrical probing possible

Plenoptic cameras are a valuable instrument for the inspections of MEMS because of its unique advantages at their competitive price.

References

1. Edmund Optics Ltd: 20× Mitutoyo Plan Apo Infinity Corrected Long WD Objective. Edmund Optics Ltd. (2019). https://www.edmundoptics.de/p/20x-mitutoyo-plan-apo-infinity-correc ted-long-wd-objective/6625/. Accessed 16 Sept 2019
2. Ens, J., Lawrence, P.: An investigation of methods for determining depth from focus. IEEE Trans. Pattern Anal. Mach. Intell. **15**(2), 97–108 (1993)
3. Wilburn, B., et al.: High performance imaging using large camera arrays. ACM Trans. Graph. **24**(3), 765–776 (2005)
4. Ensenso GmbH: www.ensenso.com. Ensenso GmbH (2018). https://www.ensenso.com/. Accessed 12 Sept 2019
5. Callen, D.: Vision-Spectra.com: Coherent Inc., May 2017. https://www.photonics.com/Art icle.aspx?AID=62061. Accessed 11 Sept 2019
6. Micro-Epsilon: Micro Epsilon Laser Triangulation system. MICRO-EPSILON UK & Ireland Ltd. (2019). https://www.micro-epsilon.co.uk/service/glossar/Laser-Triangulation.html
7. Gustafson, M.G.L.: Surpassing the lateral resolution limit by a factor of two using structured illumination microscopy. J. Microsc. **198**(2), 82–87 (2000)
8. Geng, J.: Structured-light 3D surface imaging: a tutorial. Adv. Opt. Photonics **3**(2), 128–160 (2011)
9. Lyncée Tec: www.lynceetec.com. https://www.lynceetec.com/. Accessed 11 Sept 2019
10. Pagliarulo, V., Russo, T., Miccio, L., Ferraro, P.: Numerical tools for the characterization of microelectromechanical systems by digital holographic microscopy. J. Micro/Nanolithogr. MEMS MOEMS **14**(4), (2015)
11. Wikipedia Contributors: Digital holographic microscopy. Wikipedia, The Free Encyclope-dia, 28 August 2019. https://en.wikipedia.org/w/index.php?title=Digital_holographic_micr oscopy&oldid=912841452. Accessed 12 Sept 2019
12. Wikipedia Contributors: Optical coherence tomography. Wikipedia, The Free Encyclopedia, 11 July 2019. https://en.wikipedia.org/w/index.php?title=Optical_coherence_tomography& oldid=905735980. Accessed 12 Sept 2019
13. Heliotis AG: www.heliotis.ch. https://www.heliotis.ch/index.html. Accessed 12 Sept 2019
14. Dunsby, C., Gu, Y., French, P.M.W.: Single-shot phase-stepped wide-field coherence-gated imaging. Opt. Express **11**(2), 105–115 (2003)

15. LightField Forum: History of light field photography (timeline). http://lightfield-forum.com/what-is-the-lightfield/history-of-light-field-photography-timeline/. Accessed 13 Sept 2019

16. Lippmann, G.: Épreuves réversibles donnant la sensation du relief. J. Phys. Theor. Appl. **7**(1), 821–825 (1908)

17. Adelson, E.H., Wang, J.Y.A.: Single lens stereo with a plenoptic camera. IEEE Trans. Pattern Anal. Mach. Intell. **14**(2), 99–106 (1992)

18. Lumsdaine, A., Georgiev, T.: Full resolution lightfield rendering. Indiana University and Adobe Systems (2008)

19. Perwass, C., Wietzke, L.: Single lens 3D-camera with extended depth-of-field. Proc. SPIE **8291**, 4- (2012)

20. Ammann, S., Gilson, O.: Pattern Illumination for Lightfield Camera. Interstaatliche Hochschule für Technik Buchs, Buchs (2019)

16

Context-Aware Plug and Produce for Robotic Aerospace Assembly

David Sanderson[1]([⊠]) [iD], Emma Shires[1], Jack C. Chaplin[2] [iD], Harvey Brookes[3],
Amer Liaqat[3], and Svetan Ratchev[2] [iD]

[1] Centre for Aerospace Manufacturing, University of Nottingham, Nottingham NG7 2PX, UK
{david.sanderson,emma.shires}@nottingham.ac.uk
[2] Institute for Advanced Manufacturing, University of Nottingham, Nottingham NG8 1BB, UK
{jack.chaplin,svetan.ratchev}@nottingham.ac.uk
[3] Airbus, Bristol, UK
{harvey.brookes,amer.liaqat}@airbus.com

Abstract. Aerospace production systems face increasing requirements for flexibility and reconfiguration, along with considerations of cost, utilisation, and efficiency. This drives a need for systems with a small number of automation platforms (e.g. industrial robots) that can make use of a larger number of end effectors that are potentially flexible or multifunctional. This leads to the challenge of ensuring that the configuration and location of each end effector is tracked by the system at all times, even in the face of manual adjustments, to ensure that the correct processes are applied to the product at the right time. We present a solution based on a Data Distribution Service that provides the system with full awareness of the context of its automation platforms and end effectors. The solution is grounded with an example use case from WingLIFT, a research programme led by a large aerospace manufacturer. The WingLIFT project in which this solution was developed builds on the adaptive systems approach from the Evolvable Assembly Systems project, with focus on extending and increasing the aerospace industrial applicability of plug and produce techniques. The design of this software solution is described from multiple perspectives, and accompanied by details of a physical demonstration cell that is in the process of being commissioned.

Keywords: Aerospace assembly · Context awareness · Distributed data service · Flexible manufacturing systems · Manufacturing service bus · Multi-agent systems · Plug and produce · Robotic assembly

1 Introduction

Global air travel has seen significant growth in recent decades, doubling every 15 years and demonstrating strong demand for new aircraft. This delivers a challenge to aircraft manufacturers to ramp up production to higher rates in order to keep pace with demand. One of the biggest challenges to the introduction of a new product is industrialising the new automation technologies that enable the required ramp up to full production rate. The industrialisation process requires the development and validation of a wide variety of technologies in a short period of time. This can be accomplished at a reduced cost through flexible, reconfigurable, and modular production systems that enable multiple processes to be evaluated concurrently without large commissioning efforts. Such systems also enable reduction in cost by enabling adaptation in the automated system to cope with component variation and process uncertainty. This supports delivery of automated assembly processes (e.g. drilling, fastening etc.) to the correct location on the actual product. Such technology contributes to reduction in manufacturing costs, both non-recurring (e.g. production systems design and commissioning) and recurring (e.g. reduction in changeover, human intervention, and cycle time).

The WingLIFT project [1] has identified a number of specific aims in support of the industry requirements when considering the assembly of aircraft wings. One aspect of these aims is the application of innovative information management technology to optimise flow and distribution of both internal and external information across a wing sub-assembly factory. Intelligent assembly systems are required to monitor the key parameters of the entire manufacturing system, which supports quality assurance, geometric deviation awareness and control, and data feedback for real-time continuous improvement.

The work presented in this paper contributes to this technology solution specifically by monitoring the configuration of the system in real time. This technology is grounded in a specific use case that describes an automated assembly cell containing a set of process end effectors, each with a potentially large set of possible configurations, that are shared between a relatively small number of automation platforms.

This paper is organised as follows: Sect. 2 provides an overview of the current state of the art in flexibility in manufacturing systems, with particular reference to previous projects carried out at this institution in the area on which WingLIFT builds. Section 3 describes the motivating use case for the work, before Sect. 4 develops the architectural concept for WingLIFT. Section 5 specifies the demonstration scenario that will be used to validate the work, along with an outline of the solution developed. Finally, Sect. 6 summarises the work presented.

2 Flexibility in Manufacturing Systems

2.1 Flexible and Reconfigurable Manufacturing Systems

In a manufacturing sector characterised by market unpredictability, increased global labour costs, and growing consumer demand for highly personalised goods and services, producers are naturally pushed to remain competitive by maintaining shorter times to market, increased product diversity and specialisation, and shorter product life-cycles. This has resulted in a growing body of research into production systems that can incorporate new technologies and provide high levels of robustness, resilience, and responsiveness.

There are a number of approaches to delivering these characteristics, including flexible manufacturing systems [2, 3], reconfigurable manufacturing systems [4], automatic and adaptive control [5], and manufacturing systems modelling and simulation [6]. One specific technology that has been developed in this area is "plug and produce" [7], named by analogy to the concept of "plug and play" in computing. The EU FP7 PRIME project

[8] developed a multi-agent approach to plug and produce with commercially available components for simple robotic assembly tasks in a fixed system dealing with dynamic product changes and unexpected disruptions [9–11].

2.2 Evolvable Assembly Systems, Context Awareness, and WingLIFT

EPSRC Evolvable Assembly Systems (EAS) [12] was a fundamental research project following on from PRIME. It aimed to deliver adaptable and cost effective manufacture by enabling a compressed product life cycle through the delivery of robust and compliant manufacturing systems that can be rapidly configured and optimised. In turn, this should enable the reduction of production ramp-up times and programme switchovers. In summary the project proposed a multi-agent system [13] to provide manufacturing control systems with the characteristics of agility, multi-functionality, adaptability, and resilience. Further information on the EAS project can be found elsewhere [14–17], but the remainder of this section focusses on how EAS viewed the concept of context-awareness in terms of intelligent production systems. One product of the EAS project was the concept of a context-aware cyber-physical production system, shown in Fig. 1 and discussed in more detail in [18].

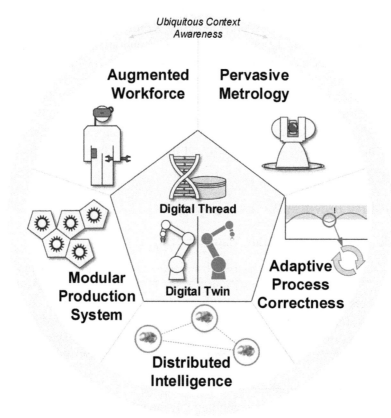

Fig. 1. Conceptual framework for context-aware cyber-physical production systems

The basis of the concept is that of a shared context for the system, where the context is knowledge about the system and its current state. This context allows all the elements of the system to share the relevant knowledge and information required to accomplish the system function. The foundation of the context is the digital information concerning the system, starting with the information created at design and commissioning ("digital twin"), and added to throughout life by the operation of the system ("digital thread"). This contextual information is gathered and handled by distributed intelligence across a set of modular system components. Pervasive metrology[1] allows for the highest quality information at all times. The information can be used to allow the system to self-adapt and maintain its correct functioning. The final aspect of the concept allows for the human workforce and the automation to work together most effectively by assigning decision-making and operations in a hybrid manner to best allocate responsibilities. In summary, the context-aware cyber-physical production systems concept enables the smart integration of all equipment in order to best leverage the available information and thereby accomplish the production aims in the most efficient manner possible with the available resources.

WingLIFT focusses on a specific instantiation of part of this concept in order to prove its applicability in an industrial environment. The WingLIFT approach involves the aspects of data sharing that enable smart integration of dynamic modular production systems through the use of distributed intelligence. This distributed intelligence is presumed to be based on multi-agent technology, but an agent is not a "hard requirement" for every resource in the system, as will be discussed later. Other parts of the WingLIFT project include some aspects of pervasive metrology, but they will not be included in this paper.

3 Use Case

3.1 High-Level Use Case Motivation

The high-level use case identified in the WingLIFT project for this work is as follows. A semi-automated aerospace assembly cell exists in which a small number of automation platforms (e.g. industrial robots) share a larger number of process end effectors (e.g. end effectors designed to either drill, fasten, seal, or position components). Each end effector may have a large number of possible configurations (e.g. for the drilling end effector, there may be a variety of cutting tool sizes; for the fastening end effector there may be a variety of fastener diameters and lengths; and so on). These configurations may be changed dynamically during operations either by the automation control system, or by the operator. Both the automation platforms and end effectors are expected to be moveable around the cell through the use of automatic tool changers and either rails or moveable platforms. The system therefore requires some method for maintaining knowledge of the current configuration state of the whole system, including the hardware configurations and positions of both automation platforms and end effectors, and the software configuration of the control system.

---

[1] Pervasive metrology is where metrology is used throughout the system, named by analogy with pervasive computing [31], an offshoot of ubiquitous computing [32].

3.2 Specific Use Case Scenarios

Further developing the high-level use case described above, the project defines a set of specific use case scenarios. The scenarios are as follows:

- Resource addition and resource removal
- End effector pick-up and end effector drop-off
- Configuration change (hardware) and configuration change (software)

For the purposes of this paper, we will describe in detail the end effector pick-up use case and a generalised "configuration change" use case that combines both hardware and software changes. The project utilises a multifunctional UML approach (i.e. according to the Object Management Group's Unified Modeling Language [19]) to describe the use cases and solution; for this paper we will describe each use case with a table.

End Effector Pick-Up. The end effector pick-up use case scenario shown in Table 1 describes a situation where the system is required to change the currently equipped end effector on a given automation platform (in this case a robot) to a specific end effector. This requires that the system is aware of the locations of the robot and end effector, and also the current and desired configurations of the end effector.

Table 1. End effector pick-up use case scenario in tabular format

Name: End effector pick-up

Actors
• Existing production system • Existing robot requiring end effector • Existing end effector to be picked up • Operator/integrator

Pre-conditions
• System and all relevant resources are functioning correctly, support plug & produce, and have compatible interfaces • Robot is part of production system, is functioning correctly and has interfaces compatible with the end effector • End effector is part of production system, is functioning correctly and has interfaces compatible with the robot • End effector is not already on (any) robot, but is in a known location that is reachable by robot • End effector has (or can be given) definition of capabilities and configuration

Basic flow

1. Start: System requires end effector to be added to robot
2. System identifies current (or last known) location of end effector
3. Robot and end effector are brought to the same location and connected together. Details of this physical process are out of scope, but this could happen in three ways:
  a. Robot moves to end effector and picks it up
  b. End effector is brought to robot, which picks it up
  c. Robot and end effector move to same location, where robot picks up end effector
4. Robot/system reads current configuration setting of end effector. The system becomes aware of the end effector configuration. The "Change Configuration" use case is executed – the configuration change is the joining of the robot and end effector
5. Robot and end effector are now considered "joined"
6. System checks that end effector configuration matches expected configuration and notifies operator of successful pick up. Either:
  a. Configuration is as expected – success
  b. Configuration is not as expected – a change is required
7. Completion: The end effector in the internal representation of the production system has been set as being joined to the representation of the robot: all resources in the system should be aware of the new capabilities/configuration and location/connectivity of the joint robot with end effector

Post-conditions
• The new end effector is part of the production system (attached to the robot); system and all relevant resources are functioning correctly, support plug & produce, and have compatible interfaces • All resources in the system should be aware of the new end effector's capabilities/configuration and location/connectivity • The new end effector can be given commands and generate output as expected

Configuration Change. The configuration change use case scenario shown in Table 2 shows a situation where a change has been made to a resource (e.g. end effector) in the system that must be communicated to the rest of the system. Examples of this change could include an end effector being mounted to a given robot (which updates both the robot configuration and the end effector configuration), an end effector being placed in a tool rack (which updates the "location" configuration of the end effector), or an end effector setting being changed (for example the size of fastener being held).

Table 2. Configuration change use case scenario in tabular format

Name: Configuration change
Actors
• Existing production system • Existing resource to be configured • Operator/integrator
Pre-conditions
• System and all relevant resources are functioning correctly and support being configured • Resource to be configured is part of production system and is functioning correctly, but is not in the correct configuration • Resource to be configured can be given definition of capabilities and configuration • The change to the configuration is such that the rest of the system needs to be made aware of the change (i.e. it will impact planning or production processes)
Basic flow

1. Start: A change is made to the configuration of a resource in the system that is significant enough to be communicated to the rest of the system. The details of what this configuration change is are out of scope. It may include changes to the settings on an end effector (e.g. which size bolt is loaded)
2. Resource reads new configuration. The details of this are out of scope, but examples include:
  a. Some resource in the system – or the system controller – requested a configuration change be applied, so already communicated the change to the resource
  b. The resource automatically detects the configuration change; this could be through specific sensors or because the resource automatically determined the required configuration change so is already aware of it
  c. The operator adjusts hardware selector switches on the resource, which are read by the resource controller
  d. The operator inputs the configuration change on an HMI, which is read by the resource controller or system (which would then pass it to the resource controller)
3. The resource updates its internal representation to reflect the new configuration
4. The resource communicates its new configuration to the system, which notifies all relevant resources and incorporates the change into its internal representation
5. Completion: The resource has its new configuration reflected in its internal representation. The system and all relevant resources are aware of the new configuration. This new information may be used by other resources as a trigger for other processes

Post-conditions
• System and all relevant resources functioning correctly and support configuration • Resource has new configuration; remainder of system is aware of new configuration as appropriate • Resource to be configured can be given definition of capabilities and configuration

4 Reference Architecture Concept

4.1 Generic Process Flow

Based on the use cases developed in the project discussed in Sect. 3, a generic process flow has been identified and is presented diagrammatically in Fig. 2 using the example of the "end effector pick-up" use case. This generic process flow allows a solution to be designed that will address the range of problem scenarios facing the system, where each use case is a specific example, rather than designing a solution specifically for each use case and then attempting to combine them.

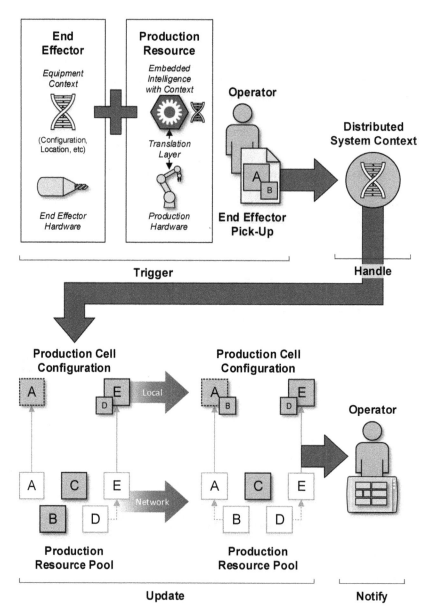

Fig. 2. Generic use case flow for WingLIFT, using the example of end effector pick-up

Each use case follows the following process:

1. **Trigger**: An event occurs to trigger the use case. In this case it is a requirement for the end effector B to be fitted to the robot A.
2. **Handle**: An entity in the system either chooses to handle the event, or is assigned to handle it. In this case the WingLIFT software will gather the required data (e.g. end effector location) from the distributed system context and assign the specific required processes to the relevant robot controller.

3. **Update**: The system configuration is updated. This happens both at the local level by each individual resource, and at the network level where the shared context is updated. The robot controller configuration will be updated to include the new end effector, and the end effector context will reflect its new location and configuration.

4. **Notify**: Once the use case has been completed, one or more entities in the system are notified of the success or failure of the process. In this case, the operator is notified through an HMI.

4.2 Architectural Concept

Placing some of the terms used in the previous section into context, the top-level agent-oriented architectural concept, based on that of the EAS project, is shown in Fig. 3. Each resource maintains a local internal model for low-level decision-making and control. All resources in the system are connected to a shared context which forms a "joint model" from the many local internal models. High-level decision-making can be performed on this joint model. The shared context is also the link to the wider enterprise and any additional external data sources or storage locations.

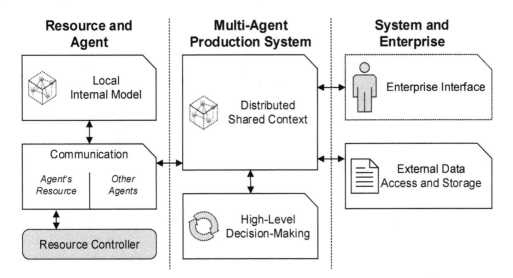

Fig. 3. Top-level agent-oriented architectural concept

Building on the EAS project, it is assumed that the majority of the resources in the system will be controlled by intelligent agents [13]. In Sect. 4.4, integration cases will be discussed where no agent is present.

4.3 Data Communications Concept

The "distributed shared context" in the system is transmitted over a databus that performs the functions of both a Manufacturing Service Bus and of an Enterprise Service Bus (a hybrid "manufacturing/enterprise service bus"). This "shared context" is effectively all relevant data that is collected from the system; it is a joint model of the system context that is generated by the collection of the internal models of all the system elements. Once on the bus, this data can be used as required by the actors in the system, or stored for later use.

In terms of implementation, all inter-agent (or inter-resource) communication in the system is handled by a publish-subscribe databus implemented as a Data Distribution Service (DDS, as specified by the Object Management Group (OMG) DDS standard) [20]. The publish-subscribe approach is one in which, rather than the data publisher sending data to one or more specific recipients, the data is published to a channel. The data subscribers subscribe to a channel and receive data from that channel. This frees publishers from keeping track of who is interested in their data, and subscribers from keeping track of data sources. The channel can also take care of communication implementation details, rather than requiring the agents to do so. Such details may include quality of service requirements, caching or persistence, and so on.

4.4 Hardware/Software Stack

Physical hardware resources in the WingLIFT architecture are usually controlled by intelligent agents deployed on embedded computers. Each agent is connected to the resource using a resource-specific translation layer and to the rest of the system using a DDS. In the EAS project this was the most common type of stack, but WingLIFT aims to address a wider range of resource types. Figure 4 shows this more complete view: the physical resource may provide a software interface, or may require a hardware interface; the system can also interface with humans though software running on portable devices; and the system may include software services running on other computing hardware. There should be no difference to the architecture whether the resource being managed is physical automation, a human, or a software service.

Also shown in Fig. 4 are the data flows from the resources up to the databus, the options for where each piece of functionality is deployed in hardware terms, and the likely division between provided and developed functionality. Resource hardware is controlled by its own controller as normal. That controller then interfaces with the system databus either through an agent on an embedded computer, an agent deployed directly on the controller (in the case of a software PLC for example), or directly through its own network application programming interface (API). In most cases some translation will be required from vendor specific semantics to open common semantics for use on the databus. Some resource hardware will provide an API and open communication standards for interfacing with. Some "legacy" resource hardware may require a more complex translation layer that features hardware technical interconnectivity as well as semantic translation. Human resources communicate with resource agents via human-machine interfaces (HMIs). In the case of resources that directly connect to the databus through their own network API without an agent, they can only act as publishers and/or subscribers of data. If any decision-making takes place, it must either be handled entirely inside the resource, or a separate agent must be deployed on the databus to act on the data published and/or subscribed to by the resource.

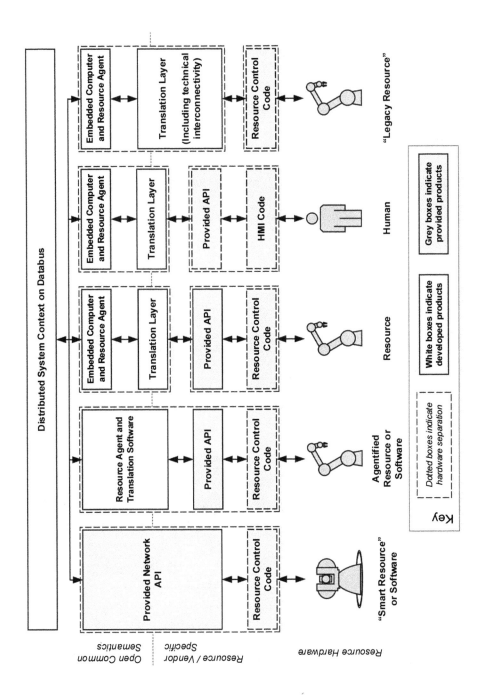

Fig. 4. Integration approaches for different resources types

5   Validation

5.1   Demonstration Scenario

In order to validate the proposed solution, we have developed a demonstration scenario based around the project use cases. In this scenario, two robots share a number of end effectors through the use of automatic tool changers as described in Sect. 3.1.

The aim of the demonstrator is to show how the two robots can share the end effectors and how the system can maintain awareness of the current configuration of both the robots and the end effectors in the face of manual changes. A visual representation of an example usage flow of the demonstrator is given in Fig. 5 in the format of a UML activity diagram.

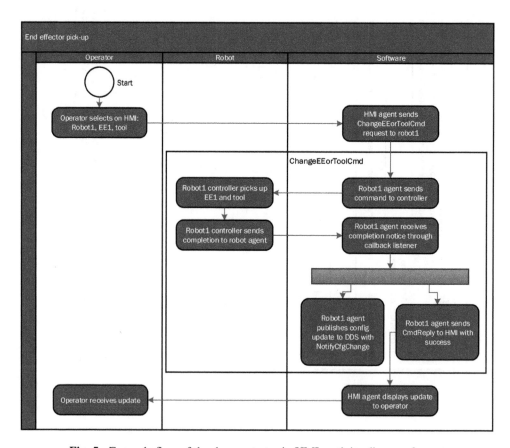

Fig. 5.   Example flow of the demonstrator in UML activity diagram format

This shows the example of an end effector pick-up: first the use case is **triggered** by the operator making a selection on the HMI. This is **handled** by the software once it receives the ChangeEEorToolCmd request. Once the end effector has been picked up, the status is **updated** locally (by the robot once the task is complete) and at the network level (when the robot publishes the context update). Finally, the operator is **notified** once the change is complete.

5.2 Outline Solution

Based on the WingLIFT architecture, databus concept, and integration approaches all described in Sect. 4, Fig. 6 shows the overall logical structure of the demonstration cell described in this section. Each robot is controlled by its own controller, which is in turn connected to a WingLIFT agent that is connected to the DDS databus. Also connected to the databus is an HMI for the operator, and an agent connected to each end effector. The end effector information is transmitted onto the bus through this agent. The bus carries all configuration and state information for all resources in the cell: the location of the robots and end effectors, the configuration state of all end effectors, and which end effector is connected to each robot. The remainder of this section describes the implementation of the cell in some more detail.

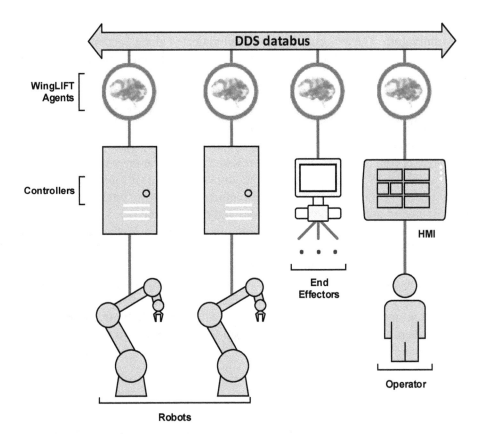

Fig. 6. WingLIFT demonstration cell architecture

Resource, Controller, and Code. Production resources must be orchestrated by the WingLIFT software. This is effectively a case of virtualising or servitising the production resource. Various approaches are possible, depending on the specific situation

[21–23]: Industry 4.0 suggests an "administration shell" wrapper around the existing control approach for example [24–26]. Some modern resources may already have suitable interfaces. Others may facilitate the addition of a custom interface (e.g. a soft PLC on which a module can be installed to communicate with the agent). WingLIFT uses an intelligent agent to virtualise each resource.

Agent. The WingLIFT architecture uses an agent-based approach to integrate resources that do not support intelligent integration. Each agent is based around a streamlined version of the JADE agent platform [27]. The JADE Abstract Architecture and Application frameworks have been utilized, but the Agent Communication and Agent Message Transport has been replaced by the RTI Connext DDS Pro publish-subscribe databus. Each WingLIFT agent extends the abstract JADE agent class, to provide structure for agent data management and behaviours.

Communication. The WingLIFT agent communicates along two main channels: via the agent-resource translation layer, and via the inter-agent communication method (e.g. DDS):

- Agent-resource translation layer: This translation layer allows the agent to communicate with the resource it is controlling. Where the resource is an HMI, it also allows the system to communicate with the human operator. While the agent side of this translation layer is common to all agents, the resource side of the layer must be customised to some degree to the specific (type/brand/make/model of) resource. This allows the agent to deal with the specific datatypes required by whatever interface is available in the resource in order to trigger operations and receive data.
- Inter-agent communication: Agents communicate with each other across a publish-subscribe RTI Connext DDS Pro databus [28]. This is based on the OMG DDS standard [20], with individual message formats defined in turn using the OMG Interface Definition Language (IDL) [29], part of Common Object Request Broker Architecture (CORBA) [30]. Connext Pro allows both the use of standard publish-subscribe communication and also request-reply messaging patterns as well. We use the request-reply pattern where appropriate, for example when sending commands to specific resources and receiving the responses.

6   Summary

This paper has presented the WingLIFT approach to context-aware plug and produce for flexible robotic aerospace assembly based on a Data Distribution Service. This approach allows the system to accurately and dynamically track the configuration and status of the process end effectors in a flexible and reconfigurable production cell. This is grounded in an industrial use case where the potential end effector configurations far outnumber the available automation platforms. The solution is presented as a set of design specifications along with a summary of a physical demonstration cell based at the University of Nottingham.

Acknowledgements. The authors gratefully acknowledge the support provided by Innovate UK through the Aerospace Technology Institute WingLIFT project (project reference 113162).

References

1. UK Research and Innovation: Wing Lean Innovative Future Technology (Wing LIFT) - project reference 113162 (2017)
2. Sethi, A., Sethi, S.: Flexibility in manufacturing: a survey. Int. J. Flex. Manuf. Syst. **2**, 289–328 (1990). https://doi.org/10.1007/BF00186471
3. Browne, J., Dubois, D., Rathmill, K., et al.: Classification of flexible manufacturing systems. FMS Mag. **2**, 114–117 (1984)
4. Koren, Y., Heisel, U., Jovane, F., et al.: Reconfigurable manufacturing systems. CIRP Ann. – Manuf. Technol. **48**, 527–540 (1999). https://doi.org/10.1016/S0007-8506(07)63232-6
5. Monostori, L., Csáji, B.C., Kádár, B., et al.: Towards adaptive and digital manufacturing. Annu. Rev. Control **34**, 118–128 (2010). https://doi.org/10.1016/j.arcontrol.2010.02.007
6. ElMaraghy, H., AlGeddawy, T., Azab, A.: Modelling evolution in manufacturing: a biological analogy. CIRP Ann. – Manuf. Technol. **57**, 467–472 (2008). https://doi.org/10.1016/j.cirp.2008.03.136
7. Arai, T., Aiyama, Y., Maeda, Y., et al.: Agile assembly system by "plug and produce". CIRP Ann. – Manuf. Technol. **49**, 1–4 (2000). https://doi.org/10.1016/S0007-8506(07)62883-2
8. PRIME: PRIME project website (2014). http://www.prime-eu.com. Accessed 15 Nov 2014
9. Antzoulatos, N., Castro, E., Scrimieri, D., Ratchev, S.: A multi-agent architecture for plug and produce on an industrial assembly platform. Prod. Eng. **8**, 773–781 (2014). https://doi.org/10.1007/s11740-014-0571-x
10. Antzoulatos, N., Rocha, A., Castro, E., et al.: Towards a capability-based framework for reconfiguring industrial production systems. In: Proceedings of the 15th IFAC/IEEE/IFIP/IFORS Symposium INCOM 2015 on Information Control Problems in Manufacturing, pp 2145–2150 (2015)
11. Antzoulatos, N., Castro, E., de Silva, L., Ratchev, S.: Interfacing agents with an industrial assembly system for "plug and produce": (demonstration). In: Proceedings of the 2015 International Conference on Autonomous Agents and Multiagent Systems. International Foundation for Autonomous Agents and Multiagent Systems, Richland, pp 1957–1958 (2015)
12. Ratchev, S.: Evolvable assembly systems - towards open, adaptable, and context-aware equipment and systems (grant reference EP/K018205/1) (2012)
13. Wooldridge, M., Jennings, N.R.: Intelligent agents: theory and practice. Knowl. Eng. Rev. **10**, 115–152 (1995)
14. Chaplin, J.C., Ratchev, S.: Deployment of a distributed multi-agent architecture for transformable assembly. In: Ratchev, S. (ed.) IPAS 2018. IAICT, vol. 530, pp. 15–28. Springer, Cham (2019). https://doi.org/10.1007/978-3-030-05931-6_2
15. Chaplin, J.C., Bakker, O.J., de Silva, L., et al.: Evolvable assembly systems: a distributed architecture for intelligent manufacturing. IFAC-PapersOnLine **48**, 2065–2070 (2015). https://doi.org/10.1016/j.ifacol.2015.06.393

16. Sanderson, D., Chaplin, J.C., Ratchev, S.: Functional modelling in evolvable assembly systems. In: Ratchev, S. (ed.) IPAS 2018. IAICT, vol. 530, pp. 40–48. Springer, Cham (2019). https://doi.org/10.1007/978-3-030-05931-6_4
17. de Silva, L., Felli, P., Chaplin, J.C., et al.: Synthesising industry-standard manufacturing process controllers. In: Proceedings of the International Joint Conference on Autonomous Agents and Multiagent Systems, AAMAS. International Foundation for Autonomous Agents and Multiagent Systems, pp 1811–1813 (2017)
18. Sanderson, D., Chaplin, J.C., Ratchev, S.: Conceptual framework for ubiquitous cyber-physical assembly systems in airframe assembly. IFAC-PapersOnLine **51**, 417–422 (2018). https://doi.org/10.1016/J.IFACOL.2018.08.331
19. Object Management Group Unified Modeling Language, UML. http://www.uml.org
20. Object Management Group Data Distribution Service Specification (current). http://www.omg.org/spec/DDS/Current
21. Van Brussel, H., Wyns, J., Valckenaers, P., et al.: Reference architecture for holonic manufacturing systems: PROSA. Comput. Ind. **37**, 255–274 (1998). https://doi.org/10.1016/S0166-3615(98)00102-X
22. Leitão, P., Restivo, F.: ADACOR: a holonic architecture for agile and adaptive manufacturing control. Comput. Ind. **57**, 121–130 (2006). https://doi.org/10.1016/j.compind.2005.05.005
23. Alam, K.M., El Saddik, A.: C2PS: a digital twin architecture reference model for the cloud-based cyber-physical systems. IEEE Access (2017). https://doi.org/10.1109/ACCESS.2017.2657006
24. Bundesministerium für Bildung und Forschung: Industrie 4.0 - Innovationen für die Produktion von morgen (2014)
25. Wagner, C., Grothoff, J., Epple, U., et al.: The role of the Industry 4.0 asset administration shell and the digital twin during the life cycle of a plant. In: IEEE International Conference on Emerging Technologies and Factory Automation, ETFA, pp 1–8 (2018)
26. Contreras, J.D., Garcia, J.I., Pastrana, J.D.: Developing of Industry 4.0 applications. Int. J. Online Eng. **13**, 30–47 (2017). https://doi.org/10.3991/ijoe.v13i10.7331
27. Bellifemine, F., Poggi, A., Rimassa, G.: JADE—a FIPA-compliant agent framework. In: Proceedings of the Fourth International Conference on Practical Applications Intelligent Agents and Multi-Agent Technology (1999)
28. RTI RTI Connext DDS Professional. https://www.rti.com/products/connext-dds-professional. Accessed 16 Sept 2019
29. Object Management Group: Interface Definition Language Specification v4.2 (2018). https://www.omg.org/spec/IDL/4.2/PDF. Accessed 16 Sept 2019
30. Object Management Group OMG IDL—CORBA. https://www.corba.org/omg_idl.htm. Accessed 16 Sept 2019
31. Henricksen, K., Indulska, J., Rakotonirainy, A.: Modeling context information in pervasive computing systems. In: Mattern, F., Naghshineh, M. (eds.) Pervasive 2002. LNCS, vol. 2414, pp. 167–180. Springer, Heidelberg (2002). https://doi.org/10.1007/3-540-45866-2_14
32. Weiser, M.: The computer for the 21st century. Sci. Am. **265**, 94–104 (1991)

Permissions

The contributors of this book come from diverse backgrounds, making this book a truly international effort. This book will bring forth new frontiers with its revolutionizing research information and detailed analysis of the nascent developments around the world.

We would like to thank all the contributing authors for lending their expertise to make the book truly unique. They have played a crucial role in the development of this book. Without their invaluable contributions this book wouldn't have been possible. They have made vital efforts to compile up to date information on the varied aspects of this subject to make this book a valuable addition to the collection of many professionals and students.

This book was conceptualized with the vision of imparting up-to-date information and advanced data in this field. To ensure the same, a matchless editorial board was set up. Every individual on the board went through rigorous rounds of assessment to prove their worth. After which they invested a large part of their time researching and compiling the most relevant data for our readers.

The editorial board has been involved in producing this book since its inception. They have spent rigorous hours researching and exploring the diverse topics which have resulted in the successful publishing of this book. They have passed on their knowledge of decades through this book. To expedite this challenging task, the publisher supported the team at every step. A small team of assistant editors was also appointed to further simplify the editing procedure and attain best results for the readers.

Apart from the editorial board, the designing team has also invested a significant amount of their time in understanding the subject and creating the most relevant covers. They scrutinized every image to scout for the most suitable representation of the subject and create an appropriate cover for the book.

The publishing team has been an ardent support to the editorial, designing and production team. Their endless efforts to recruit the best for this project, has resulted in the accomplishment of this book. They are a veteran in the field of academics and their pool of knowledge is as vast as their experience in printing. Their expertise and guidance has proved useful at every step. Their uncompromising quality standards have made this book an exceptional effort. Their encouragement from time to time has been an inspiration for everyone.

The publisher and the editorial board hope that this book will prove to be a valuable piece of knowledge for researchers, students, practitioners and scholars across the globe.

List of Contributors

Marcello Valori, Vito Basile and Simone Pio Negri
Institute of Intelligent Industrial Technologies and Systems for Advanced Manufacturing, National Research Council, Via P. Lembo, 38/F, 70124 Bari, Italy

Paolo Scalmati and Chiara Renghini
Somacis S.p.A, Via del Lauro, 7, 20121 Milan, Italy

Irene Fassi
Institute of Intelligent Industrial Technologies and Systems for Advanced Manufacturing, National Research Council, Via A. Corti, 12, 20133 Milan, Italy

Niko Siltala, Eeva Järvenpää and Minna Lanz
Tampere University, Korkeakoulunkatu 6, 33014 Tampere, Finland

Torge Kolditz, Caner-Veli Ince and Annika Raatz
Institute of Assembly Technology, Leibniz Universitaet Hannover, 30823 Garbsen, Germany

Geraldine S. Cheok, Marek Franaszek and Jeremy A. Marvel
National Institute of Standards and Technology, Gaithersburg, MD 20899, USA

Karl Van Wyk
National Institute of Standards and Technology, Gaithersburg, MD 20899, USA
NVIDIA, 4545 Roosevelt Way, Seattle, WA 98105, USA

Robert Brownbill and Peter Whiteside
Electroimpact UK Ltd., Manor Lane, Hawarden, Deeside CH5 3ST, UK

Philip Silk and Harry Burroughes
The Advanced Manufacturing Research Centre - The AMRC, University of Sheffield, Factory 2050, Sheffield S9 1ZA, UK

Windo Hutabarat
Department of Automatic Control and System Engineering, University of Sheffield, Portobello Street, Sheffield S1 3JD, UK

M. Dalle Mura and G. Dini
Department of Civil and Industrial Engineering, University of Pisa, 56122 Pisa, Italy

Emil Tochev, Harald Pfifer and Svetan Ratchev
University of Nottingham, Nottingham, UK

Jun Huang, Duc Truong Pham, Ruiya Li, Kaiwen Jiang, Dalong Lyu and Chunqian Ji
Department of Mechanical Engineering, School of Engineering, University of Birmingham, Birmingham B15 2TT, UK

Gerhard Reisinger, Philipp Hold and Wilfried Sihn
Fraunhofer Austria Research GmbH, Theresianumgasse 7, 1040 Vienna, Austria
Institute of Management Sciences, Vienna University of Technology, Theresianumgasse 27, 1040 Vienna, Austria

Lucas Paletta
DIGITAL – Institute for Information and Communication Technologies, JOANNEUM RESEARCH Forschungsgesellschaft MbH, 8010 Graz, Austria

Robert Brownbill and Adam Roberts
Electroimpact UK Ltd., Hawarden, UK

Konstantinos Bacharoudis, Atanas Popov and Svetan Ratchev
University of Nottingham, Nottingham NG7 2RD, UK

Christian Kittl
Evolaris Next Level GmbH, Graz, Austria

Markus Streibl
Know-Center GmbH, Research Center for Data-Driven Business and Big Data Analytics, Graz, Austria

Wernher Behrendt and Felix Strohmeier
Salzburg Research, Salzburg, Austria

Moritz A. Kirschmann, Jörg Pierer, Alexander Steinecker and Philipp Schmid
CSEM SA, Gründlistrasse 1, 6055 Alpnach Dorf, Switzerland

Arne Erdmann
Raytrix GmbH, Schauenburgerstr. 116, 24118 Kiel, Germany

David Sanderson and Emma Shires
Centre for Aerospace Manufacturing, University of Nottingham, Nottingham NG7 2PX, UK

Jack C. Chaplin and Svetan Ratchev
Institute for Advanced Manufacturing, University of Nottingham, Nottingham NG8 1BB, UK

Harvey Brookes and Amer Liaqat
Airbus, Bristol, UK

Index

Printed in the USA
CPSIA information can be obtained
at www.ICGtesting.com
JSHW051351221024
72173JS00006B/1304